The Woman Question and George Gissing

James Haydock

AuthorHouse™
1663 Liberty Drive
Bloomington, IN 47403
www.authorhouse.com
Phone: 1 (800) 839-8640

Published by AuthorHouse 03/12/2015

ISBN: 978-1-4969-7198-2 (sc)
ISBN: 978-1-4969-7197-5 (e)

Library of Congress Control Number: 2015903002

Print information available on the last page.

This book is printed on acid-free paper.

Also by James Haydock:

Stormbirds
Victorian Sages
Beacon's River
Portraits in Charcoal: George Gissing's Women
On a Darkling Plain: Victorian Poetry and Thought
Searching in Shadow: Victorian Prose and Thought
Against the Grain
Mose in Bondage
A Tinker in Blue Anchor

Contents

Chapter 1

The Womanly Woman

The Victorian Era, called a fast-moving age of transition as early as 1858, spawned an abundance of movements. Each of these tried in its own way to improve existing conditions by solving a question. The woman question was the nucleus of an important movement that spanned the century and brought lasting results. Historians of the movement have treated its phases in great detail. While their work is indispensable in any study of the changing status of woman in nineteenth-century England, my intention here is to focus more on the question than the movement and then show how it became a major theme in the fiction of George Gissing. Before "the Woman Question" came into existence the English ideal of womanhood was that of the womanly woman. Then as the feminist movement gathered steam the woman in revolt made herself known. Near the end of the century the new woman appeared on the scene. In the last two decades of the century three distinct types were present: the womanly woman, the woman in revolt, and the new woman.

Throughout the century a flood of conduct books, written expressly for women, poured from the presses of the day. All of them had one purpose: to instruct young women in the ideals of "true womanhood." As the feminist movement gained in power and influence, these books became even more numerous. Not altogether anti-feminist, yet belonging unmistakably to the conservative camp in a state of siege, they set forth in clear detail the duties and responsibilities of the entire sex: *"A grown-up daughter ought to nurse her mother if she is ill, or teach her little brother to read. Whenever she can't find something important and constructive to do, her duty is to dress as well as she can and play on the pianoforte."* The books stressed self-repression, patience, woman's inherent inferiority to man, polite manners, and the trivial round of duties deemed suitable for young ladies of the upper middle class. Though hastily prepared and poorly written by a bevy of semi-skilled women, they were enormously popular.

Sharing the popularity and quoted respectfully for half a century were the writings of Mrs. Sarah Stickney Ellis, whose *Women of England*, *Daughters of England*, *Wives of England*, and *Mothers of England* became standard manuals. Each one of these titles promulgated with as much force as possible the notion that man is superior to woman. *"The first thing of importance,"* so the daughters of England were told, *"is to be content to be inferior to men – inferior in mental power in the same proportion that you are inferior in bodily strength."* Because their inferiority was a self-evident law of nature, young women couldn't expect or desire the same education as men or the same knowledge of the world as men. Anything beyond a few genteel accomplishments in the name of education was deemed not only unnecessary but unwise.

According to Mrs. Ellis, the education suitable for women fell into three categories: cleverness, learning, and knowledge. Cleverness she defined as "dexterity and aptness in doing everything that falls within the sphere of ordinary duty." Young women in the middle social rank, she allowed, were more apt to require cleverness than women of wealth who could do without it. Learning she viewed as "skill in language or science," confessing even as she established this classification that acquiring a foreign language appeared to be of little value to women sequestered in the home. However, they might learn enough science to become "intelligent listeners." Knowledge, she said, is *"that acquaintance with facts, which in connection with the proper exercise of a healthy mind will necessarily lead to general illumination."* Yet women must be careful to keep their knowledge under wraps, never letting it become objectionable.

As for the duties of the womanly wife, Mrs. Ellis unabashedly promoted the dogma of the wife's inferiority: *"It is the privilege of a married woman to be able to show by the most delicate attentions how much she feels her husband's superiority to herself, not by mere personal services but by a respectful deference to his opinion, and a willingly imposed silence when he speaks."* Responsibilities other than a few duties in the home would overwhelm the average middle-class woman, or so this self-elected prophet announced, and work would make her ill. A dutiful wife had to be sheltered, protected, indulged; and her justification for being was the fact that she was the wife, daughter, or mother of some man. The man of the house, going into the crass world to make a living, suffered vulgarity at every turn to degrade his moral tone. His wife was on hand to "raise the tone of his mind from low anxieties and vulgar cares" to a higher plane, to "a state of existence beyond this present life." In other words, she must lift the sinner to salvation.

Brought up on flapdoodle of this sort, most women yearned to marry and most were afterwards duly submissive. Of the three conceptions of woman current at the time, the best known was the submissive wife as Mrs. Ellis described her, a mousy little woman whose only reason for living was to love, honor, obey, and amuse her lord and master. Her foremost duty was to manage her lord's estate and bring up his children. Tennyson, the undisputed voice of Victorianism, defined her role in *The Princess* (1847):

> Man for the field and woman for the hearth;
> Man for the sword, and for the needle she;
> Man to command, and woman to obey;
> All else confusion.

But even in the forties a more radical conception of woman's role had arisen to oppose this traditional view. Princess Ida in Tennyson's poem represents the advanced thought on the subject. Dissatisfied with her legal and social bondage, she yearns for equal rights with men – for equal footing in the home and equal opportunity in other areas of life. Between these two poles was another school of thought tinged with a mawkish benevolence that soon became "woman worship." This middle position, reflecting the Victorian spirit of compromise, held that "more breadth of culture" should be the right of all women even though they were not ready for higher education, the vote, and professional careers.

However, this woman worship as it came to be called was not by any means universal. It was not endorsed by such men as Macaulay, Carlyle, Trollope, Mill, Arnold, or Huxley. In "Emancipation Black and White" (1865), Huxley spoke out against *"the new woman-worship which so many sentimentalists and some philosophers are desirous of setting up."* But Coventry Patmore, as shown in his most famous poem "Angel in the House," was an ardent supporter. Charlotte Mary Yonge's *Womankind,* one of more than 160 books she published before her death in 1901, was a showcase of conservative opinion on Young Ladyhood, Wives, and Strong-Minded Women; all chapter titles. Although her thoughts were similar to those of Patmore, they fell short of actual worship. Trenchant criticism of this sentimental view of woman came from several sources: John Stuart Mill's *The Subjection of Women* (1869), Annie Besant's *Marriage As It Is, As It Was, As It Should Be* (1879), and George Bernard Shaw's, *Quintessence of Ibsenism* (1891). Even so, both Tennyson and Ruskin, powerful voices of the time, held the traditional view.

A woman must be careful not to harm her "distinctive womanhood," observes Tennyson in *The Princess* (1847). This talk of equality is pernicious because woman was made to be the helpmate of man. Let her perform the sacred duty of redeeming certain defects in her man, and let her be as he described her forty years later in "Locksley Hall Sixty Years After" (1884) —

> Strong in will and rich in wisdom, Edith, yet so lowly sweet,
> Woman to her inmost heart, and woman to her tender feet,
> Very woman of very woman, nurse of ailing body and mind,
> She that linked the broken chain that bound me to my kind.

John Ruskin in "Of Queen's Gardens" (1864) rambled along the same path. Rejecting the notion that woman owes her lord "a thoughtless and servile obedience," he declared that her true function is to guide and uplift: *"His intellect is for speculation and invention; his energy for adventure, for war, and for conquest, wherever war is just, wherever conquest is necessary. But the woman's power is for rule, not for battle, and her intellect is not for invention or creation, but for sweet ordering, arrangement, and decision."* With woman's role defined, Ruskin moved on to describe the home and its importance in Victorian life.

The home, he pontificated, is the source of virtues and emotions to be found nowhere else, least of all in the soul-soiling pursuits of men. It is a place radically different from the world at large. Much more than a mere house where a man may find escape from his work, it should be a place apart, a walled garden or sanctuary where one may be refreshed and strengthened by virtues too easily crushed by the commerce of life. *"It is the place of Peace, the shelter not only from all injury, but from all terror, doubt, and division. In so far as it is not this, it is not home; so far as the anxieties of the outer life penetrate into it, and the hostile society of the outer world is allowed by either husband or wife to cross the threshold, it ceases to be home."* It is a shelter for those values which the commercial and critical forces of the time were threatening to destroy. It is, moreover, a sacred place, a temple. Reigning in this sacred place and exerting a positive presence is woman.

Indeed, the moral elevation of man became so closely identified with "the angel in the house" that some of both sexes were willing to lay the blame on woman when man went astray. A fiery dissenting preacher complained in chapel in 1866 that women themselves had succumbed to mean desires for wealth and power. A few, he went on to say in well-attended sermons, had even been seduced by that "ridiculous phantom of woman's rights." Clearly, woman's place was the home and her sacred duty, according to Ruskin, was to solace and strengthen her man: *"I know women whose hearts are an unfailing fountain of courage and inspiration to the hard-pressed man, who but for them must be worsted in life's battle and who send forth husband or brother each morning with new strength for his conflict."* In an age of greed, commercialism, and competition the angel in the house was expected to preserve, quicken, and strengthen the moral fiber of her man.

This theoretical deification of woman accounts in part for the extensive and fierce hostility to her emancipation. Feminist claims to intellectual equality with men were attacked not only by conservatives but by the liberals as well. The fear of competition, as some women claimed, was perhaps the least of it. Most male opponents wanted to prevent what they honestly believed would be the loss of a vital moral influence in their lives. If woman left her home to rub shoulders with the world, it was thought she would inevitably lose those womanly virtues upon which man depended for his moral support. And so we have Lancelot Smith in Charles Kingsley's *Yeast* (1848) eager to assert his mental superiority even while venerating Argemone as *"infallible and inspired on all questions of morality, taste, and feeling."* It's his aim to convince her that *"the heart, and not the brain, enshrines the priceless pearl of womanhood."*

The men differed as to what they wanted in a wife, but most agreed that ambition, achievement, and independence were not on the table for women they hoped to marry. They looked for obedience, humility, and self sacrifice as the most desirable traits, to say nothing of purity. Though any talk of sex among the Victorians was reduced to a murmur, every groom expected his bride to be a virgin. Discovering she was not could be grounds for immediate separation and even divorce for those who could afford it. Many young women approaching marriage confused purity with prudery, and with every step toward candor they suffered agonies of conscience. The fear of being unladylike or unmaidenly was a genuine restriction, for almost everything worthwhile appeared to be either one or the other. Even to own a dog could bring hesitation, for dogs they agreed with a flutter of embarrassment have plumbing and use it. Also to look a man in the face while speaking to him was frowned upon. The delicate maiden was expected to cast her eyes downward. In the fifties and sixties and indeed for the rest of the century an enormous number of girls wanted to do something with their lives, but to oppose the dictates of convention required courage.

Lacking the ability to do something that frightens one – their definition of courage – most women sank into a plaintive way of life that brought no income and begged support by male relatives. An uncomfortable consequence of this state of affairs was the existence of superfluous women growing more numerous as the century progressed. A girl could identify herself as some man's daughter only so long as he lived. After that if she had not succeeded in becoming some man's wife, she was adrift. With the laws of inheritance favoring the sons of the family, the single woman was frequently left with no means of support, or very narrow means. Possessing no skills by which to earn a living, she was often reduced to being dependent on male relatives. Without that dependence, as it sometimes happened, she did whatever she could. It was not uncommon to find a lady serving as a housekeeper or working even as a charwoman. In times of desperation a woman alone took whatever she could get.

Among the lower classes conditions were not quite the same. From an early age working-class girls were taught that some day they would perhaps have to earn their own living. They often worked before marriage and after, even when pregnant, but were paid much less than men on the same jobs. Unlike women in the classes above them, most of them could expect to marry and hope against hope the marriage would be a good one. According to Charles Booth, a prominent social scientist of the day, when huge numbers of higher-class women were remaining unmarried, the working girl was able to find a husband. *"Every girl in the lowest classes in the East End can get married, and with hardly any exceptions every girl does marry. This is not true of the middle classes."* As those in the middle class, working-class wives were thought to be vastly inferior to their husbands and were treated like property. If a working man became displeased with his wife's conduct, he had the right to beat her with a stick (provided it was not thicker than his own thumb), and that right he practiced often.

Nor was wife-beating confined solely to the lower classes. To keep some women in line as the century drew to a close, captains of industry and owners of huge estates were sometimes forced to lay down the law with a stick to the rump. Gissing, who grew up believing he could never fish because the hook would hurt the fish, was driven several times to thinking his second wife needed a sound beating. On each occasion he managed to calm himself and draw back, allowing fictional characters to do it for him. In later years he came to believe that wife-beating for a particular type of woman was perhaps not a bad thing. It was said that when a man is too weak to control a woman, she finds ingenious ways to make his life miserable. To control a rebellious wife meant pummeling her.

Among the upper classes, as the century grew older, it became increasingly difficult for a woman to find a husband. One can't really blame the poor woman who wrote to a ladies' magazine in a tone of pique born of disappointment: *"Be good-natured, do, and tell us how to look fascinating, or at least good-looking."* In times of keen competition, with dowries becoming almost non-existent and men less prone to marry, a young woman could rely on little more than a bright personality and a good figure albeit hidden by clothing that reached to the ankles. Towards the end of the sixties as the crinoline shrank and became looped up behind in a bunch, the skirt was drawn with extreme tightness across the hips. This focused attention on the lower parts of the female anatomy, particularly the stomach, and brought into fashion "a certain rotundity of form" that attracted the male eye. Women lacking in natural rotundity were aided by an artificial protuberance that made them look four months' pregnant.

In 1867 *London Society* reported an incident involving a fashionable lady when first introduced to one of these devices. With plenty of money to spend, she went to buy a gown at the shop of "the most eminent dressmaker in Paris." Looking her up and down, he exclaimed in suave and silvery French, a language she had some difficulty understanding, "Mais, Madame, vous n'avez pas de ventre!" Pausing for a translation, she was astonished and felt insulted when he said in English, "You have no belly!" Without the artificial belly, he explained, no gown would fit her. *"The lady had never been aware till then of such a want. She had always been satisfied with the supply which nature had given her, and could not see any necessity for the intervention of art."* When the dressmaker insisted –"Il faut absolument!" – she submitted, had the dress strained over the contrivance, paid the man a handsome fee, and walked into the street plump and comely with a smile on her face but with an uncertain stride.

Invention also aided the female in other areas. French fashion writers directed ladies to special stores where artificial breasts were for sale. It was hard to find these items in England, and yet by 1849 a "Registered Bust Improver" was being advertised. *"To the present time pads made of Cotton and Wool have been much used for improving the Bust. This invention is far superior. The advantages to be obtained by it are alluring Development, a perfect Fit of the Dress, and comfort in the Wear."* A similar advertisement appeared in 1881: *"Ideal for perfecting Thin Figures. Words cannot describe its charming effect, which is unattainable by any other Corset in the World. Softly padded Regulators regulate a beautiful Bust."*

It was a near disaster for an Englishwoman of this period to expose her legs, but the deliberate exposure of the breasts was considered fashionable. At the Opera, where ladies flaunted extreme décolletage, a gentleman staring at a comely woman was heard to remark: *"Did you ever see such a thing?"* Pausing for a moment, his companion replied: *"Not since I was weaned!"* Even the pages of *Punch* had drawings of women in fancy gowns with the division between the breasts clearly shown. And a wag writing to a friend in Australia said this: "*She wore a rose in the centre between certain hills of snow which were naked to the visible eye – I mean visible to the naked eye, and the said rose was encircled by many leaves. Old Osborne advanced, as he always does, and looking at the rose and its leaves, said with a twinkle in blue eyes: 'Pardon me, Madam, but I really do believe you wear your fig leaf rather high!'"* The ladies' magazines were observant of the trend and didn't hesitate to comment on it. In 1867 one of their contributors, surely a womanly woman of the old ideal, huffed: *"The low-necked dress and bold look of the wearer are signs of the present fast, frivolous, and indecorous age."* They were actually signs of not-so-quiet desperation in the mating game.

Competition in the marriage market was fierce. This certainly influenced the way women dressed, accenting the feminine form and revealing uninhibited expanses of bosom. The low-necked dress had become the article of choice because no designer had dared to raise the hems of long and voluminous skirts that went to the top of one's shoes and often swept the ground. Hips, belly, and breasts had become fair game because female legs and buttocks were off limits. "Certain hills of snow" assailed the male eye even as other parts of the female anatomy were kept under wraps, and they served well to attract the opposite sex. Dress is often more seductive than nudity, but in the cause of sexual selection women throughout the century didn't hesitate to expose whatever treasure they had whenever they could. They knew very well the power of various stages of undress artfully employed to attract libidinous men. Sketches and photographs of severe young women clothed from chin to toe with not even a seductive wrist exposed are concealing the truth.

When she unwillingly found herself in "the marriage war," as the fierce competition came to be called, a woman's body was her best weapon. The girls with youth and beauty on their side entered the fray with eagerness and confidence. Those older and plainer retreated from the front lines and became battle-worn before their mettle could even be tried. Confronted with the awesome figures their elders were so fond of marshalling, thousands reeled and retreated. In 1860 young women of the middle class were told that only one girl in three, who was still single at twenty-one, could expect to marry. At twenty-five her chances had withered to one in six, and at thirty to one in sixteen. As the century unfolded, this state of affairs became even worse, so that by the 1880's huge numbers were remaining unmarried. Many eligible men who might have married young and gentle spinsters believed that living alone was better than marriage. The lonely spinster was no match for her male counterpart, the bachelor. While she hadn't been able to find a mate and was obliged to live out her life in disappointment, he on the other hand had chosen, possibly for economic reasons, to remain single.

Marriage, of course, was no assurance of a happy life. Indeed in many cases, despite the untiring efforts of those who tried to establish woman worship as a way of life, the married woman was often miserable. In 1871, after holding her tongue for more than two decades, a long-suffering wife spoke her mind: *"I have borne for twenty-two years with humility and gentleness of spirit all the insults of a coarse nature. I have been a devoted slave to the man I swore to love and obey. I have borne insults and hard work and words without a murmur, but my blood boils when I see my gentle, innocent girls tremble at the sound of their father's voice."* The editor of the magazine that published her letter replied: *"As he is the breadwinner, you must bear it with meek and quiet spirit."* In the next issue several readers wrote to express dismay over such *"a violent and vicious letter against a hard-working husband."* The issue had become a little drama expressing the agony of unfortunate wives in England and the opprobrium of those more fortunate.

Remaining unmarried when a woman yearned for marriage and children and a rewarding domestic life was perhaps even worse than living in turmoil with a domineering husband. It too made for sadness and misery and loss of hope. In 1868 a spinster on the brink of self destruction confessed: *"The position of a single woman of thirty in the middle class is horrible. Her cares are to be properly dressed, to drive or walk or pay calls with Mamma, to work miracles of embroidery as she sits in idleness, or to play the piano when guests arrive. But what good is all this? What justifies our will to live? What we want is something to do, something to live for each and every day."* Clearly the times were ripe for a sweeping change in the status of women in England, a change long delayed, and also in those English speaking countries closely related to England.

Chapter 2

The Women in Revolt

For centuries the subordinate position of woman was accepted as within the natural order of things: the Almighty made man to inhabit the earth and woman to serve man as helpmate. For countless generations women had tolerated this self-evident truth, yet the restless nineteenth century saw the emergence of a genuine female revolt. Perhaps the impulse for the revolt came from the French Revolution with is rallying cry of *liberté, egalité, fraternité.* Though a wag claimed the true cry of the revolution was *n'oubliez pas retourner vos livres a la bibliothèque,* his witty remark was lost in time until recently. In the unrest that followed this historic upheaval seeds of rebellion were sown among a number of thoughtful women. Inspired by the idea of equal human rights, Mary Wollstonecraft published *A Vindication of the Rights of Women* as early as 1792. The book set forth the essence of what was to become a long struggle. It became the manifesto of a movement that went on into the twenty-first century.

Though the phrase was later extended to mean equal rights in all areas of life, "the rights of women" referred at first to legal rights. In the first half of the nineteenth century the legal position of grown women was comparable to that of children. The law in fact looked upon a married woman as little more than a half-witted child. *"By marriage,"* an eminent lawyer explained, *"the very being or legal existence of a woman is suspended, or at least incorporated into that of the husband, under whose wing, protection, and cover she performs everything; she is therefore called in our law a femme covert."* This meant that the property, earnings, personal liberty, and even the conscience of a wife belonged to her husband. Moreover, even the children she was expected to bear belonged body and soul to him.

Not until 1882 with the Married Woman's Property Act did the law grant married women full possession of property owned before marriage and earnings after. The right of a man to imprison his wife in his own house was not questioned until 1891, and the presumption that a woman who commits a crime in the presence of her husband is guiltless was not abolished until 1925. As to the guardianship of children, mothers had no rights whatever before 1839. If a woman's husband proved himself to be a self-centered thug demanding more of her than she could give, her life might easily be shattered. Under the law with few rights to protect her, she was at a severe disadvantage. Since divorce before 1857 was practically unheard of except among a few in high society, there was no escape short of death. The women in revolt sought to correct these abuses.

The first legislative attempt to improve the position of women was inspired by Caroline Norton. A woman more sinned against than sinning, she was not a feminist by any means, but personal suffering eventually drove her to action. A few years before Victoria came to the throne, Caroline was married at nineteen to Richard Norton and became at once a glittering hostess of the first rank in London society. Her house in Storey's Gate was frequented not only by literary, artistic, and fashionable people, but also by politicians of high place such as Lord Melbourne and several Whig ministers. The granddaughter of Richard Sheridan, the famous dramatist and statesman, she inherited his reason and wit and her mother's beauty. Just as Sheridan was famous for doing in the eighteenth century, Caroline and her husband lived above their means. The stress of not having enough money to support their way of life led in time to bickering that culminated in a hard slap to the cheek that left her stunned.

Shortly afterwards she left their home and took refuge with relatives, who complained of Richard's boorish behavior. A series of battles followed and in time Richard seized the children by force and spirited them off to an undisclosed location. At this point Caroline realized that if her husband so decreed, she might never see her children again. Alarmed even by the thought of losing them to the man she now detested, she sought help from powerful friends. That led to Richard accusing Lord Melbourne of "criminal conversation" with Caroline, who couldn't be sued for adultery. The case against Melbourne came to trial in June of 1836. It was dismissed on grounds of insufficient evidence and caused no damage to either Melbourne or Caroline. However, it taught her that she had practically no legal standing at all in a court of law. As a married woman she could neither sue nor be sued, and she could not be represented by counsel.

After the trial her husband refused her permission to see the children, refused to give her an allowance to live on, and kept in his possession all the property that was hers when they married. All this made the woman bristle with anger, and she exclaimed to friends that if the law would not allow her even to visit her children, she would change the law. She then set about writing a series of fiery pamphlets that found their way into the hands of influential people. Then to her dismay she discovered her husband owned the copyright to all the pamphlets. Fuming with anger she penned the following: "*I abjure all other writing till I see these laws altered; it is the cause of all women of England. If I could be justified and happy as soon as tomorrow, I would still strive and labour in it. And if I were to die tomorrow it would still be a satisfaction to me that I had so striven. Meanwhile, my husband has a legal lien (as he has publicly proved) on the copyright of my works! Let him, if in his greed he so desires, claim the copyright of THIS!!*"

When Thomas Noon Talfourd, Lamb's executor, introduced in Parliament the Custody of Infants Bill, it was evident that Caroline Norton's "works" had brought results. Talfourd met Caroline in 1837 and was in her company often to discuss the progress of the Bill. Their being together so often, at once considered suspicious by those who sided with her husband, incited a magazine to publish an attack on

Caroline. The writer not only called the woman a "she-devil" and a "she-beast," but implied that she and Talfourd were having adulterous relations. In a fury the maligned woman made up her mind to sue, only to realize the law would not permit her. She was at the center of a scandal that ran far and wide, even touching the shores of France, but she had no right to defend herself or even explain her position. In spite of scandal, however, the Infants Custody Act went its way in slow steps. It reached the House of Lords at the close of 1838 and became a law in the summer of 1839. It allowed mothers against whom adultery was not proven to have custody of their children under seven with access to older children. Caroline had won her battle, but only in part. Not until 1925 when Parliament passed an equal-guardianship act was her victory complete. Her agitation, grown out of pain and suffering, was very important. It called to the attention of politicians the not-so-pretty grievances of women and wives. In later years Caroline Norton was a staunch defender of women's rights in all areas of life.

She was a contemporary of those who were to spearhead the women's movement in Britain. It may be of some value to name these leaders here and show their ages in the pivotal year 1839 —

Harriet Martineau	37
John Stuart Mill	33
Elizabeth Barrett	33
Mary Carpenter	32

Caroline Norton	32
Charlotte Brontë	23
George Eliot	20
Louisa Twining	19
Anne Clough	19
Florence Nightingale	19
Frances Power Cobb	17
Barbara Lee Smith	12
Frances Mary Buss	12
Josephine Grey	11
Emily Davis	9
Elizabeth Garrett	3

To a person each of these remarkable women would work with untiring energy for the emancipation of women. It would be a struggle that wasn't over when the century ended. It would go on with new leaders and workers well into the twentieth century and beyond.

At the heart of the movement was the will and desire to correct abuses and demand unequivocally specific rights. One faction within the feminist movement wanted equal educational opportunity. Another sought free entrance to the learned professions. A third wanted work for women that for centuries had been available only to men. Another continued the work begun by Caroline Norton, demanding a share in the government of the country and an equal right to vote. Still another agitated for a new feminine morality – for greater freedom in dress, manners, social behavior, speech, and mode of living.

In 1847 several strong-minded women known for their "forward-thinking" were aided by Frederick Maurice and Charles Kingsley in setting up a series of "Lectures to Ladies." A specific aim was to improve the education of governesses, and they acted under the auspices of the Governesses' Benevolent Institution founded in 1841. The lectures, delivered by a group of professors at King's College London, soon developed into an institution, and in 1848 Queen's College for Women was established in London. The object of the college, housed in one small building, was to teach "all branches of female knowledge." The trouble with that statement of purpose, however, was that few people had even the slightest notion of what constituted "female knowledge." The comic press carried squibs about *"Professors of Bead-Purse Making, Basket Weaving Par Excellence, and Degrees in Crochet Work."* People snickered, of course, but the young women who came to improve their skills as governesses or to gain jobs as teachers blithely ignored the ridicule.

They were hungry young women, these eager first students who thronged to the classes of the new college. They clamored for knowledge, but most of them were ignorant even of rudimentary grammar and arithmetic. Before many months had gone buy it became apparent that "female knowledge" was just another term for the ordinary working equipment of a schoolboy. Most of the professors, some with doubtful qualifications, settled down to a curriculum of elementary subjects. A few held out for advanced lectures in social science, English literature, French as a spoken language, and philosophy. Also some lectures in the physical sciences were offered, and to everyone's surprise they were eagerly attended.

This seeking of knowledge on the part of women was a sign of the times. In the year after Queen's College opened its doors, Bedford College London was founded. In 1871 Newham College was established at Cambridge, and in the summer of 1873 Girton College came into being. It remained a college for women only for more than a hundred years, and the Girton Girl became famous. Male undergraduates were finally allowed in 1979. By 1873 twenty-two of the thirty-four professors at Cambridge were admitting women to their lectures. At Oxford acceptance of women in higher education was slower. But during the decade of the seventies when Oxford was in a ferment over Italian art and architecture, working-class movements, the pre-Raphaelites, Browning and the new poetry, culture as opposed to anarchy, the new science, and the higher criticism of the Bible, Oxford University was concerned also with higher education made available to young women.

When the first female students arrived in the autumn of 1879, few lectures were open to them; yet by 1884 they were attending lectures in almost every school. When London University granted full membership to women in 1878, with the chance to earn degrees (including the crucial medical degree), the fight for equal educational opportunity was over. Although some courses were altered in the belief that anatomical details might offend, women were now receiving essentially the same education as men. In defiance of the many conduct books preaching the doctrine that too much mental activity, study in a university classroom, could bring on nervous collapse, they proved themselves equal to men as students or better. With education they became in the argot of the day "strong-minded," "advanced," "forward-thinking," and extended the female revolt.

One of the earliest of the women in revolt was Florence Nightingale. Receiving her "call to duty" on February 7, 1837, she broke away from the stultified surroundings of proper young ladyhood and eventually became a nurse. Her work in the ill-equipped and poorly staffed hospitals of the Crimea in 1854 made her famous, and for the remainder of her long career she worked valiantly to improve hospital nursing. However, she was never a feminist. She had an active distaste for the feminist propaganda that multiplied so rapidly during her lifetime, and she believed too many women hadn't recognized the importance of her own work. In 1861 she wrote to Harriet Martineau, by then an influential writer and one of the first female sociologists, expressing disappointment in the struggle for equal rights: *"I am brutally indifferent to the rights and wrongs of my sex."* Clearly, she was not in sympathy with the women's movement, and yet her persistence securing practical reform in medicine and her insistence on more women becoming nurses helped a great deal.

In the same year that Florence Nightingale began to "do something" another pioneer, Frances Power Cobbe, was at a very select school for young ladies at Brighton. Her parents thought she was having the time of her life in that school, filling her bright mind with all sorts of good things. Later she was able to convince them that while the school had its charm she had been miserable there. *"In the curriculum of this school,"* she told them, *"at the bottom of the scale were morals and religion, at the top music and drawing – miserably poor music too."* Home again in Dublin, she announced that her "female education" had rendered her impatient of things intellectual and perhaps unable to gain knowledge in depth, and so she would never again attempt to learn anything. For the rest of her life she would do nothing but "read novels and enjoy myself." All that was said in moments of pique. Later she was reading books on science, philosophy, politics, and religion. Her reading ultimately led to a close study of religion with the result that she became a Deist and remained so until she died at eighty-one. An ardent social reformer advocating equal rights for women in all areas, she founded in 1875 the Society for the Protection of Animals Liable to Vivisection.

Some pioneers of the movement who received their training at Queen's College were Frances Mary Buss, Dorothea Beal, and Sophia Jex-Blake. The latter, born in 1840, became a pioneer in opening the medical profession to women. When she enrolled against her parents' wishes in Queen's College in 1858, she wanted to become "the best teacher in England." By 1860 she had decided to become a doctor. Undaunted by staggering obstacles in both England and the United States, she struggled for more than a decade to gain medical knowledge and finally sat for examinations in 1872 at Edinburgh. She failed her final examinations, but only because she had spent too much time arguing the female students' cause and too little time for study. Dismissing the setback, she went on working with petitions and legal precedents but found time to read her textbooks. Eventually in 1877 she passed her exams, received her degree, and put her name triumphantly upon the Medical Register of Great Britain. The following year London University began to offer the coveted medical degree to women, and so another long battle was won.

Meanwhile, other groups were demanding a share in the government. They studied politics with the same enthusiasm given to other activity, and with gratitude they read John Stuart Mill's *Representative Government* (1861) in which female suffrage was unmistakably advocated. In the same year that this book appeared, Mill began work on another which he called *The Subjection of Women* (1869). With the exception perhaps of *On Liberty* (1859), the book on women became the most famous of his works even though eight years passed before it saw the light of day. In those eight years a formal woman's suffrage movement had come into existence, and Mill himself brought the matter forward in the House of Commons. Afterwards agitation for the vote seemed to be making some progress, and many suffragists thought their great opportunity had arrived when the Reform Bill of 1884 was introduced. However, Prime Minister Gladstone was not in sympathy with woman's suffrage. His Bill had no mention of women, and the suffrage amendment was roundly defeated.

In subsequent years what seemed to be a vital cause made little headway. Though only the masculine half of the population had the vote, Demos appeared satisfied. Agricultural laborers were now enfranchised, and it would be years before one could expect another extension of the franchise laws. In the last decade of Victoria's reign, the women in revolt continued to seek the ballot, but it was not until 1918 that they achieved their aims with certain restrictions. In the spring of 1928 those restrictions were abolished, and women at long last were granted equal voting privileges. It had taken almost a hundred years to gain that goal, but the last glaring inequality in the legal position of women was now removed.

Meanwhile in the 1890's the feminist movement was extending itself in many directions. New ideas and new methods had been introduced, and open antagonism to male domination had markedly increased. In the propaganda of the nineties one found a tone of bitterness that to a large extent had been missing in earlier decades. There was also an element of emotionalism, sometimes bordering on hysteria, that was characteristic of more radical women who came to be called "militants." By the nineties and later the feminist movement, referred to in these years simply as "the Cause," included hundreds of women who merely desired excitement. H. G. Wells in *Ann Veronica* (1909), drew a memorable picture of feminists in the militant phase. *"I so long for jail time,"* one exclaims, *"I pray for it each and every night."* Although it now seems quite tame, the novel was considered a scandalous work in its day and was denounced by *The Spectator* as *"capable of poisoning the minds of those who read it."*

George Gissing died before the militant phase reached its climax, and yet he lived to see the meek and submissive Victorian woman become assertive and aggressive. Before his death more women were revolting than ever before, and against more things. The work of Josephine Grey Butler among "fallen women," and her campaign protesting the regulation of prostitution, had opened the eyes of numerous women. They learned with horror that thousands of women in London's West End were cooped up in brothels, exploited, bullied and abused by pimps, ill-treated by all around them, but tolerated and "protected" by the police. Women of the upper classes lived in another world and had no contact with the sordid world of the prostitute even though men could and did pass freely between them. Clearly, it was time to protest this double moral standard.

With some women deciding what to do about gender became almost an obsession. A peculiar facet of the movement was its "sex extinction" phase, the cry to put down sex altogether. If women were ever to attain full equality with men, adherents of this view held, they would have to repress those instincts that made them womanly. In some quarters they gained the reputation of becoming hysterical, so much so that journalists were calling them "the shrieking sisterhood." Though in full control of her emotions at all times, Rhoda Nunn in Gissing's *The Odd Women* (1893) is a feminist belonging to the fringes of this group. All movements, she believes, must go through a period of asceticism before achieving their aims. Christianity is a good example. In her own words: *"I am seriously convinced that before the female sex can be raised from its low level there will have to be a wide-spread revolt against sexual instinct. Christianity couldn't spread over the world without help of the ascetic ideal, and this great movement for woman's emancipation must also have its ascetics.*" Having a major character express thoughts like these proves that Gissing had studied and understood the women's movement.

Though the influence of the militants was tempered by more tolerant feminists, their speeches, writings, and public demonstrations made young women of every class restless and discontented. The daughters of England, denied the freedom they believed was their inherent right, began to see themselves as martyrs under the yoke of brutes. Soon nearly every home had at least one rebellious daughter, and the desire to escape male tyranny led to overt acts. Often the rebellious daughter was of a type widely different from those who were striving to obtain greater opportunity. She had as a rule only vague ideas as to what she wanted to do with her life, but above all, as illustrated by Wells's Anne Veronica, she wanted to be free of parental control. On occasion her discontent was strong enough to cause her to leave home, but then she found that without special training no jobs were open to her. And if she borrowed money from a wealthy man, as did Anne Veronica, she could find herself the victim of unwanted advances. In the struggle for existence the unmarried girl with no income was under the lion's paw.

If the rebellious daughter ruffled the feathers of the late-Victorian paterfamilias, the rebellious wife was even more a problem. Some wives, according to Charlotte Mary Yonge, a well-known contemporary novelist, began their rebellion with the marriage ceremony. In *Womankind* (1877), the conservative Miss Yonge who never in her life was able to meet a man to match her father, revealed facts that startled readers: *"The new lights contemn the vow of obedience. Some clergymen say that they find brides trying to slur over the word obey; and the advanced school are said to prefer a civil marriage because it can thus be avoided."* Brides were deliberately glossing over the word *obey*? Perhaps it was happening with a few but certainly not with many before the 1890's. In earlier decades most young women on that special day were eager to pronounce as clearly as they could and by rote the traditional and very old marriage vows.

Although it was generally bruited about that Ibsen's *A Doll's House* (1879) first incited wives to rebellion, evidence of this sort indicates otherwise. The play was produced in England in 1889 and exerted much influence in the nineties, but revolt was already in the air when the short-haired women and the long-haired men went to see Ibsen's drama and applauded it enthusiastically. To them it was not so much a play as a piece of propaganda, a doctrinaire dissertation on what a sinned-against wife had to do to go on living. They made up only a small part of those in attendance, but their raucous reaction to Nora's decision to walk away from home, slamming the door behind her, affected (or infected) the entire audience.

Thomas Hardy declared that Ibsen's message to women was too obvious, and yet the feminists liked it that way. Though he was more concerned with broader issues, Ibsen was hailed as a champion of the woman's cause in Europe and England. His play in three acts was dissected and discussed by scores of women happy to find an ally in a skillful dramatist. They praised the work, based on an incident in real life, as a powerful plea for the emancipation of women. Though his conversion was not immediately evident, David Lloyd George asserted that Ibsen had made him a feminist. As Prime Minister he was dominant in securing the vote for women in 1918. Those indifferent to the women's cause saw the propaganda as a detraction from the artistic merit of the play while opponents of the movement attacked Ibsen for poisoning the minds of women. The "new morality" inspired by Ibsen was seen in some quarters as downright dangerous.

Walter Besant, well-known as a novelist and historian, was convinced that Ibsen's message was something less than wholesome. In an article titled "The Doll's House and After," which appeared in the *English Illustrated Magazine* at the beginning of 1890, he took up the story where Ibsen left off and gave a dismal synopsis of what happened to Nora's family after she left home. Robbed of her womanly influence, her husband degenerates into a raging drunkard; her son becomes a good-for-nothing deadbeat and forger; and her daughter, shamed by her brother's crime, commits suicide. It was satire to be sure, but few readers laughed. Most of them agreed with Besant that many homes would come to this if women were encouraged in their wicked demand for personal independence. An uncertain number also agreed with Henry Arthur Jones, who called Nora *"the first of the tiresome hussies,"* and said the play should have ended with the husband Torvald exclaiming, *"Thank God she's gone!"*

Ibsen, of course, cannot be said to have generated entirely the keen public interest in the rights and duties of married women in the nineties. And yet his play seems to have served as a point of departure for much discussion of the subject. Much of what Gissing says about marriage, though traumatized by two failed marriages, has the echo of Ibsen. Moreover, other writers on the contemporary scene were writing diatribes exploring or explaining marital problems and insisting that marriage in most cases led irrevocably to misery. From 1888 to 1894 Mona Caird published in the *Westminster Review* a series of articles on "The Morality of Marriage." When they attracted the public's attention and became the kernel of endless conversation, *the Daily Telegraph* took up the subject. For almost a year a huge number of letters from subscribers appeared in its columns under the heading, "Is Marriage a Failure?" In those letters and those published in other journals, "the horrors of marriage" were exposed to the public with a frankness many deemed shocking. Hundreds, even thousands, of public letters prove that Gissing was not the only husband in England suffering marital disaster in the 1890's.

In that decade as well as earlier in the century, those of a more conservative bent didn't hesitate to attack the women in revolt. Prominent women in particular were persuaded to announce in a public forum their opposition to female suffrage and other aims of the movement. "An Appeal Against Female Suffrage" was published in *The Nineteenth Century* near the end of 1889 and signed by a hundred women of means, including the wives of Thomas Huxley, Leslie Stephen, Matthew Arnold, and Walter Bagehot. They were not exactly enemies of the movement and were more tolerant by far than Mrs. Eliza Lynn Linton, who became the first female salaried journalist of the era and author of over twenty novels. Though she wanted equal education for women, she deplored some of the other goals of the women's movement and the methods used to achieve them.

She began attacking the movement in the 1860's in articles and novels harsh and bitter. As late as 1898 before she died at seventy-six in July of that year, she was implacable as ever. Her articles crucifying "the wild women" were answered effectively by Mona Caird. She said Mrs. Linton, whose husband lived in America after 1867, divided women into two classes: *"the good, beautiful, submissive, charming, noble, and wise"* on the one hand, and *"the bad, ugly, rebellious, ungenerous, foolish, and liberty-demanding"* on the other. A severe critic of the feminist movement, Linton's most famous social essay on the subject was "The Girl of the Period," published in *The Saturday Review* in 1868 and reprinted more than once. It caused an uproar, and so did some of her novels that came from her pen later.

There is little doubt that some of the women in revolt were as Eliza Lynn Linton described them, but most of them were sensible women who had a job to do and did it. As to physical appearance, unless their portraits flatter them exceedingly, Mary Wollstonecraft, Caroline Norton, Florence Nightingale, and Josephine Butler were attractive women by any standard. Dr. Sophia Jex-Blake grew fat in her later years but was admired for her open and honest face. Frances Cobbe also grew hefty in middle age, but Elizabeth Garrett who became a prominent physician was tall, dignified, shapely, and serene. Women not so attractive were equally valuable to the cause that produced "the New Woman." Before the century was out she could be seen performing her daily work just about everywhere.

Chapter 3

The New Woman

In the last two decades of the nineteenth century, mainly from the feminist revolt, a woman of a new type emerged. A person of so-called advanced opinions, she went about advocating the independence of her sex, defying convention, and calling attention to herself. Observing quite plainly that she was thinking and acting in marked contrast to the traditional behavior of women, the public and press began to call her "the New Woman." In the nineties the term was used as a synonym for "the emancipated woman" and "the enlightened woman," but for some unknown reason it was always placed in capitals. At the end of the century a new set of ideals was before English women, and to describe the change the phrase "new womanhood" (without capitals) was commonly used. In Gissing's *The Crown of Life* (1899), Piers Otway is commissioned by a Russian journal to write an article on the "New Womanhood in England." As early as 1880 Gissing himself had been asked to write a series of articles for the same magazine, *Vyestnik Evropy*.

The novelist and most of his contemporaries viewed the new woman as too aggressive, as making herself conspicuous and absurd by loudly demanding refinement of rights that had already been won. The stereotype included the domineering wife, a sharp-tongued new woman who gadded about on her bicycle while her hen-pecked husband did the housework. It was generally thought that she was single by choice and bitter in her estimate of men. She claimed that for generations men had willfully abused her kind: *"Man deprived us of all knowledge. He narrowed our outlook on life so that our view of it should be all distorted, and then declared that our mistaken impression of it proved us to be senseless creatures. He cramped our minds so that there was no room for reason in them, and then made merry at our want of logic."* Now in this latter part of the nineteenth century the new woman had courageously thrown off her shackles and broken free. Because the struggle had been harsh and painful, how could she respect any man?

Yet while professing to despise men, in many instances the new woman's behavior seemed to be in deliberate imitation of them. She often dressed in a masculine way, minimizing her breasts, and displayed in her manner and conversation qualities that could hardly be called feminine. At times she smoked cigarettes in public carriages or dared to speak of female legs in print. *"A man's idea of beauty threatens always to be satisfied with the ballet dancer's legs, pretty things enough in their way,"* wrote Sarah Grand who prided herself on being a new woman. Maria Louise Ramé, who wrote under the pen name Ouida, made answer to Grand in 1894: *"The elegant epithet of cow-woman implies the contempt with which maternity is viewed by the New Woman who thinks it something fine to vote at vestries, shout at meetings, lay bare the spines of living animals, haul the gasping salmon from the river pool, and hustle male students off the benches of amphitheatres."* Though often quite attractive, the new woman nonetheless was considered unlovely and unfeminine. Responding to criticism, as the century closed she was becoming less extreme and was winning wide acceptance.

It is unlikely that Queen Victoria had much to do with the emergence of the new woman, but the mere fact that a woman was on the throne wielded some influence. Victoria had little sympathy for the women's movement and spoke out against it as it gained momentum. In a letter sent to a friend in 1860, she said: *"The Queen is most anxious to enlist everyone who can speak or write to join in checking this mad wicked folly of Women's Rights, with all it attendant horrors, on which her poor, feeble sex is bent, forgetting every sense of womanly feeling and propriety."* This was her precept, her thinking on the matter and her incipient alarm, and yet her example to some extent inspired the innovators. In the government of her country she was more than a figurehead; she took an active interest in ruling the nation in spite of agencies that limited her rule. Her precept seems to have guided conventional women while her example encouraged the rebellious ones.

These in turn encouraged greater freedom of behavior in young girls not directly a part of the movement. For years the term "fast" had been an epithet of disapproval. A magazine of the sixties, revealing distinctive bias, supplied a definition: *"In the sense now applied, 'Fast' is an Americanism and extremely vulgar, as are all Americanisms."* It was fast to attend a skating rink without the protection of a male relative; fast to cross the road to speak to a male acquaintance or look him full in the eyes; fast to wear a hat instead of a bonnet to church; fast to chew food with open lips or take more than one helping at table; and fast for a young lady to sing comic songs on Sunday. Near the end of the sixties and for the remainder of the century, many young women ignored these injunctions to live their lives with more freedom. That in turn led conservative voices to accuse them of extreme vulgarity. A leading figure, Eliza Lynn Linton, cried out that greater freedom for women was making them coarse and vulgar.

The behavior of these girls and women stirred up a stream of protest, but in this protest we get a glimpse of woman's changing position. A flabbergasted observer said a fast young woman, already beginning to show herself as a new woman, has *"an inordinate love of gaiety, a bold determined manner, a flippant style of conversation, and a glaring and sometimes immodest mode of dress."* She was speaking of costumes that revealed too much of the female anatomy, especially in summer, even though skirts were long and cumbersome. Girls in their teens were wearing less, showing disrespect for their parents, speaking ugly slang in the company of other girls, *"so repulsive in a feminine mouth,"* and riding horseback clad in pantaloons. Older fast women were shooting billiards in the company of men and smoking cigarettes sub rosa. The time all this was taking place was as early as the 1860's. Thirty years later such behavior was fairly common.

In 1868 the *Saturday Review* published a series of articles on "The Girl of the Period." Though unsigned, most readers came to know the author as straight-laced Eliza Lynn Linton. The articles were even more offensive than the attacks made upon the new woman in her novels. They were meant to show the baneful effects that the cry of emancipation was having upon the female sex in general. "The Girls of the Period," the undisclosed author wrote, *"is a creature who dyes her hair and paints her face as the first article of her personal religion; whose sole excuse for living is plenty of fun and luxury. What the demimonde does in its frantic efforts to excite attention, she also does in imitation."* That a way of life led to slang, bold talk, unseemly jesting, love of pleasure, indifference to duty, an inordinate materialism, and a horror of useful work. The writer further charged that because the modern English girl was no longer tender, loving, or domestic, she had much difficulty finding a husband: *"All men whose opinion is worth having prefer the simple and genuine girl of the past with her tender little ways and bashful modesties."* But the taste of freedom was sweet, and the girl of the period would never again return to the stultifying ideal of the past.

In the same magazine a later article described that type of woman whose cries for equality were an influence on the young girls of the time. Intellectual or at least pretending to be, *"she entrenches herself in the 'ologies; adores Mr. Kingsley because he is earnest; takes up the grievances of her sex; pronounces old men fogies and young men intolerable. Her character like her face is rigid and osseous; she plunges into science and cuts her hair short to be in proper trim for Professor Huxley's lectures."* In later decades this ossified woman (as Mrs. Linton would have her) would crowd into college classrooms throughout the land and read *Sesame and Lilies* (1871) with a frozen frown on her face. Though she could appreciate Ruskin's poetic style, his romantic-chivalric view of women would rub her the wrong way. Archly she would declare the book *"rather stodgy, dull, and top-heavy with old-fashioned opinion."*

In George Gissing's *Thyrza* (1887) Annabel Newthorpe, who belongs to a higher class than the workgirl of the title, is seen reading Ruskin's *Sesame and Lilies* (1865) in moments of leisure. When asked what she thinks of the book, she replies: "I think it very beautiful and very noble." Her remark surprises no one because she isn't one of Gissing's emancipated women. The young women of "advanced" opinion in his work like to show off scientific volumes whether they've read them or not. Nancy Lord of *In the Year of Jubilee*, trying hard to impress others as a new woman, places a book on evolution on the drawing-room table simply for show. When she and Lionel Tarrant visit the library, she selects from the shelf Hermann von Helmholtz's *Lectures on Scientific Subjects*. Its author was one of the great scientists of the day. Ironically he died in the year *Jubilee* was published (1894), and yet by then his most valuable work had been translated into English.

With unusual perception a few intellectuals were calling the girl of the 1870's "the coming woman." The Girton girl, for example, was obtaining a higher education equal to that of men, and she was beginning to show off her knowledge. In 1879 a gentleman complained that he had chanced to sit next to such a girl at dinner. *"She was so amazingly scientific and profoundly intellectual that I was appalled. Repelling my ordinary remarks with a freezing stare, she started volubly on Comtism, Darwinism, and Bathybism and paid no attention to my discomfort."* Bathybism? The gentleman could have meant the girl spoke of bathybates, a genus of predatory cichlids endemic to Lake Tanganyika in east Africa. Or maybe she wanted her listener to know about sea depth. Brightness of intellect and a tendency to display it regardless of the consequences were dominant traits of the new woman.

Education and the new womanhood were inseparable. To become well-educated or at least well-read was the ambition of every new woman. A journalist for a daily newspaper in 1886 based his vivid description on information gleaned from interviews: *"She is highly educated, attends lectures and concerts. She reads Morris and Rossetti and Walter Pater. In lighter moments she reads Ouida and Miss Braddon, for Dickens is out of date. She learns carving and fretwork and paints on china. She is devoted to her brothers in a somewhat condescending way. An admirable tennis player, she has been known to get the better of them at tennis. She knows quite well what she is about, and is absolutely sincere in her likes and dislikes, which she is apt to express with considerable candour."* Ouida, whose real name was Maria Louise Ramé, was not in sympathy with the new woman. She was, however, a well-known novelist, a celebrity of the time, and the friend of many influential people. Oscar Wilde, Algernon Swinburne, Robert Browning, Wilkie Collins, and the artist John Millais attended her soirées for evenings of music and good conversation. Mary Elizabeth Braddon was a popular novelist best known for *Lady Audley's Secret* (1862). A prolific writer, she produced more than eighty novels with inventive plots now in the dust bin of history.

Formerly the English girl had been carefully guarded in what she read, but Ruskin instructed parents to let her loose in the library "as you do a fawn in a field." By the 1880's the daughters of England were reading in all directions, causing alarm among their mothers who were unable to accept Ruskin's advice. One of them complained in 1885: *"I can't tell what is coming to the girls nowadays. I was never allowed to read such books; I never talked of such things; why my mother would have fainted if I had even heard of such gossip as the girls discuss nowadays."* Others grumbled that while Mudie's Lending Library was careful not to bring a blush to a maiden's face, the book stores were full of pernicious stuff to seduce innocent girls, *"novels with which no pure-minded woman ought to soil her fingers."* While Mudie tried his best to offer exclusively innocuous books (to the detriment of authors wanting realism in their work), the new woman found his fare too bland. She was strong-minded rather than pure-minded, and she deliberately sought books that Mudie wouldn't stock.

This could explain Gissing's popularity among female readers. In 1895 he wrote to his German friend Bertz: *"It is strange how many letters I get from women, asking for sympathy and advice. I really can't understand what it is in my work that attracts the female mind."* A definition of the strong-minded woman was supplied by Charlotte Yonge in 1882: *"A strong-minded woman is a term for one who is either ungentle or unwilling to be bound by the restrictions of her sex. It is a piece of modern slang and does not reflect true feminine strength of mind."* Education brought strength of mind. It was of utmost importance to the new women because it also opened doors to allow them to be independent. Many of them understood that they would never be able to marry, and through education they could prepare themselves for useful lives independent of men. Before the middle of the 1880's young girls were beginning to understand they need not look to marriage as their only goal. Marriage was elusive and they were no longer content to idle away the best years of their lives waiting for a future that might never materialize. So they made it their business to "know everything," to read anything available to them, anything from suspect French novels of romance and intrigue to the evening papers.

It must not be supposed that all the new women were bluestockings, intellectuals spending most of their time in the Reading Room of the British Museum. In the 1860's Ouida was said to have written many of her novels in bed by candlelight with curtains drawn and surrounded by purple flowers. By the time the 1870's came on the scene, the new female writers knew full well that physical exercise was good for them and seldom lounged in bed. Some were up at the break of day wandering the streets of London, even visiting dangerous neighborhoods, for literary material. Others when they could afford it traveled far and wide or played tennis. Some among the new women had come across Juvenal's phrase *mens sana in corpore sano* and quickly decided as they improved their minds they couldn't neglect their bodies. As a consequence they began to engage in sports more strenuous than the croquet of the sixties, and displayed more and more physical activity that became a sign of the times. In the eighties the trend continued, and in the nineties it culminated in the bicycle riding that swept the nation.

Physicians were so vociferous in pointing out the healthful effects of riding bicycles that even sedentary Gissing was persuaded to try it. H. G. Wells introduced Gissing to the machine. Experimenting with autobiography, he wrote a delightful account of the day they went riding: *"He talked very much of ill health and I tried to make him a cyclist, for he took no exercise at all except walking, and I thought it might be pleasant to explore Surrey and Sussex with him, but he was far too nervous and excitable to ride. It was curious to see this well-built Viking blowing and funking as he hopped behind his machine. 'Get on your ironmongery,' said I. He mounted, wobbled a few yards, and fell off shrieking with laughter. 'Ironmongery!' he gasped, and lay in the grass at the roadside helpless with mirth."* The warm and pleasant passage came from a man who often found fault with the people who listed themselves as his friends.

Among the feminists the bicycle was as an important instrument of emancipation, for it widened the horizons of women. It wasn't until the early nineties that women began to entertain the idea that moving about freely on any conveyance at their command was not only a pleasant activity but good for their health. When they saw men riding bicycles, they asked why can't we do it too? When a few tried it and found it "incredibly venturous," others followed suit even though observers, looking at them with jaundiced eye, found them shocking. The shock was intensified by the fact that in the early days, when there were only men's bicycles, riding had to be done in bloomers. It was a costume introduced in England as early as 1851 by Amelia Jenks Bloomer, an American feminist and temperance worker. It consisted of a jacket with tight sleeves, a skirt reaching a little below the knees, and a pair of Turkish pantaloons secured by elastic bands around the waist and ankles. The costume was certainly an improvement over the cumbersome garments then in fashion, and though adopted by a number of women, it failed to hold its own against prejudice and ridicule.

One striking innovation (the bicycle) compounded with another (bloomers) was more than the public could tolerate. Those who insisted on giving both a good try were hooted in the streets, and little boys flung mud at their legs. Yet the new women, having long since learned to ignore ridicule, found much pleasure in riding. Moreover, the bicycle brought a physical freedom they had never known before. They were no longer confined by duties to their respective homes;

they could spin off whenever they felt like it as far as half a dozen miles from home. Although female use of the new machines brought acute opposition from a large portion of the population, the feminists urged their followers to conquer the world on wheels. A bevy of new women wrote lyrical books on the subject. Lady Henry Somerset gave Frances Willard a bicycle. She called it "Gladys" and referred to it as *"that harbinger of health and happiness."* Doctors advocated cycling as a remedy for *"dyspepsia, torpid liver, incipient consumption, nervous exhaustion, rheumatism, and melancholia."* Moreover, it got women out of doors, eased *"their nervous troubles,"* and made them strong.

After a time certain modifications were made to allow women in skirts to ride the bicycle. But even the modified machines pointed up the need for more sensible female dress. Inevitably as women became more active their dress became less voluminous. In the next century they would free themselves of ankle-length skirts, and the hems would get shorter and shorter. Their clothing would become more simple, lighter, and more comfortable, and that brought more activity and better health. Their hair, trimmed by a few as early as the late sixties, would become universally short except among older women. The new womanhood would gradually be accepted by virtually all women. Sporadic attempts would be made from time to time to reinstate the old ideal but with little success. The new woman was alive and well and on the scene to stay.

Chapter 4

Gissing's Womanly Women

During his career as a novelist, a time spanning the last two decades of the nineteenth century, George Gissing gave much attention to the role of women in society. Early in 1882 he wrote to his sister Ellen, expecting her to convey his remarks to their older sister Margaret: *"You girls nowadays have astonishing advantages over your mothers and grandmothers; it is only to be hoped you will make use of it for the only real end of education – improvement of character. If you only could know how much of the wretchedness of humanity is occasioned by the folly, pigheadedness, ignorance and incapacity of women you would rejoice to think of all these new opportunities for mental and moral training."* After the publication of *The Odd Women* in 1893, he revealed identical sentiments in a letter to his German friend, Eduard Bertz: *"I doubt whether we are greatly at variance in our views of the woman question. My demand for female 'equality' simply means that I am convinced there will be no social peace until women are intellectually trained very much as men are. More than half the misery of life is due to the ignorance and childishness of women. I am driven frantic by the crass imbecility of the typical woman. That type must disappear, or at all events become altogether subordinate."*

Convinced that the old ideal of the womanly woman in Victorian life was injurious not only to women but to society as a whole, as he struggled to make a name for himself he vehemently opposed that view. However, as with other major issues as he entered the 1890's, a time when innovation and change were in the air, his thoughts on the subject moved into a state of flux. The position he had taken on the woman question in the early years of his career had changed considerably by 1894, but the change was not complete until 1901. To the end, however, he believed education would bring about a better woman in English life, and that belief was confirmed in the woman from France, Gabrielle Fleury, whom he met in 1898.

When Gissing settled in London in 1878 after spending a year in America, he began to write long letters to his sisters, Margaret and Ellen, advising them to read substantial books and take their studies seriously. He wanted them to become self-dependent, sensible, educated women as opposed to the ignorant clinging vine promoted by the old Victorian ideal of woman. In his letters he is much concerned with opening to them the precepts of the new education then available to women. In May of 1880 he said to them that a girl's education should be general and liberal in character, designed to expand intelligence rather than impart thorough knowledge of any one subject. It seems obvious he was influenced by Ruskin's thought, but he went beyond that to believe a woman could become enlightened if at first her mind were free of dogma and expanded.

Should his sisters fail to reach that goal, they could at least develop into self-reliant young women. To Ellen he wrote at the end of 1886: *"I daresay you are quite old enough to travel by yourself. Of course it would be better if you had someone with you, but after all the self-reliant woman is the best, one that would go from here to San Francisco with perfect ease and simplicity. It becomes a woman to have knowledge of the world, and not to be a helpless puppet."* Then in 1887 he placed before Ellen the Renaissance ideal of education: *"I often think of that story of Lady Jane Grey sitting on a summer's morning reading Plato. A strange thing that it has taken these centuries to get back, to begin to get back, to the ideal of woman's education which the Elizabethans had."* At about the same time he observed that one of his students had an intense desire to read Homer in the original – he was earning a few shillings as a tutor – and he hinted that he wanted his sisters to develop a love of the classics.

They should also read the great English and European writers, Shakespeare in particular: *"A woman is a mere duffer if she is not able to read Shakespeare with perfect intelligence of his vocabulary."* They could even dip into some of the greater works of American literature, as he had done himself, and go beyond fiction. In addition to creative and imaginative literature, they should become acquainted with the best currents of intellectual opinion and be able to discuss in a social setting the prevailing ideas of the day. With emphasis he declared they should read anything that would broaden their minds and lead them away from sour little religious books. Of these he had no sympathy whatever but feared they would somehow fasten upon the minds of his sisters and corrupt them. Ellen was younger and more open of mind than Margaret whose piety irritated him. Her reading habits were also a source of vexation, for when he relaxed with Ovid when on a summer holiday together, she busied herself with *"some dirty little pietistic work"* and could speak only of facts.

To his dismay he was to discover later that Ellen too was a victim of the Puritanical bent. When *The Emancipated* came out in 1890, she accused him in an angry letter of using her as the model for Miriam Baske. He replied immediately, attempting in well-chosen words to pacify her: *"It is a delusion to suppose that I identify you with Miriam. Nothing of the kind. You have grown up in a far more liberal atmosphere."* Even so, he confided to his commonplace book that it was impossible to talk with either of his sisters about *"the inner things of one's heart and mind."* A deep-seated Puritanism didn't allow them to talk about sex or sexual relations *"even to the extent permissible in other English households."* Any time he and Ellen ventured on the subject – it couldn't be done at all with Margaret – they found themselves in a ridiculous game of cat and mouse and exhausted all their ingenuity devising vagueness of speech. He was surely thinking of his sisters when he spoke in admiration of a character in *The Odd*

Women (1893): *"No Grundyism in Rhoda Nunn; no simpering, no mincing of phrases."*

When *Born in Exile* was published in 1892, both sisters expressed regret that Gissing had strayed so far from the Church. Margaret's letter, reeking with unadulterated piety, left him disgusted and irritated and trying to understand how she could send him such nonsense in the wake of his publishing another good book. While he was in the act of trying to enjoy his achievement, his sister professing deepest love for him – and she was deeply sincere – was taking it upon herself to chastise him for his loss of faith in the old-time religion. All he could do was shake his head as he read: *"Apropos of* '*Born in Exile,*' Madge writes to me – '*It is a pity you should write on a subject you so little understand as Christianity. It would be as reasonable for me to deny the existence of all the beautiful things you have seen and told me of in foreign countries, simply because I have not seen them, as it is for you to deny spiritual things you have never seen or felt, when there are thousands of people who have seen them; and are therefore as certain of them as of their own existence. How anyone can disbelieve the Bible merely because it is not written in the latest scientific language seems remarkable.*'" His reaction: *"How impossible to reply to such stuff as this!"*

Though he fought against it, he was beginning to feel that the long years of tutoring his sisters by mail had been wasted. They had been reared in a stronghold of Puritanism and had not been able to throw off the mantle of dogma. Before the decade was over, however, he was believing that maybe their faith in God and the afterlife had kept them sane, and maybe their piety wasn't so bad after all. Despite his efforts to enlighten them, they remained virginal womanly women going to church each Sunday and eventually opening a school of their own. While they in time became rather prudish old maids, at least they escaped the stigma of being deemed superfluous.

How far his sisters failed to meet the best ideal of the womanly woman can be seen in *Isabel Clarendon* (1886). Isabel is an orthodox woman with a traditional education, but living in the midst of wealth and leisure she has cultivated the most desirable of those traits that men for generations have admired as womanly, and Gissing himself admired her. In *Demos* (1886) Adela Waltham is another womanly woman he admired. When the book was about to come from the press, he wrote to Ellen: *"The heroine, by name Adela, you will think delightful, or so she seems to me at all events."* Later after reading the reviews of the new novel, he said: *"I regret that few people seem to understand and appreciate Adela Waltham. I fancy she will always be a great favourite of mine."* Perhaps Gissing was deceived by his own creation. Adela is obedient, self-sacrificing, and goody-goody to be sure, but in most instances as the story unfolds she proves herself more tiresome than delightful. That was the opinion of his sisters.

In his next novel, *Thyrza* (1887) Gissing imparted qualities of the womanly woman to an idealized portrait of a working girl, and again he fell in love with his own creation: *"Thyrza herself is one of the most beautiful dreams I ever had or shall have."* In Emily Hood of *A Life's Morning* (1888) he created another womanly woman, but again he confused conventional womanhood with saintliness. By now he was beginning to realize that his idea of the womanly woman, when translated to paper, seemed as idealistic and as unreal as Ruskin's. *"It is quite certain,"* he confided to Bertz, *"that some of my own girls and women err on the side of goodness. It is easy to tell an author that his women don't please one's critical sense, but damnably hard to sit down and represent the women one has in mind."* Already he had decided to leave off attempting to portray the womanly woman as an angel-woman. In later novels he would place her opposite the emancipated woman, and she would lose in the comparison. Near the end of his career he would make a show of returning to his earlier position.

In the middle of the 1880's he was becoming increasingly interested in the feminist movement but didn't begin to show that interest in his work until the beginning of the next decade. In September of 1888 he went to Paris and from there to Italy. On October 2, at the Salle des Conférences, he attended a lecture by Clémence Louise Michel, a well-known feminist, on the role of women in the world. In his diary he didn't mention the trouble he surely had understanding the woman's rapid French. Apparently he understood enough of what she said, for her message impressed him even though her looks left much to be desired: *"I had expected to see a face with more refinement in it; she looks painfully like a fishwife. Dressed with excessive plainness in black and wearing an ugly bonnet. Much fluency, of course, and signs of intellect. Demanded absolute equality of women with men in education and rights."* The fact that Gissing went to such a lecture during the crowded days of his first journey abroad is ample evidence of a healthy and growing interest in the woman question.

Shortly afterwards he would begin writing *The Emancipated* (1890) in which he would show a remarkable womanly woman with flaws that when corrected would leave her emancipated. Miriam Baske is a beautiful young widow of narrow Puritan persuasion and smitten by spiritual pride. We first see her writing letters beside a window that looks out on the Bay of Naples. Stunning in its beauty, the bay doesn't stir her interest at all; she doesn't bother to notice it: *"You need not envy me the beauty of Naples, for it gives me no pleasure."* The tone of the letters addressed to friends in the midland town of Bartles is petulant, vindictive, and gloomy: *"I have a very good mind to write to Mr. Higginson and beg him to suspend the girl from his employment until she becomes regular in her attendance at worship. She and her mother ought to be punished in some way. Speak to them sternly."* Eleanor Spence, a relative, has broken away from "the bondage of dogma" and isn't certain what to make of Miriam: *"I don't profess to understand her. Her character is not easily sounded. But no doubt she has the Puritanical spirit in a rather rare degree. She doesn't really live in Naples. From the first day she has shown herself bent on resisting every influence of the place. She won't admit that the climate benefits her; she won't allow interest in anything Italian."* Her doctrine will not permit her even to enjoy the fine weather. On Sundays there must be no piano playing and no reading for entertainment. At the dinner table no one must laugh or crack a joke.

At eighteen Miriam was married to *"one Mr. Baske, a pietistic mill-owner, aged fifty."* When he died two years later, he left her an enviable income of eight hundred pounds a year. Her wealth brought her power and she became a leader among the dissenters in Bartles. Now she is planning to pull down her expensive house and build in its place a bigger and better chapel. It is spiritual pride rather than religious zeal that drives her to make these plans. Moreover, her leadership is threatened by another woman with money, and so she must act promptly. The blueprints for the new chapel she brings with her to Naples, expecting to study them and make decisions. When she puts them out of sight, we have the first indication she is beginning to throw off the mantle of Puritanism. After a month in Italy she is reading Dante on Sunday and beginning to enjoy the sunshine. The movement is from strict Hebraism to enlightened Hellenism.

As time passes a spiritual change occurs in the young woman. As she begins to feel the allurement of Italy she takes pleasure in resting her eyes upon form and color. Instead of sitting bolt upright in a carriage, she relaxes on the cushions and develops a longing for the sound of music. Her costume gives way to a dash of color and even her appetite improves: *"The abundant fruits of the season became a temptation to her palate."* For the first time she begins to taste the pleasure of books. Earlier she *"had never read a book that would not pass her mother's censorship,"* and that lady approved only of sour little works of piety. She discovers she has a brain and can use it, learns Italian, and reads poetry for the first time. As time passes she begins to look younger, dresses in clothing adapted to the country, and gives up her plans to build a chapel in Bartles. In three years Miriam's transformation is complete although *"sculpture still alarms her."* Unable to come to terms with nudity, the nude statues in Italy bring a feeling of shame and disgust. In Bartles again she builds a public bath instead of a chapel. Entirely emancipated, her spiritual voyage has taken her from the hebraic ideal as defined by Matthew Arnold to to the hellenic ideal.

While Miriam Baske is a dynamic character in the process of changing from "womanly" to "new," the six Madden sisters in *The Odd Women* (1893) are presented as weak, static, and conventional. Trained in the old ways, they are incapable of adjusting to changing times. Their education consists of those genteel accomplishments traditionally expected of young ladies of the upper-middle class: learning to read passably, learning to write without spelling errors, and learning by rote a few pieces of music for the piano. The house has many books and their father has encouraged them to read, but it has never occurred to him that his daughters should prepare for good jobs should he not be able to support them. Their education, therefore, has no practical value and doesn't fit them for the world. So when Dr. Madden dies of an accident and they have to support themselves, they feel helpless and terribly afraid. Half of their number quickly perish, leaving the remaining three to survive any way they can. Since they are not able to marry, they can only become governesses at low salaries, companions at even lower wages, or shopgirls in a lower social class.

Their story illustrates Gissing's interest in the economic problems of the woman question, specifically the problems confronting conventionally trained women who were not able to marry and thus had to support themselves. Repeatedly asking middle-class parents to provide their daughters with an education they can use in a practical way, his earliest instruction on this subject appears in *Isabel Clarendon* (1886): *"Of no greater unkindness can parents be guilty than to train as if for a life of leisure children whose lot will inevitably be to earn a livelihood by day-long toil. It is to sow in them the seeds of despair. Do not heed the folly of those who say that culture is always a blessing; the truth is that, save under special circumstances, it is an unmitigated curse."* The Madden sisters are presented as odd women, superfluous women, because they are victims of the older ideal of womanhood. Perhaps the most famous of Gissing's conventional women, they are unwanted by a crass and commercial society and unwanted by any eligible man in marriage because they are plain, except for Monica, and have no money.

Because a full discussion of the Madden sisters appears in a later chapter, it's unnecessary to say more about them here.

I should note, however, that upon publication contemporary critics acclaimed *The Odd Women* (1893) the best of Gissing's books, and today it ranks as one of his best. But Gissing himself had a low opinion of the book. He wrote it in six weeks in the autumn of 1892, and because the task of writing went much faster than any of his former novels, he believed his preparation had been rather shaddy with not enough indisputable thought going into the story. On the last day of 1892 he noted in his diary that the year had not been a good one. He said it had been a year of domestic misery and discomfort and profitless except for the one book done in record time. When he finished the last chapter of *The Odd Women* on October 4, 1892, he noted: *"I have written it very quickly but the writing has been as severe a struggle as ever I knew. Not an hour when I was really at peace in mind. A bitter struggle."*

The remark came as no surprise to his sisters. Every novel that saw the light of day was the result of long, hard labor. He complained that he often threw away more paper, as he struggled to write, than he used. Although writing fiction didn't come easy for George Gissing, from the time he published his first novel in 1880 until his death in 1903, he authored an average of one book a year. In 1895 he published as many as three short novels. It wasn't long before his readers began to appreciate him as a novelist probing social issues, and before his untimely death he had gained a reputation as more than a petty scribbler.

Chapter 5

The Marriage Market

Many young women in Gissing's work are so eager to marry they can talk of nothing else. In *A Life's Morning* (1888) the five nubile Cartwright sisters are so preoccupied with attracting a male they can think of nothing else. Though ready to marry, the supply of marriageable men is not a good one, and so the chance to realize their dream is small indeed. They live in a dull little town called Dunfield and must compete with maidens better looking and better off financially. With neither money nor beauty – *"a parcel of schoolboys would have been as provocative"* – they can only dream of romance and talk incessantly of love-making and flirtation. Of the five, Jessie Cartwright is more man-crazy than the others. By means of subtle suggestion – Mrs. Grundy wouldn't allow him to do more – Gissing implies the girl is feeling sexual urges that lead her to prattle constantly about men and marriage. Whenever the subject changes in conversation, she returns to her favorite subject within a few minutes. *"I can't see what else there is to talk about,"* she tells Emily Hood. *"What a grown-up girl has to do is look out for a husband. How you can be satisfied with books is more than I can make out."*

It seems hard to believe, but the supply of young women was so large and the demand so small that many were willing quite literally to sell themselves into marriage. In *The Odd Women* (1893) a mature female character tells Widdowson that she knows half a dozen young women off hand who would jump at the chance to marry a man with his money. *"Don't you know, dear boy, that there are heaps of ladies, real ladies, waiting to marry the first decent man who offers them five or six hundred a year?"* Impractical and out of tune with the times, Widdowson can't believe what he's hearing: *"Do you seriously tell me there are ladies in good society who would have married me just because I have a few hundreds a year?"* The woman replies that she could get together *"a round dozen in two or three days. Girls who would make good, faithful wives in mere gratitude to the man who saved them from horrors."* This question of "immoral morality," as Gissing called it, generated much discussion. When a girl married solely for economic security, couldn't it be said she was no better than the women who stood under the street lamps? Emily Hood in *A Life's Morning* (1888) believes that a woman who sells herself with ecclesiastical sanction differs "only in degree of impurity" from the one plying her trade on the pavement. In *Denzil Quarrier* (1892), Gissing poses an ethical question: Who is to be accused of immoral behavior, Lilian for giving herself out of wedlock to Quarrier or the Mumbrays, married but despising each other?

Plainly, English girls were not willing to marry if it meant living in poverty. On this score alone thousands refrained from marrying eligible and willing young men. The laws of primogeniture held that the eldest son received most of a father's wealth at time of death, and this situation left the younger sons almost penniless. Some of them went into the military, business, or the professions, but the time needed for a man to "arrive" was much longer than in previous centuries. Also the cost of living was going up steadily, and lacking effective birth control, numerous men hesitated to marry for fear of creating a large family. It was cheaper to satisfy sexual appetite in a brothel. So while many nubile young women pined away for lack of husband and home, prostitution flourished. Biffen in *New Grub Street* (1891) would like nothing better than to marry but doesn't dare even to think about it because of his poverty: *"Already thirty-five years old, he had no prospect of even being rich enough to assure himself a daily dinner; marriage was wildly out of the question."* Later when Biffen is on the brink of suicide, it is said of him: *"He could not bear to walk the street where the faces of beautiful women would encounter him. He must die without having known the touch of a loving woman's hand."* Again, though striving for realism, Gissing couldn't resist ubiquitous Victorian pathos.

Whelpdale in the same novel has been engaged to marry four times, but *"every time the girl has got out of it at the last moment."* They jilted him because he was honest enough to tell them he was poor. On the other hand, numerous men were unwilling to marry women who didn't have money. Milvain in *New Grub Street* (1891) repeatedly declares that but for Marian Yule's poverty he would gladly marry her. Winifred Haven in *The Odd Women* (1893) is good looking and personable, but lacking a dowry she finds it difficult to marry: *"She has no money but what she can earn, and such girls, unless they are exceptionally beautiful, are very likely indeed to remain unsought."* Winifred Chittle of *In the Year of Jubilee* (1894) is plain, insipid, spoiled, and indiscreet; but since she will soon become an heiress, her chances to marry are excellent. In the same novel Stephen Lord worries that "some plotting, greedy fellow" will marry his daughter Nancy for the money he plans to leave her. These fortune hunters roamed through all levels of society. In the leisure class Vincent Lacour of *Isabel Clarendon* (1886) tries without success to marry Ada Warren for the inheritance she will soon receive. In *Demos* (1886) Alice Mutimer of the working class comes into money and wishes to keep it a secret because she knows a girl with money gets chased after by men who care nothing for her but much about the money.

The girl with money had no trouble whatever finding a mate, but the girl without it was faced with enormous competition. In *The Odd Women* (1893) Gissing referred to this state of affairs, all too common in his day, as "the marriage war." This severe competition made English girls extremely prejudiced of foreign women. Some considered it almost a crime for a man to marry a woman from another country and bring her home to England. In *Demos* (1886) when Adela Waltham believes Hubert Eldon is planning to marry a foreign woman, she becomes *"cold as ice, not a spark of love in all her being."* In *A Life's Morning* (1888) Philip Athel *"wedded his Italian maiden, brought her to England, and fought down prejudices."* Later he comes to believe he should have given his love to an English lady. Of more than 400 female characters in Gissing's fiction, fewer than a dozen appear to be of foreign extraction. His fictional characters, both male and female, are almost exclusively English. He was concerned with the problems of England and how a thinking person might find solutions.

As we have seen, a sure index of the keen competition in the marriage market could be found in the attire of women. With no wealth to lure a man, a girl had to resort to the allurements of physical beauty accented by suggestive clothing. Worldly Lady Kent in *Isabel Clarendon* (1886) urges Isabel's mother to allow her to debut in society while the bloom of youth is still radiant on her cheek: *"She had just been 'finished off' with the ordinary accomplishments, and if she now 'came out' there was much probability of her attracting a suitable husband. What was the use of beauty to a girl if not to get her an establishment in life? There was no disgrace in standing up and proclaiming oneself to be disposed of; the folly and the danger would lie in trying to keep out of sight."* In the same novel an incident involving a friend of Isabel's throws light on how far women were willing to expose themselves in the hunt for a mate: *"It fell to Asquith to take down to dinner a certain miss Pye, a tall young lady with a long thin nose, simply dressed in white with much exposure of bust. This décolleté costume was a thing Robert found it impossible to get used to; he felt if he went on dining with ladies for another five and twenty years, there would still arrive in him the same sensation of amazement. Singular questions of social economy invariably suggested themselves. How far was this fashion a consequence of severe competition in the marriage market?"* Beatrice Redwing in *A Life's Morning* (1888) is resplendent in a dark blue gown with *"bosom and arms radiant in bare loveliness."*

Bodily exposure was one way to attract a man, but a more subtle expression was the use of delicate perfumes or in some instances mere soap and water. In *Born in Exile* (1892), after Janet Moxey leaves a group of people, *"There lingered behind her that peculiar fragrance of modern womanhood, refreshing, inspiriting, which is so entirely different from the merely feminine perfume, however exquisite."* Though Janet has become a physician, it is unlikely the aroma trailing behind her is from the clinic. The fragrance is that of feminine cleanliness accomplished by ample use of scented soap and water. Concerned more with success in her profession than with marriage, she doesn't find it necessary to use perfume or wear revealing clothing.

The sexual lure was meant to arouse the interest of a man, and then with the carrot dangling before him he could be led to the altar. But some girls in a desperate bid for marriage deliberately allowed the carrot to be eaten beforehand. By means of inverse seduction a few desperate women tried to force a man into matrimony. Despicable Harriet Smales in

The Unclassed (1884) lures Julian Casti into "a man trap" and seduces him through lies and trickery. Clara Hewett in *The Nether World* uses her expertise as an actress to snare Sidney Kirkwood. Since her face has been burned with acid, she is careful to set the scene in a darkened, private room where she may show herself to best advantage. Her skillful acting strikes dormant chords of sympathy and sentiment in the guileless Kirkwood, who falls into her trap and fails to escape. Another victim of this inverse seduction is Everard Barfoot in *The Odd Women* (1893), but showing himself as shrewd as his seducer, he manages to wiggle free.

Later he tells a friend that a girl named Amy Drake got him in a private railway car and literally threw herself on him. She hoped that by becoming pregnant he would marry her without resistance. He got her pregnant but agreed only to support the child. When the incident became known, his family and friends expressed disapproval of the way he treated the girl. To Rhoda Nunn he explains: "*What those good people didn't understand was the girl's character. They thought her a helpless innocent; she was a -----, I'll spare you the word. She simply planned to get me into her power, thought I would marry her. It's the kind of thing that happens far oftener than you would suppose.*" In the novel published a year later, *In the Year of Jubilee* (1894), Nancy Lord allows herself to be seduced by Lionel Tarrant, the man she hopes to marry. When the sexual act is over and the two are relaxing, Tarrant muses at length over what has happened and whether the conquest was his or hers. The incident becomes an exercise in ratiocinative give and take. At times he thinks too much, at other times too little.

In life and in art the Victorian womanly woman competed more readily in the marriage market than the emancipated woman. From girlhood she had been taught that marriage was her ultimate goal, and when it became very difficult for a girl in the middle classes to marry, it was necessary to compete with whatever means she could muster. The feminists, on the other hand, claimed they could live full and useful lives independent of men. While most of Gissing's strong-minded women are strongly sexed, they manage to steer clear of marriage. Those who do marry, for example Cecil Doran of *The Emancipated* (1890), are afterwards quite miserable. The conventional girl with youth, beauty, and money could marry and usually did, but lacking these enticements many remained unmarried. A major aim of the feminists was to find ways to help women who couldn't marry.

Though many young women in Gissing's novels yearn to marry, those who do often find marriage intolerable. Gissing's work, taken as a whole, amounts to a severe indictment of one of the most cherished of Victorian institutions. We may wonder why, and we may find the answer in Gissing's own experience. His first marriage was a horror and so was his second. Although he managed to free himself of both, domestic misery over several years left emotional scars not to be erased. The hurt he was feeling inevitably came into the novels he wrote when married and also when unattached.

Only near the end did he find an anodyne in a symbolic marriage to Gabrielle Fleury. She tried hard to heal his wounds but with only varying degrees of success. The damage had been done and the novels show it. Adela Waltham's marriage to Richard Mutimer in *Demos* (1886) soon becomes "an unnatural horror," and she thinks of flight: *"There were hours when Adela's soul was like a bird of the woods cage-pent: it dashed itself against the bars of fate, and in anguish conceived the most desperate attempts for freedom."* Her Puritan conscience, however, will not allow her to forsake her husband, and so she accepts her lot without complaint.

Adela believes there is no other way to please her husband than submitting to him entirely, losing her identity in his: *"She very seldom turned her eyes to his but there was humility in her bent look. If ever he and she began to speak at the same time, she checked herself instantly and Mutimer had no thought of giving her precedence. This behaviour in his wife struck him as altogether becoming."* But as time passes her maudlin servility irritates him and he becomes nasty. When Mutimer accuses her of infidelity, he manages to make her angry enough to say their marriage is over. A moment later she is making her husband a cup of tea, justifying her meek surrender with these thoughts: *"As helpless in his hands as though he had purchased her in a slave market, of what avail to sit like a perverse child?"* Improbably admired by Gissing, Adela is shown as a womanly woman content to be owned by a domineering husband. Her characteristics are patience, self-sacrifice, and a willingness to submit her will to one that is stronger. To do so, she believes, is in the order of things. Disrupting order in a marriage inevitably brings chaos, and that she will avoid at all cost.

In the same novel Alice Mutimer, ironically the sister of Adela's brutish mate, must submit also to a domineering husband. Called "the Princess" because of her good looks and haughty behavior, she scorns the proposal of the mild Mr. Keene to accept Rodman. The name alone describes him, an inflexible man hard as steel who must always have his way. His little wife is completely under his thumb: *"You've got to learn that when I tell you to do a thing, you do it or I'll know the reason why!"* To emphasize the injunction, he seizes her by the wrist *"in a clutch that seemed to crush the muscles"* and flings her back on a chair. Five years later in 1891 Gissing remarked that just such an action as this would have saved, at least temporarily, the marriage of Edwin Reardon in *New Grub Street* (1891): *"He had but to do one thing, seize her by the arm, drag her up from the chair, dash her back again with all his force – there, the transformation would be complete, they would stand towards each other on the natural footing."* Some writers on Gissing have said this is the first time this idea appears in his work, but they are in error. Using force on a rebellious wife occurs as early as the first novel, *Workers in the Dawn* (1880). When his wife tries to shoot him, Waghorn brutally flings her to the floor.

Long-suffering Alice Mutimer, the Princess, not only must endure physical abuse from Rodman, but mental and emotional abuse as well. When she complains of boredom one afternoon, he calls her names and taunts her, saying any beauty she ever had is fading fast: *"I'll tell you one thing, old girl, you're losing your good looks. Nothing like what you were when I married you."* When friends suggest he married her only for her money, she denies it and defends him. However, he runs through her inheritance in no time at all and baits her with the suggestion that she might have to take in washing or set up a sewing machine. Insisting they will be living in poverty soon, he asks what she will do to prevent it. Calmly she replies she has full confidence in his ability to bring them plenty of money: *"There's nothing you can't do."* Shortly afterwards, finding her husband away from home almost all the time, Alice sinks into feeble-mindedness and amuses herself with childish games. Too late she learns Rodman has a second wife. On an unscrupulous bigamist she has thrown away her youth and a rare feminine beauty that justified her nickname.

Paula Tyrrell in *Thyrza* (1887) is another example of the feminine will trampled and subdued by the male ego, and so is Pennyloaf Candy in *The Nether World* (1889). Though some readers have said Victor Dalmaine is a nineteenth-century Petruchio who tames his clever wife quickly, the remark is misleading. Paula is seldom clever and she is certainly no shrew. Gissing clearly shows that she is susceptible to stronger personalities. As a girl her father's ideas had always been her own, and married to the hard-headed, no-nonsense politician his ideas are hers. But when she repeats anecdotes potentially harmful to his career, he calls her to task: *"I mustn't have people associating my name with all kinds of nonsensical chatter. I have a career before me, Paula."* Despotically, he tells her what she can and what she cannot talk about: *"Cultivate talk of a light, fashionable kind, keep to the sphere which is distinctly womanly."* Then pausing, he looks her over and utters a compliment to please her: *"How well you look in that dress!"*

Dalmaine's attitude is exactly that of Torvald Helmer in Ibsen's *A Doll's House* (1879). There is, however, no influence here. Gissing didn't read Ibsen until 1888, a full year after *Thyrza* was published. Moreover, while Nora rebelled and left home, Paula meekly assents to being treated as a doll. Slowly she allows her politician-husband to remake her in his own image, and she exalts his name whenever she can. Pennyloaf Candy, a denizen of the nether world and without rights of any kind, is also abused by a callous husband. On their wedding day they go to the Crystal Palace to have fun, and there he squanders their money on himself, ignores her with brutal indifference, and flirts with other girls. Soon afterwards he abandons her to live elsewhere in London but returns like clockwork to get her pregnant every spring. Her name, a corruption of Penelope, is classically descriptive. She is frequently seen in ragged clothes on the stoop of their squalid dwelling, a baby in her arms and surrounded by other babies, waiting for her wandering husband to return home.

The Victorian ideal of marriage and its failure to satisfy the demands of modern life is perhaps best illustrated by the union of Monica Madden and Edmund Widdowson in *The Odd Women* (1893). Though Widdowson is eccentric and much older than Monica, she agrees to marry him for several reasons: younger men have paid no attention to her; Widdowson has money and can offer her security; she won't have to work many hours each day as a shopgirl. Also she won't sink to a lower station in life but will be able to live in comfort in the middle class again. She doesn't love him, and so all these reasons amount to "unspeakable folly." As soon as they are married, her husband begins to act much older, mumbles platitudes that show old-fashioned ideas concerning wives, and displays inordinate jealousy. With chapter fifteen of the novel Gissing presents a meticulous case study of the doomed May-December marriage.

Step by step he shows its gradual disintegration, at the same time commenting on what is causing the ruin. Not a week goes by before Widdowson begins to concern himself with every movement his wife makes. He will not allow her to go anywhere alone, and though her youth irritates him, he wishes to be with her every minute of the day. He stands in contrast to Harvey Rolfe in *The Whirlpool* (1897). Widdowson's marriage shrivels and dies because he can't allow Monica enough freedom, Rolfe's because Alma has too much freedom. Without meaning to hurt his young wife in any way, Widdowson proves to be the most complete despot she has ever known. He is constantly harping on her duties as a wife, treats her much as a child to be guided, keeps her always under control and much of the time at home, and delights in seeing her in pretty dresses. For him, as with Helmer in *A Doll's House* (1879), his wife is little more than a doll, an object of decoration. It has never occurred to him that when a woman becomes a wife, she remains an individual with rights and obligations and a life of her own.

Widdowson takes it for granted that his duty is to command and direct, hers to obey and be guided. His views on women and their place in the world are radically out of date, for he has fallen out of touch with the life and times around him. *"Woman's sphere is the home, Monica. Unfortunately girls are often obliged to go out and earn their living, but this is unnatural, a necessity which advanced civilization will altogether abolish. You shall read John Ruskin; every word he says about women is good and precious."* His wife appears to listen attentively but is already beginning to think her own thoughts. She is becoming stifled by so little freedom of movement and like Ibsen's Nora, she is tired of being treated as a doll. In what is now Gissing's most famous novel, *New Grub Street* (1891), Dora Milvain in a moment of pique complains to Whelpdale whom she will later marry: *"You have so often spoken like this. I have really no ambition to be a doll of such superfine wax."* Dora's portrayal seems undoubtedly influenced by Ibsen, and yet the doll analogy was popular among writers long before Ibsen. As early as 1817 Thomas Love Peacock used it in *Nightmare Abbey*, having a young man speak of women as musical dolls for sale in the toy shop of society. His father replies: *"Your idea of a musical doll is good. I bought one myself, but it was confoundedly out of tune."*

When Monica complains of the strict seclusion imposed upon her, Widdowson again seeks Ruskin as an ally. Grumpily he tells her she is defying "the natural law" that places a woman in the home under the thumb of her husband. Eventually his tyranny drives her into open rebellion. Astonished that his union with this bright and pretty girl has brought only misery and failure, he re-examines his thoughts on women but reaches no viable conclusion. He seeks reconciliation, but she replies that will never happen because he can never see her as a free and equal companion. In less than a year Widdowson has learned that the old Victorian ideal of marriage is no longer viable in changing times. But not able to change, he loses the only woman he ever loved, a woman too young for him who dies in childbirth at twenty-two. His inability to accept the new thinking and adjust to it illustrates one of the dominant themes of the book. Monica's persistent rebellion is part of that theme.

Chapter 6

Edith and Echoes of Edith

Monica's rebellion against a gentle husband who tries to understand her needs but can't prompts a discussion of Gissing's stormy second marriage. After returning from his first trip to Italy, he suffered intensely from loneliness and isolation and went home to Wakefield. Early in August of 1890 he met a Wakefield girl, Connie Ash, and imagined he had fallen in love with her. On August 11, he recorded in his diary: *"Met Mr. and Mrs. Ash, Connie, younger sister Gertie, a pretty, dark girl, and boy Norman. Had much music. Gertie plays the mandolin. Connie sang a good deal, and beautifully. I am in love with her."* With some hesitation he went again to Connie's home on August 14, but after this date her name is no longer mentioned. Apparently the girl didn't receive his overtures, or more likely he was too timid to make it known to her that he liked her. Henry Shergold in the short story, *"A Lodger in Maze Pond"* (1894), speaks for Gissing when he says: *"Perhaps it is my long years of squalid existence. Perhaps I have come to regard myself as doomed to life on a lower level. I find it an impossible thing to imagine myself offering marriage, making love, to a girl such as those I meet in the big houses."* Gissing often let his characters speak for him.

On August 15, 1890 in obvious pain he wrote to his friend Bertz: *"This solitude is killing me. I can't endure it any longer. In London I must resume my old search for some decent work-girl who will come and live with me. I am too poor to marry an equal, and cannot live alone."* Bertz agreed that celibacy for Gissing was detrimental to his health but urged his friend to think twice before marrying just anyone. Gissing replied that insufficient income would keep him from making a truly desirable match. In 1890, with eight full-length novels to his credit, he earned only 150 pounds. By 1892 his annual income had risen to slightly more than 274 pounds, but he couldn't expect so much as that each and every year. His income depended on how much he could write, how much he could publish, how much the publishers were willing to pay for his work, and how many readers would buy it. He was not working in an office or factory where he could depend on a stable income month after month. In the early years he supplemented his income tutoring the sons of well-to-do people, but in the middle years and after he worked only at his writing.

So even to marry an English girl of the middle class was out of the question. To Bertz he said: *"Educated English girls will not face poverty. They remain unmarried in hundreds of thousands rather than accept poor men. I know that my danger, if I become connected with a tolerable girl of low position, is very great: I am weak in these matters. But then, reflect: there is no real hope of my ever marrying any one of a better kind, no real hope whatever! I say it with gravest conviction."* Then on October 25, 1890, he informed Bertz that he had made the acquaintance of *"a work-girl who will perhaps come to live with me when I leave this place at Christmas. But everything is dark and almost hopeless. I must consider nothing but mere physical needs. I feel weak and miserable, and can only recover something of my old self by the change of life I have referred to. Otherwise, there is nothing before me but lapse into mental and bodily ruin."* About a month earlier, according to his diary, Gissing had met a girl of the working class named Edith Underwood. A few months later she would become his second wife.

Exactly where he met Edith Underwood will probably never be known. Morley Roberts, his friend and first biographer, tells us in the book he published in 1912, *The Private Life of Henry Maitland*, that it was probably in or near a chandler's shop. It was located in the Marylebone Road in London, a neighborhood not entirely respectable and known to be dangerous at night. Gissing supposedly told Roberts he rushed out and spoke to the first woman he came across. He admitted that Edith was not particularly attractive but possibly delightful in intimacy, and that was all that mattered. His diary shows that she didn't hesitate to come to his rooms unchaperoned. But when he urged her to come live with him, she refused unless he married her. He wanted her to become his grisette, his working-class lover in a free bohemian relationship like those of Murger and Musset, but a note in his commonplace book reveals his disappointment: *"With the English character, the 'Vie de Bohème' is impossible. In English girls there is first conscience and secondly stupidity, keeping them from this ideal."* So to Bertz he wrote at the beginning of 1891: *"Our relations are as yet platonic. If anything is to come of our connection it will have to be marriage."*

They married near the end of February in 1891. A terse entry in his diary records the event: *"Married to Edith Underwood at Register Office, S. Pancras. Drove in fog to Paddington and caught the 11:45 for Exeter."* He must have surely spoken of the ceremony in letters to his family, though apparently none have survived. He knew, and perhaps they knew as well, that he married Edith not for love but for physical release. For a time he had loved his first wife with desperate intensity, but for Edith he had no feeling other than sexual. Yet the relief he gained was so invigorating that he grew tender toward his bride and even became optimistic about educating her. While she couldn't be introduced to the family until her speech and deportment improved, he felt it would take only a short time. After a week he confided to Bertz that he was in *"vastly better health and spirits,"* but a month later he was sounding a vague complaint to Ellen: *"Intellectual converse is of course wholly out of the question."* Days later he wrote again to say positive things about Edith's housekeeping: *"We have a great deal of cleanliness and comfort, though of course only the plainest and meanest of food."*

Then near the end of 1891, without intending to do so, he spoke of his wife as though she were a servant: *"Edith does very well, improves much in every way. I am more than satisfied with her. The house is orderly, everything punctual. She has many very good qualities."* He was beginning to display a condescending attitude toward this girl of the people that would eventually infuriate her. That and the fact that he refused to introduce her to his friends and family slowly changed the pliable young woman into a raging shrew. Before the end of their second year of marriage Edith had become rebellious, and for reasons not wholly unjustified. Though she had earlier shown "a certain refinement," she now bombarded her husband with language so fowl he could only stare at her in amazement. When she failed to score verbally, in moments of fury she hurled crockery at him. Shocked and saddened, Gissing was forced to admit he had gambled a second time choosing a partner and had lost. On the last day of 1892, he noted in his diary that the year was fraught with *"domestic misery and discomfort."* And there was little he could do about it.

His diary carefully describes the jockeying for position between himself and his wife, the constant bickering on her part, and the daily increase in virulence. When he saw he could no longer weather the storm under his roof, he sought the aid of Eliza Orme and Clara Collet. The former was a friend of his publisher and the latter a social scientist making a name for herself. *"We see but one visitor,"* he said to Ellen at the end of 1895, *"Miss Collet who knows the extraordinary circumstances of the establishment and puts up with everything."* Clara Collet tried hard to help but may have done more harm than good. Even the birth of two healthy sons, Walter Leonard in 1891 and Alfred Charles in 1896, couldn't mitigate Edith's wrath. Before long Gissing was driven "vixen-haunted" from home. In February of 1897 he wrote to his brother Algernon: *"I have simply been driven from home — chased away with furious insult."*

The friendship with Clara Collet, begun in 1893, continued to Gissing's death and was extended to Gabrielle Fleury Gissing. During the troubled years of 1893 to 1898, Clara Elizabeth Collet was often the only person whom Gissing could talk with of things that interested him. She provided the intellectual stimulation he sorely needed and couldn't find in his marriage. After his death in 1903, as one of the executors of his will, she struggled without succeeding to get publishers to bring out a complete edition of his work. Later she took it upon herself to oversee the education of his sons. She was a professional social scientist who worked first as a researcher for Charles Booth in 1886 and went on to publish books and articles on the work of women. By the time Gissing met her, she was a well-known authority on the subject of working women. At the turn of the century she had become the principal authority on women's occupations in Britain. Gissing chose his friends very carefully and had only a few. Clara Collet was certainly one of the most valuable of them all and may have loved him, but only as a friend.

His health beginning to break and under the care of a physician named Philip Pye-Smith, Gissing went back to Edith near the middle of June, 1897. In compliance with the doctor's orders, they moved at the end of July to Yorkshire. They were both looking forward to a better life, but the diary indicates their life together continued to be miserably unhappy. After describing what appeared to be a pleasant family outing near the end of summer, Gissing observed: *"Of course everything spoilt by E's frenzy of ill temper. I merely note the fact, lest anyone reading this should be misled and imagine a day of real enjoyment."* Even in misery he was conscious of posterity and the need to finish current literary projects. In less than a month he had fled from Edith again. This time he decided rather suddenly to go to Italy for a second time. His older son Walter was now at Wakefield with the family, but little Alfred was with his mother in London lodgings. Gissing would never live with her or his sons again.

He wrote to Bertz that he would leave England on September 22. For several months, until April 14, 1898, he was in Italy. On leaving that country he spent four days in Potsdam with Bertz. Then he returned to England on April 20 as spring was coming. While in Rome he wrote to H. G. Wells: *"Things are going very badly. My wife has carried uproar into the house of the friend [Eliza Orme] who was kind enough to take her; insult and fury are her return for infinite kindness and good-will; it seems impossible for her to remain there much longer. It wouldn't matter in the least but for the poor little child who is with her; she might go where she liked and rage to her heart's content. As it is, I fear I may be obliged to return to England much sooner than I meant to."* In the same letter he said Miss Orme could place her in the house of a working-class woman: *"With people of the educated class she cannot live; their proximity simply maddens her."* He worried about Alfred, a toddler and helpless, for by this time he believed Edith was mad: *"He might just as well be in the care of a drunkard or a lunatic as of this furious and hateful woman."*

Back in England and afraid Edith would hunt him down, he went into hiding in Dorking. In Potsdam he had told Bertz all about his problems with the woman, and on May 17, 1898, he wrote: *"Of course I must hide myself, in constant fear of attack by that savage."* He had heard from his family that she was determined to find him, and he feared that any moment she would pound on his door screaming abuse. *"Nothing settled yet about my wife and the little child,"* he wrote to Bertz on the first of July. *"She does not know where I am, but is trying hard to discover and threatens to give all possible trouble. The Solicitor cannot persuade her to sign a deed of separation. Meanwhile, the people in whose house she is living have given her notice to quit, owing to her bad behaviour."* He had thought that if Edith went to live with a working-class family, her temper would improve; but in this as in other assumptions he was wrong. When they gave her notice to move, she became more violent than ever and assaulted her landlady.

She was now living in unknown lodgings with Alfred. Gissing's lawyer was trying to get possession of the child but with no success whatever. *"It seems I cannot take the child from her,"* he said to Bertz in September. *"They say I have neither legal nor moral right. Well, I fear his life is sacrificed – my own fault. The marriage was criminal."* In similar vein he wrote to Morley Roberts: *"All work impossible owing to ceaseless reports of mad behaviour in London. That woman was all but given in charge the other day for assaulting her landlady with a stick!"* A few days later Edith discovered Gissing's hiding place and went directly there, bringing Alfred with her. He expected her to fly into a rage when he refused to take her back, but she was strangely calm. When he refused even to discuss the matter, he thought surely she would lose all control and create a violent scene. To his surprise, with eyes flashing but saying nothing, she turned on her heel and marched away, dragging Alfred with her. Later, recalling what had happened, he remembered he had not acknowledged his little son, had not even glanced at the child.

At the beginning of 1898, in uttermost resignation, Gissing revealed to Ellen that Edith had told him she was planning to go before a magistrate and declare he had deserted his family. He was outraged by her behavior and added sadly: *"I am really afraid she will end in the lunatic asylum."* Four years later, at the end of February in 1902, he informed Bertz that Edith had been arrested for serious ill-treatment of her little son. On further examination the authorities had deemed her insane and removed her to an asylum. *"Well, this has surprised nobody. Miss Orme always believed that she was not in her right mind. Happily, the landlady of her lodgings had the good sense and humanity to interfere (after many warnings) to protect the poor little child. I need not tell you that, on the whole, I regard this as a good thing. The poor woman will now be taken care of in a proper way at less expense to me than before. Little Alfred is to be sent to a farmhouse in Cornwall. He will now have a chance to grow up in healthy and decent circumstances. I cannot tell you how greatly I am relieved."* Walter, the older son, was killed in World War I. Alfred came out of the war with the rank of Captain. He married, fathered three children, lived until 1975, and became an author in his own right.

Gissing had predicted that Edith would end her days in an insane asylum. From the time of her commitment in 1902 until her death in 1917, she remained in confinement at the asylum, receiving no visitors but wearing her wedding ring day and night. According to her death certificate, she died of "organic brain disease." That was a catch-all phrase used by doctors who couldn't determine exactly the cause of death. Her age was given as forty-five, and she was described as the wife of "---- Gissing, occupation unknown." It has been suggested that if the disease had already set in shortly after marriage, neither she nor her husband can be blamed for the turmoil and misery they suffered, but that is too facile a conclusion. A more credible theory is that of Dr. Harry Hick, who believed Gissing's refusal to allow Edith to move among his friends and family caused most of the difficulty in the marriage.

His first wife deeply resented this same behavior, and even his third complained that he tried to keep her too much in seclusion. Edith, his second, was sensitive about her position in life. Her instinctive dislike of higher-class people flamed into hatred when she thought they were looking down on her. The attitude was exacerbated by her husband's aristocratic temperament in conflict with her democratic outlook. Moreover, she associated learning, culture, professional position, and refinement with wealth. Because Gissing was never wealthy, she found it difficult to believe he was anything but a pretender. Without wealth one shouldn't presume to speak and act like a gentleman, as Gissing invariably did. Certainly if one's economic position were no better than that of his neighbors, one shouldn't snub them, as Gissing invariably did. His attitude toward Edith was similar to Alfred Yule's in *New Grub Street* (1891); the fictional wife suffered in silence, but not the real one.

Since the wooing of Edith Underwood coincided with the writing of *New Grub Street* (l891), echoes of Edith run helter-skelter through the novel. Some take the form of self-examination, of head in argument with heart. The issue is whether Gissing is doing the right thing as he plans to marry a girl of the working class. By precept and by example he justifies the step he is about to take. The question at the heart of the debate is whether a struggling writer with no money should marry a woman of his own class or one of a lower class. Edwin Reardon's marriage to a woman of the upper-middle class is on the brink of failure because the man is poor and can't supply his wife with the luxury she expects. As Reardon's marriage disintegrates and falls into ruin, in juxtaposition is the marriage of Alfred Yule to a working-class woman. Although Yule is dissatisfied with his lower-class wife and can see only her faults, Gissing is careful to show that she has in fact many admirable qualities. A good woman, she stands by him in spite of the abuse he heaps upon her. The gist of the matter is presented in Milvain's remark about Reardon: *"A man in his position, if he marry at all, must take either a work-girl or an heiress, and in many ways the work-girl is preferable."*

In 1889 young and handsome Gissing – he was only thirty-two – could have likely married Edith Sichel, an heiress with £20,000, material property, intellect and education, and high social standing. However, his conscience wouldn't allow him to marry for money and be supported by his wife. So in the final analysis a workgirl was preferable, the sort of girl Alfred Yule married. He met the girl in a chandler's shop, *"and before long she consented to be his wife and share his garret."* He didn't love the girl but the time had come when he couldn't do without a wife. He sought an untaught woman who would take pity on his loneliness, and he found her: *"Many a man with brains but no money has been compelled to the same step. Educated girls have a pronounced distaste for London garrets; not one in fifty thousand would share poverty with the brightest genius ever born."* Gissing himself is speaking, repeating sentiments we've heard already. A few pages later he declares that a number of poor Grub-Street writers are *"men with unpresentable wives."* Mr. Hinks lives in harmony with *"the daughter of a laundress."* Mr. Gorbutt has a wife who rues the day she married a man of letters, for had she waited just a bit longer she might have married a prosperous tradesman. Mr. Christopherson, married to the daughter of a butcher, wrangles with her constantly but shows affection for her. Then with caustic irony Gissing comments: *"These men were capable of better things; they should have waited; they might have married a social equal at something between fifty and sixty."* The side of Gissing telling him not to marry was losing the debate.

Yet before making up his mind he decided to balance a man who had married a working girl with one who had married a social equal. If the former turned out better, he would know he was doing the right thing. Alfred Yule has struggled all his life to become a successful man of letters, but has reaped only bitter disappointment. For this he blames having married beneath himself: *"Look at Fadge. He married a woman of good social position; she brought him friends and influence. How has it been with me? I live here like an animal in its hole and go blinking about if by chance I find myself among the people with whom I ought naturally to associate."* Then Gissing comments: *"Alfred Yule was not so grateful as he might have been. He might have found himself united to a vulgar shrew, whereas the girl had the great virtues of humility and kindliness."* If he were to marry such as woman as Mrs. Yule, Gissing couldn't expect euphoric happiness, but if she were kind and affectionate, he could put up with her, live with her, and find contentment.

But what if he were able to marry one of his own class, a girl of education, refinement, intellect? Edwin Reardon has married such a girl, but after one child and two years of marriage it's all over. As the promise of his becoming a successful author fades, his wife becomes impatient and unsupportive. *"I love you with all my heart,"* she tells him. *"But I am so afraid of the future. I can't bear poverty, and I dread to think of your becoming only an ordinary man."* He has won a sympathetic woman's love but can't retain it because his pockets are empty. By now Gissing knows exactly what he must do. Narrow circumstances and the uncertainty of his trade tell him he can't hope to marry a girl of the middle class. All of them want their husbands to have a higher income than he can even dream of, much less deliver. He must look to a lower level and hope for the best. Mrs. Yule represents Edith Underwood as Gissing hoped she would be. However, before the end of 1892, when he was writing *The Odd Women* (1893), life with Edith had turned sour. In that novel the echoes of Edith are sour and cynical. His second wife had become an open wound in his side to fester and cause endless pain. The hurt went into his creative effort.

When Everard Barfoot of *The Odd Women* returns from the Orient, he learns that his friend Mr. Poppleton has been committed to a lunatic asylum. His cousin, Mary Barfoot, tells him that Poppleton went insane because of business troubles, but Everard believes he was driven crazy by having to explain his jokes to an inordinately stupid wife. *"Mrs. Poppleton not only never made a joke, but couldn't understand what joking meant. Only the flattest literalism was intelligible to her; she could follow nothing but the very macadam of conversation, had no palate for anything but the suet-pudding of talk."* Though Mrs. Poppleton is said to have come of a very good family, her denseness suggests an embittered view of Edith, particularly her inability to understand the subtly of certain witticisms Gissing was fond of uttering. Another friend, a Mr. Orchard, has forsaken his wife for no apparent reason, and Barfoot offers an explanation for this too. A very imaginative man, Orchard had married a practical, pedestrian, utilitarian woman with no appreciation whatever for beauty. While viewing a natural landscape at Tintern Abbey, a scene that took away the breath of her husband, she complained incessantly of her servants. Like Edith, she was immersed in mundane trivialities, and she insisted on imposing them upon a husband who was trying to do literary work.

All of this is an echo of Gissing's life with Edith, but the woman herself is mirrored in the reprehensible Mrs. Tom Barfoot. Everard says his brother once showed promise of becoming a genius, *"but marriage has blighted the hope, I fear."* Mrs. Barfoot is selfish beyond belief, and though uxorious Tom fails to please her; she has no feeling for him other than contempt. The man suffers from poor health that might be improved in a better climate, but that she will not allow: *"she must live in London, her pure native air."* When the Gissings were living in Exeter, a quiet, restful, and beautiful place, Edith complained constantly. A woman of the streets and squares of the big city, she couldn't abide the country. When Tom Barfoot dies, his loathsome wife tells anyone who will listen that Everard Barfoot caused his death, charging him with deliberate fratricide and vilifying his reputation. Though the situation in real life was not so dramatic, when Gissing left Edith she behaved much the same way, stunning his relatives with crude accusation.

The stark portrayal of Mrs. Tom Barfoot was conceived five years before Gissing's final severance from Edith in 1897. In 1892 he still had vague hopes of salvaging his marriage, but in the next year when he was at work on *In the Year of Jubilee* (1894), his disillusionment was complete. Ada Peachey in that novel is the vivid embodiment of all the defects he had found in Edith. Ada is vulgar, pretentious, selfish, and ignorant. What is more, she has a violent temper which she vents at a moment's notice upon her husband, servants, and sisters. Her fury is most evident in the climactic scene which forces her husband to flee. Arthur Peachey is so uncomfortable in his wretched home that he spends most of his time at the office. But on the evening in question he returns home earlier than usual, dreading calamity and finding a scene worse than he ever expected. *"You're just in time,"* Ada screams, *"to see this beast taken to the lock-up. Perhaps you'll believe me now!"* She is speaking of Emma, the nurse-girl, and she tells Arthur the girl has stolen marked money. She had been suspected of petty thefts before this, but in gratitude for her devotion to his child Peachey had defended and befriended her. Now his wife is screaming charges based on proof, and he is powerless to help the girl. She is sent upstairs to put her coat on. When she doesn't come down immediately, Ada finds her in a pool of blood with her throat cut. In her terror the servant has used a pair of scissors in a clumsy attempt at suicide. Ada stands over her, snorting in disgust.

Then as Emma is being restored to consciousness, the enraged shrew turns upon her husband, screaming abuse, and accusing him of immoral relations with the servant. *"You wouldn't have her sent away, oh no! She was so good to the child, and so good to somebody else! A dirty servant! I'd choose someone better than that, if I was a man. How much has she cost you? As much, no doubt, as one of the swell women in Piccadilly Circus!"* Peachey gains enough courage to thrust her from the room. Outside she rails at him in *"the language of the gutter and the brothel."* He cringes beside the bed, hands over his ears, his child screaming in terror. At length Arthur opens the door to hear voices below in quiet conversation. He seizes the moment to dress his three-year-old son and run with him from the house. When Ada returns from the police station, *"haggard and faint with excitement but supported by the anticipation of fresh attacks upon her husband,"* she can hardly believe he has left her. Discovering he has also taken the child, she flies into a frenzy and begins to smash every breakable object in the bedroom.

Escaping the clutches of the furious woman proves only temporary. At first Ada flings at Arthur as much trouble as she can, and then pretends repentance in an effort to get him back under the same roof. Against his better judgment he consents to return. All calm and sweetness as he settles down to living with her again, she reasserts her physical hold upon him. As soon as she knows with certainty that she is pregnant, she believes he won't leave her again and rapidly reverts to the foul virago of earlier times, becoming even nastier than before. Only then does Arthur summon the courage to leave her once and for all, never to return. Peachey's troubles are a blueprint of Gissing's own. Both men must leave their wives twice before the separation takes effect. The vividness of detail in depicting Ada Peachey and her miserable husband points to a substratum of personal experience. Gissing himself had been tormented by just such a woman. Though rendered more intense than in life, the painful story of Arthur and Ada Peachey is substantially Gissing's own. However, the final severance from Edith didn't come until three years later. As with his first marriage, Gissing has anticipated with the accuracy of prophecy the outcome of his second.

Less than a month after his separation from Edith in 1897, he was hard at work on the book that became *Charles Dickens: A Critical Study* (1898). In the chapter on Dickens's women and children, he concerned himself mainly with his author's "foolish, ridiculous, or offensive women," and he described them in a vein of bitterness. *"These remarkable creatures,"* he wrote with Edith in mind, *"belong for the most part to one rank of life, that which we vaguely designate as the lower middle class. In general, their circumstances are comfortable; they are treated by their male kindred with great, often with extraordinary consideration. Yet their characteristic is acidity of temper and boundless license of querulous or insulting talk. The real business of their lives is to make all about them as uncomfortable as they can. Invariably they are unintelligent and untaught; very often they are flagrantly imbecile. Among the poor folk in London such women may be observed today by any inquirer sufficiently courageous; they are a multitude that no man can number; every other house in the cheap suburbs will be found to contain at least one specimen, very often two for the advantage of quarrelling when men are not at hand. If Dickens were writing now, I believe he would have to add to his representative women the well-dressed shrew who proceeds on the slightest provocation from fury of language to violence of act."* One week before writing this Gissing had fled his home, never to return again. There can be little doubt that a rare vehemence swelling to ferocity in this chapter on Dickens's women resulted from the sordid intensity of his final separation from Edith.

Chapter 7

Gissing's Women in Revolt

The earliest of Gissing's rebellious wives is Maud *Gresham in Workers in the Dawn* (1880). A spoiled society girl, Maud marries the hard-featured John Waghorn for his money and social position. Soon afterwards she begins to live her life separately from his. When Helen Norman expresses surprise at the arrangement, Maud replies: *"Don't you know this is marriage à la mode, the way in which every matrimonial establishment with any pretension to elegance is conducted?"* It's the Victorian equivalent of what we would call an open marriage today, but before long Maud and her husband are quarreling fiercely in private: *"I want you to understand one thing. You may be as damned sulky as you please when we're alone together; for that I don't care a snap. But when we're obliged to be seen in each other's company, I'll thank you to show me a little more politeness."* Waghorn tries to dominate his spoiled wife, but she rebels by spending large sums of money as often as she can. They quarrel on this score, resort to violence, and end the marriage by getting a divorce. In novels that came later divorce was almost impossible.

Of the unhappy Elgars in *The Emancipated* (1890), he says: *"It was hateful that she should remain the wife of such as man as Elgar, but what refuge was open to her?"* The law will not allow her to get a divorce without dragging her name and his through the mud at great expense. Although Elgar has been unfaithful to his wife, she never views his infidelity as grounds for divorce. However, because she no longer respects him, she feels no need to obey him, and so without really wanting it she becomes rebellious. When she vehemently complains of his reprehensible behavior, the marriage rapidly begins to fall apart. In the same novel a rebellious wife named Mrs. Travis has left her husband because of similar infidelity: *"My husband happens to be the average man, and the average man isn't a pleasant person to talk about in this respect."* The double standard of morals allowed a man to be unfaithful so long as he was discreet in his conduct, but it rigorously condemned infidelity on the part of a wife. Lionel Tarrant of *In the Year of Jubilee* (1894) makes the standard quite clear: *"Infidelity in a woman is much worse than in a man. If a man really suspects his wife, he must leave her, that's all; then let her justify herself if she can."* Mrs. Travis insists she will never return to her unfaithful husband, but in time she yields to "natural and social laws" and finds herself under his roof again. Separation, she allows, just isn't enough to keep them apart. Though very difficult to obtain, divorce in such cases is seen as necessary.

In Gissing's next novel, *New Grub Street* (1891), Amy Reardon speaks her mind about divorce. In conversation with Edith Carter, she asks: *"Isn't it a most ridiculous thing that married people who both wish to separate can't do so and be quite free again?"* Edith replies it would probably lead to unwarranted trouble, but Amy isn't convinced. *"In America people can get divorced if they don't suit each other – at all events in some of the states – and does any harm come of it? Just the opposite I should think."* Amy is advocating divorce on grounds of incompatibility, a daring speculation for the time. Indirectly, in words often used by Gissing, she is attacking the obsolete Divorce Law of 1857. The law granted divorce at tremendous expense only when adultery could be proven. Women could bring the antiquated law up to date if those happily married would help, but they won't. Amy's husband for once agrees with her: *"If only our idiotic laws permitted us to break the legal bond, how glad both of us would be."* He would be glad because Amy has become one of the "tiresome hussies" descended from Ibsen's Nora. At various stages in the breakdown of their marriage, she openly defies her husband, creating an agony that prevents him from doing his best work, indeed any work. Separation soon becomes inevitable.

In a few years Gissing himself would be seeking a divorce and finding the task a virtual impossibility. He began to think of divorcing his second wife after meeting Gabrielle Fleury in July of 1898. He knew Edith was dead set against it but thought he might be able to get an American divorce without her knowing about it. He wrote to a friend in Baltimore, an American he had met in Italy, asking for information on the marriage and divorce laws in the various states. Also he asked Morley Roberts to find a book on the subject, but nothing of real value came to him. Moreover, he believed a divorce would incur the risk of losing all contact with his children. They were in the custody of friends who sympathized with his plight, but maybe the law would take a harsher view. So he ceased to aim at legal divorce and began to think of another way to live with Gabrielle.

If Amy Reardon is a good example of the rebellious wife in *New Grub Street* (1891), Marian Yule is an equally good portrayal of the rebellious daughter. For years Alfred Yule's wife and daughter have lived in terror of his angry, unfair outbursts of temper. Never blaming himself, he has always vented his anxieties, frustrations, and disappointments upon his family. But in time Marian resolves to have it out with him, *"to front her father's tyrannous ill-humour, and in one way or another to change the intolerable state of things."* Yule has treated his wife with flagrant injustice, and the daughter considers it her duty to interfere and make things better. Although Mrs. Yule urges Marian to do nothing, the girl exclaims: *"I must speak! We can't live in this terror!"* When her father turns glowering upon her, she feels her strength ebbing but somehow stands firm and urges him to be more civil. He is set in his ways and will not or cannot listen to her, but when he becomes nearly blind, he calms down and begins to act like a good husband and father. The rebellious daughter quickly becomes dutiful again and supports him until he dies.

Perhaps a better example of the rebellious daughter is Serena Mumbray in Gissing's next novel, *Denzil Quarrier* (1892). The girl is so uncomfortable with her parents that she finds any excuse to be absent from home many hours each day. Though not religious, she gets caught up in the revivalist movement with its appeal to rich and poor, urban and rural, men and women, and even children. She does all she can to spread the revivalist message but eventually begins to believe the women's movement with its cry of freedom is more to her liking. Her domineering mother has tried to rear Serena in strict accordance with the norms of conventional young ladyhood, but at twenty-three the young woman has a mind of her own. When her mother objects to her reading a French novel, traditionally thought of as too risqué for young ladies, Serena calmly puts down the book and begins to play the piano. This appears to pacify the older woman until her daughter cries out while continuing to play: *"You had rather have me play than read that book? That shows how little you understand of either. This is an immoral piece of music! If you knew what it meant you would scream in horror. It is immoral, and I am going to practice it day after day!"*

If Serena Mumbray was becoming more involved in the woman question, so was Gissing. Completed in 1891 and originally called "The Radical Candidate," *Denzil Quarrier* gave more pages to the woman question than any of his previous novels. As the radical candidate for membership in Parliament, Denzil Quarrier proposes to explore in a speech the aims of the feminist movement. His opening address to the Polterham voters will be an essay on "The Position of Woman in Our Time." Later changed to "Woman: Her Place in Modern Life," his speech aims to emphasize the most important issues of the woman question. In the town of Polterham the woman question is a hot subject, and the people are eager to hear what Quarrier will say about it. *"I should like to know,"* a townsman comments, *"whether Mr. Quarrier is disposed to support the Female Suffrage movement."* Another replies, *"If he is, he mustn't expect my vote. We've seen enough in Polterham lately of the Female question."* Then Gissing intrudes to add: *"The Woman Question was rather a dangerous one in Polterham just now."*

The period of Revivalism in which not a few women made fools of themselves had come and gone, and the subsequent campaign of Mrs. Hitchen, who spoke only to women audiences on "Purity," had ruffled the feathers of the townspeople and left many querulous. The older women look upon the woman question as not quite proper, and most of them, young and old, are dead set against Mrs. Wade, the town's only feminist. Since Quarrier's position has not yet been revealed, the whole community turns out to hear his speech. In the best classical manner he opens the address with an amusing anecdote. It seems that *"a certain enlightened young lady gave a lecture once to advance the theory that woman's intellect suffered from the habit of allowing her hair to grow so long."* Having gained a bit of sympathy by making his audience laugh, he becomes serious and declares that women are demanding emancipation in all areas of society as well as from *"long tresses and flowing garb."*

The reference is to an important concern of the women's movement, the cumbersome dress of women. They were also revolting against long tresses that got in the way of their work, or increased outdoor activity, so that by the end of the century short hair was the hallmark of the emancipated woman.

Another important issue presented in Quarrier's speech is female education and its relation to marriage. The ordinary girl, he declares, is sent into adult life with a mind scarcely more developed than that of a child. This is shoddy preparation for marriage, for many girls make "monstrous errors" when called upon to accept a husband. There is no scheme for rendering marriages universally happy, but judicious training can put young girls on their guard when selecting a mate. It's possible to put them on terms of equality with marriageable young men, and that should be done. To this the conservatives in the audience murmur, *"Oh, shameful! Shocking!"* But Quarrier continues: *"They must be treated not like ornaments under glass cases, but like human beings born with mental apparatus even as men are."* Education no different from that available to men should be given to women. Quarrier's views are the same as Gissing's. In conclusion, he speaks of England's many superfluous women: *"the chances are enormously against their making a marriage worthy of the name."* Then he delivers the informing idea of *The Odd Women* (1893), Gissing's next novel: *"Let women who have no family of their own devote themselves to the task of training the new female generation."* Only then, the radical candidate insists, will women become truly emancipated.

When the meeting breaks up, the people attending gather in little groups to discuss the speech. One of the more outspoken is Mr. Chown. He wants to free the female mind from the yoke of superstition and priestcraft. Give them more rights only when they have thrown off an obstructive religion. This aim to free women of a stultifying religion was one of the dominant themes of *The Emancipated* (1890). At that time and also in 1892 when the novel under discussion was published, Gissing in full agreement with Chown. By 1894 his thoughts on the subject had changed. Ada Peachey of *In the Year of Jubilee* (1894) was demonic because she had no authority to guide her in moral matters, no religion. The misery of the Peachey household and thousands like it could generally be traced to wives with no sufficient moral sense: *"There was no hope of impressing Ada with ideas of goodness, truthfulness, purity, simply because she recognised no moral authority."* The men and women surrounding Mr. Chown walk away to listen to Mrs. Wade after he delivers his final remark: *"There were good things in the lecture, but on the whole it was flabby, flabby."*

In another group Mrs. Wade the feminist is holding forth: *"Speaking for myself, I cannot pretend to agree with the whole of Mr. Quarrier's address; I think his views are frequently timid"* – laughter and hushing – *"frequently timid, and occasionally quite too masculine. I should prefer to entitle Mr. Quarrier's lecture, 'Woman From a Male Point of View.' However, it was certainly well-meaning and something for which a member of the struggling sex may reasonably be grateful."* The best part of his speech, she tells Quarrier, consisted of those remarks about young girls being trapped into monstrous marriages. She hints that she was a victim of a similar experience and goes on to say that the position of woman in society has changed little since the time of the Greeks: *"Woman is still enslaved, though men nowadays think it necessary to disguise it."* Quarrier asks why she is so insistent on getting the vote for women. She replies: *"I insist on the franchise because it symbolizes full citizenship. I won't aim at anything less than that."* Though not a militant feminist, Mrs. Wade is a suffragette. The action of the novel takes place before the Third Reform Bill of 1884. Had Mrs. Wade been working in the real world, she would have participated in the suffragist agitation that appeared to stand a chance in that year but was defeated.

Later she brings up the subject of women's dress. Pausing beside a lake, she remembers having witnessed a splendid sight at that spot. When a little girl fell off the bank into deep water, a young man dived in with his clothes on to rescue her. *"I can't tell you how I enjoyed that scene! It made me cry with delight. I liked his courage but envied his power. If we could swim well and had no foolish petticoats, we should jump in just as readily. It was the power over circumstances that I admired and envied."* A similar discussion was to take place in Gissing's next novel, *The Odd Women* (1893). Everard Barfoot is certain that Rhoda Nunn can't swim. When she asks how can he be so sure, he replies: *"Only because it's so rare for any girl to learn swimming. A man who can't swim is only half the man he might be, and to a woman I should think it must be of even more benefit. Women are trammeled by their clothes. To be able to get rid of them and move about with free and brave exertion of all the body, must tend to every kind of health."* Earlier Rhoda had observed: *"How delicious it was in one's childhood, when one ran into the sea naked! I will enjoy that sensation once more, if I have to get up at three in the morning."* Commentary of this sort eventually sparked a revolution in women's dress.

In *The Odd Women* (1893) Mary Barfoot and Rhoda Nunn, both feminists, have taken it upon themselves to train other women. Rhoda is speaking to Monica Madden: *"Do you know that there are half a million more women than men in this happy country of ours? So many odd women, no making a pair with them. The pessimists call them useless, lost, futile lives. I, naturally, being one of them myself, take another view. I look upon them as a great reserve. When one woman vanishes in matrimony, the reserve offers a substitute for the world's work. True, they are not all trained yet, far from it. I want to help in that, to train the reserve."* Rhoda is the assistant of Mary Barfoot, who has opened a school to train young women for work in offices. Of Miss Barfoot's mission, Gissing writes: *"She did not seek to become known as the leader of a 'movement.' Yet her quiet work was probably more effectual than the public career of women who propagandize for female emancipation. Her aim was to draw from the overstocked profession of teaching as many capable young women as she could and fit them for certain pursuits nowadays open to their sex. She held the conviction that whatever man could do, woman could do equally well."* The exception would be those tasks that require physical strength beyond that of women.

Gissing presents these two feminists as intelligent and thoughtful women with strong opinions, though Rhoda's views are more extreme than Mary's. Rhoda is the fiery adversary of those *"care-nothing and believe-nothing women"* who keep the world stagnant, but the danger is that her militant zeal may damage rather than help the cause. She opposes marriage, believing that few marriages turn out well: *"I would have girls taught that marriage is a thing to be avoided rather than hoped for. I would teach them that for the majority of women marriage means disgrace."* Mary sees dangerous tendencies in Rhoda's thought. *"Your zeal is eating you up,"* she cautions. *"We have no mission to prevent girls from marrying suitably – only to see that those who can't shall have a means of living with some satisfaction."* The more even-tempered Mary makes it clear to Rhoda that if people come to think of them as fanatics, their usefulness is over. *"The ideal we set up must be human."*

Mary's position is more clearly defined in the formal address she delivers to several of her students. Her topic is woman in the labor market, but she also touches on other aspects of the woman question. *"I am strenuously opposed,"* she tells them, *"to that view of us set forth in such charming language by Mr. Ruskin. Were we living in an ideal world, I think women would not go to sit all day in offices. But the fact is we live in a world as far from ideal as can be conceived. We live in a time of warfare, of revolt. If woman is no longer to be womanish, but a human being of powers and responsibilities, she must become militant, defiant."* Out of such activity will come a woman of a new type. In this last decade of the nineteenth century the Victorian ideal of womanly perfection is out of date. The ideal ignores the fact that half a million young women are without the chance to marry and must therefore support themselves. The old ideal would have women remain dependent when they have only themselves to depend upon. The time has come when women must discard the old conception of woman for a new ideal of strength, self-reliance, and independence.

What, then, should be the characteristics of the new woman, and what should be her place in society? This new type of woman should be active in every sphere of life. She should be allowed to do her share of the world's work, but not at the expense of neglecting the home. In developing her character the best of the old ideal should be retained: *"Of the old ideal virtues we can retain many, but we have to add to them those which have been thought appropriate only in men. Let a woman be gentle, but at the same time let her be strong; let her be pure of heart, but nonetheless wise and instructed."* The adoption of these so-called manly virtues will not unsex woman any more than getting a college degree has unsexed them. In fact it will be a vast improvement, not only to women but to the men as well. If any disorder is to come of the change, let the responsibility rest on those who resisted change. Although in time Gissing's opinions on these matters would become more conservative, in 1892 when he created these characters he was in full agreement with everything Mary has said.

Chapter 8

Gissing's New Women

Gissing's earliest representation of the new woman appears in *Isabel Clarendon* (1886). In that novel Ada Warren, an emancipated new woman, stands in contrast to Isabel Clarendon, a gracious womanly woman. Were there competition between the two, Ada would lose dreadfully. Isabel is beautiful, cultivated, and charming while Ada is plain and strange and too thoughtful for her own good, though possessing a hidden strength that in time makes her attractive. Bernard Kingcote, Gissing's alter-ego, notes that Isabel is *"a woman to the tips of her fingers, a womanly woman, everything that Miss Warren, for instance, is not. In fact, the latter's presence throws Mrs. Clarendon' womanliness into relief."* That overly overt statement sets up the sustaining contrast.

Though only a foil to Isabel Clarendon, Ada Warren is carefully developed as a new woman and given most of the characteristics typical of the new woman. When Kingcote comes upon her, sketching in the countryside, her eyes hold his *"with something like defiance."* Only a new woman, as Gissing saw her, would have been so bold. Conventional girls were taught to glance demurely downward in the presence of a man. At the end of the century a woman writer remembered that she and her sisters had been trained to lower their eyes when first addressing a man: *"Nor shall I ever forget the agony of our governess who believed she had succeeded in producing young women of high degree only to discover otherwise. When she observed us looking a man we knew full in the face, she was aghast. This looking at acquaintances straight in the face was a cardinal offence, for according to her a maiden's eyes should always be cast down."* Aware of this old and rather silly convention, Ada Warren deliberately catches the gaze of a stranger and holds it defiantly as he speaks to her.

Brashly intellectual, she reads deeply in subjects that stretch the mind. Scorning such frivolous society magazines as the *Queen,* she pores over the *Fortnightly Review* and the *Nineteenth Century*. Her book of the moment is a volume of Comte:

"You are a Positivist?"

"No, merely an atheist."

"That's rather dogmatic, isn't it? The word Agnostic is perhaps better."

"I believe it comes to very much the same thing. The word has been coined principally to save respectability."

"A motive with which you have small sympathy"?

"None whatever."

Ada is influenced, of course, by two dominant intellectual currents of the time, the higher criticism and the new science.

In the journals of the day she has followed the controversy over Huxley's new word, which began almost as soon as he coined it in 1869 and was still lifting eyebrows in 1889. Since the time of the novel's action is 1881, Ada can't be expected to know all the ramifications of the argument, but she is well-versed in what had been said as late as 1880. In that year the *Saturday Review* for June 26 noted: *"In nine cases out of ten Agnosticism is but old atheism writ large."*

R. H. Hutton said in 1881 that *agnostic* was suggested by Huxley at a party held previous to the formation of the Metaphysical Society in 1869. At the first meeting of the Society, Huxley defined the term. An agnostic, he said in effect, is one who holds that the existence of anything beyond and behind material phenomena is unknown and (so far as can be judged) unknowable. A First Cause and an unseen world are subjects of which we know nothing. The word differs in meaning from *atheist,* defined as one who denies or disbelieves the existence of a god. A writer for the *Spectator* said in 1876: *"Nicknames are given by opponents, but Agnostic was the name demanded by Professor Huxley for those who disclaimed atheism and believed with him in an 'unknown and unknowable' god; or in other words that the ultimate origin of all things must be some cause unknown and unknowable."* In 1882, one year after Ada Warren saw little difference between agnosticism and atheism, James Anthony Froude published Carlyle's trenchant opinion on the subject: *"The agnostic doctrines, he once said to me, were to appearance like the finest flour from which you might expect the most excellent bread; but when you came to feed on it you found it was powdered glass, and you had been eating the deadliest poison."*

Influenced also by Matthew Arnold, Miss Warren's ultimate goal, as she embarks on her intellectual journey, is culture. She seems to have read very carefully Arnold's *Culture and Anarchy* (1869) and has made its conclusions her own. She also reads Latin, is beginning to study Greek, writes short stories for entertainment, is developing critical acumen, paints a decent picture, and plays the piano. Although most of the characters in the novel see her as *"a strange specimen of womanhood,"* what they say matters little to her. Independent to the core, she goes her own way and proves herself a worthy person, gaining in the end the full sympathy of her creator.

In the same novel Hilda Meres is Gissing's earliest example of a girl influenced by the new education. Others are Nancy Lord (1894) and May Tomalin (1901). Nancy Lord is the kind of girl *"turned out in thousands every year from so-called High Schools."* Her education was concerned chiefly with names. She has heard of Keats but knows nothing whatever about his life or poetry. May Tomalin, on the other hand (deftly created for satirical effect), brightly professes to know a great deal about English poetry while really knowing nothing at all. Speaking of Lord Dymchurch, she tells Lady Ogram: *"I find he takes a great interest in Old English, and we talked about Chaucer and so on for a long time. He isn't quite so well up in it as I am; I put him right on one or two points and he seemed quite grateful."* Her starchy, practical aunt replies: *"If*

I were you, I shouldn't talk about Old English next time you see Lord Dymchurch. Men don't care to find themselves at school in a drawing-room."

Gissing's satirical bent is at its best with Hilda Meres. *"How much she knew!"* he exclaims. *"She could render you an ode of Horace, could solve a quadratic equation, could explain to you the air-pump and the laws of chemical combination, could read a page of Aelfric's 'Homilies' as if it were modern English. And all the while the very essence of her charm lay in the fact that she knew nothing at all."* Kingcote, who usually speaks for Gissing in this novel, doesn't care much for Hilda and on the whole has a distaste for young girls: *"I never met one who did not seem to me artificial, shallow, frivolous."* Here the fictional character isn't speaking for Gissing, for he likes Hilda very much: *"She crossed your path like a sunbeam."* Sixteen years old, the girl is attractive, lively, intelligent, clean-minded, fun-loving, and entering a new type of womanhood with grace and confidence. After high school she will probably become a student at Girton College, Cambridge and distinguish herself as a Girton Girl.

In similar terms, though with heavier irony, Gissing describes the education of Cecily Doran in *The Emancipated* (1890). Suave and well-educated Ross Mallard is speaking: *"Miss Doran is a young woman of her time; she ranks with the emancipated; she is as far above the Girton Girl as that interesting creature is above the product of an establishment for young ladies* [a select finishing school for the daughters of gentlemen]. *Miss*

Doran has no prejudices, and in the vulgar sense of the word no principles. She is familiar with the Latin classics and with the Parisian feuilletons; she knows all about the newest religion and can tell you Sarcey's opinion of the newest play. Miss Doran will discuss with you the merits of Sarah Bernhardt in 'La Dame aux Camélias,' or the literary theories of the brothers Goncourt. I am not sure that she knows much about Shakespeare, but her appreciation of Baudelaire is exquisite. I don't think she is naturally very cruel, but she can plead convincingly the cause of vivisection." This mention of Francisque Sarcey (1827-1899), a prominent drama critic, is a good example of how Gissing used in his novels material newly gathered from experience. Before writing this book he attended one of Sarcey's lectures in Paris and was delighted by what he heard.

In educating Cecily Doran, Mrs. Lessingham has discarded entirely the old ideal of female education in favor of the new. In her opinion the old time-tested traditional education for girls didn't impart knowledge so much as fostering a special ignorance of the facts of life. She tells us the average parent insists that his daughter be kept pure-minded in a world that is anything but pure. Middle-class girls are therefore required to wear "rose-coloured spectacles" until they marry, and then are expected to toss them aside on their wedding night. Such nonsense contributing to a fool's paradise has been done away with in the education of Cecily Doran. As the result she isn't haunted by vulgar shame that passes for modesty; and because she has seen things as they are – not as inflexible, moralistic teachers would like them to be – she will never do anything foolish. *"It's only the rose-coloured spectacles that cause stumbling."*

Later when Cecily stumbles in spite of her training, Mrs. Lessingham is at a loss to explain why, but Mallard believes the girl's education has been too rapid and too radical. He is careful to point out that Cecily's emancipation is premature. Change of that sort must come slowly, not only through education but through experience, immersion, absorption. Education and experience must work hand in hand over an extended period of time, and even then neither the process nor the result may be what one might call positive and ameliorative. Some girls, in fact, are incapable of becoming advanced women, and those who pretend fall into a painful muddle and make fools of themselves. These pretenders crop up frequently in Gissing's later novels. Two of the most memorable are Jessica Morgan (1894) and Iris Woolstan (1901). Jessica Morgan is a moving study of a girl with slight intelligence who tries to enter the ranks of clever women by becoming well-educated. After she fails an important examination, she deteriorates into frustrated despair and half-madness. Iris Woolstan believes herself to be a new woman when she is really a womanly woman in every way and eventually ceases to pretend.

Of the pretenders, the earliest in Gissing's work and perhaps the best are the Denyer sisters in *The Emancipated* (1890): *"Common to the three was a resolve to be modern, advanced, and emancipated, or perish in the attempt. Every one who spoke with them must understand that they were no everyday young ladies, imbued with notions and prejudices recognized as feminine, frittering away their lives amid the follies of the drawing-room and of the circulating library. Culture was their pursuit, heterodoxy their pride."* As accomplished pretenders each has a specific role to play.

Barbara poses as the adorer of Italy. With English people she never loses an opportunity to babble Italian phrases. Speak to her of Rome and she murmurs rapturously, "Roma, capitale d'Italia!" Mention an English writer and she professes to admire only those who have found inspiration south of the Alps. The proud mother tells a story of Barbara's going up to the wall of Casa Guidi and kissing it. Robert and Elizabeth Browning occupied the second floor, or *piano nobile,* of the fifteenth-century patrician house in Florence from 1847 to 1861. Casa Guidi is now owned and maintained by Eton College. For Barbara, ecstatic lover of Italy, the Italians can do no wrong. She loves their art and architecture. While she has never read the three-volume treatise by John Ruskin titled *The Stones of Venice* (1851-53), viewing the stones in person leave her starry-eyed.

Madeline Denyer professes a wider intellectual scope. Less naive in her enthusiasms, she has taken for her province "aesthetic criticism in its totality." She has a passable knowledge of French, and she has talked so much about learning German she believes she already knows it. She has no understanding whatever of Greek and Latin, but from modern essayists has gathered *"so much knowledge of these literatures as to be able to discourse of them with a very fluent inaccuracy."* She is familiar with all schools of painting and music and likes especially the obscure figures. For the great masters she has only a moderate interest. Anyone praising them becomes in her eyes a rather superficial person given to philistinism. And because culture is her never-ending pursuit, she has read Matthew Arnold more than once and knows all about philistines in English society.

Zillah is plainer than the other two sisters and has nothing of their vaunted cleverness. Her mind is slow and her memory unretentive, but she has a genuine desire to instruct herself in a solid way: *"She alone studied with real persistence, and by the irony of fate she alone continually exposed her ignorance, committed gross blunders, was guilty of deplorable lapses of memory. Her unhappy lot kept her in a constant state of nervousness and shame."* Zillah's specialty is "the study of the history of civilization." In some identity other than a Denyer, she would have said she studied history. At heart she's an old-fashioned woman, but out of deference to her sisters, she has smothered those impulses and believes her spiritual life rests "on the postulates of science." Later when she becomes a governess among Midland dissenters, she eagerly accepts their religion and finds peace. Barbara and Madeline remain pretenders for the rest of their lives, becoming more adept in the pretense but fooling no one but themselves.

Gissing's satirical presentation of the Denyer sisters pokes fun at those girls who believe they can achieve happiness by aping the new women. Impossible, he tells us in *Born in Exile* (1892), for the new women themselves are often exceedingly unhappy. Marcella Moxey in this novel is a dark, intense, masculine-minded young woman living in exile among traditional females and despising them. To complicate matters, she rather despises herself because she feels like an alien with no friends either male or female and no ability to make friends. In many respects she is similar to Ada Warren of *Isabel Clarendon* (1886), and were they real women living in London they might have met to become bosom companions. Both she and Ada appear to be highly sexed, as are other new women in Gissing's fiction, suggesting he viewed educated women in real life as very attractive. Far from having thrown off "the burden of sex," most of his emancipated women have fire in their veins and no means to quench it.

Marcella is a lonely and frustrated young woman but unhappy largely because she is "bitterly enlightened." Even as a girl she found pleasure in attacking Christianity. At seventeen or eighteen she was *"bitter against religion of every kind, a born atheist in the fullest sense of the word."* And yet her moral sense seems more highly developed than in most other women. Remarkably honest in everything she does, she hates falsehood, injustice, and brutality. She dies trying to prevent a brutal carter from beating his horse: *"In a steep lane she came up with a carter who was trying to make a wretched horse drag a load beyond its strength. He was beating the poor horse unmercifully. Marcella couldn't endure that kind of thing, impossible for her to pass on and say nothing. She interfered and tried to persuade the man to lighten his cart. He was insolent, attacked the horse more furiously than ever, and kicked it so violently in the stomach that it fell. Even then he wouldn't stop his brutality. Marcella tried to get between him and the animal, just as it lashed out with its heels."* She found little pleasure in her life because she could neither learn tolerance nor persuade herself to affect it, and so most people disliked her, but to the end her mind and heart kept their clearness and courage. Her brother described her well when he called her *"the one woman in ten thousand at once strong and gentle."*

In *Our Friend the Charlatan* (1901) one finds another bright and tender new woman similar to Marcella Moxey but better adjusted to her world and more productive. Described as *"a good, able girl of the best modern type,"* Constance Bride is *"one of the few women who have nothing of the baby or the idiot in them."* When his conservative mother calls her "a very unpleasant young woman," Dyce Lashmar quickly defends her, saying *"She's of the new school, you know, the result of the emancipation movement."* She is, in a word, the best example of the new woman in all of Gissing's work. Growing up as the feminist movement gained more and more of its aims, she has within her a balanced blending of the old and new. She is honest, wholesome, knowledgeable, pure-minded as well as strong-minded, and intelligent but not heavily intellectual. When Lashmar prattles about the women's movement, she tells him the woman question has become tiresome: *"I hate talk about women. We've had enough of it. A woman is a human being, not a separate species."* Then she jumps on her bicycle *("sprang into the saddle")* and spins off.

In league with all of Gissing's new women, Constance Bride keeps abreast of the most recent currents of thought. If one is astonished to find Sylvia Moorhouse reading Hugh Miller's *Testimony of the Rocks* (1857), it is a greater surprise to hear Bride and Lashmar discussing Nietzsche. In *Born in Exile* (1892) Sylvia takes up Miller's book and is much amused by it: *"It's the chapter in which he discusses with perfect gravity whether it would have been possible for Noah to collect examples of all living creatures in the ark. He decides that it wouldn't, that the deluge must have spared a portion of the earth."* The fact that Sylvia is able to laugh at Miller's treatise shows her "advanced" thinking. A devout Christian, Miller defended the doctrine of special creation and maintained that the Bible, rightly interpreted, didn't contradict geological discovery. The six days of creation mentioned in Genesis corresponded to six geological eras clearly shown in rock formations.

But what about Bride and Lashmar and Nietzsche? Although the German philosopher went mad in 1889, his books written before then were not read in England until the close of the century. Her reading very much up to date, Constance is attracted to Nietzsche's insistence on the right of the strong in human affairs. And yet she is perceptive enough to believe his writings are dangerous: *"He'll do a great deal of harm in the world,"* she tells her friend. *"The jingo impulse, and all sorts of forces making for animalism will get strength from him directly or indirectly."* His teachings if carried out on a large scale will result in *"a return to sheer barbarism, the weak trampled because of their weakness."* As she evaluates Nietzsche's dangerous philosophy, Constance Bride flashes keen insight. For a moment, as she looks into the future, her mind is Gissing's and she is speaking his thoughts.

Other emancipated women in the novels are Sibyl Carnaby, Bertha Childerstone, Bertha Cross, Beatrice French (who makes a show of smoking cigarettes), Janet Moxey (who becomes a doctor), May Rockett, Miss Rodney, Alma Rolfe, Eleanor Spence, and Stella Westlake. May Rockett's story, "A Daughter of the Lodge" (1901), collected in *The House of Cobwebs* (1906), illustrates an important social force the new women found themselves up against. An active feminist and new woman, May returns to the humble cottage of her parents on the estate of a titled gentleman. Her brain teeming with new ideas and believing the democratic spirit is now the order of the day, she attempts to behave on terms of equality with Hilda Shale, the baronet's daughter. Deeply resenting such behavior, it isn't long before Hilda and her mother, Lady Shale, force May Rockett into a scene of supreme humiliation. Virtually exiled by a feudal lord in modern times, the girl returns to London, never to visit her parents again. The do-nothing aristocracy in its cold-blooded complacency is shown nonetheless to have vast power. When the new woman comes into conflict with it, she is brought painfully to her knees.

Now what was the masculine reaction when this clever new woman with her new ideas, new view of the world around her, and new outlook on the life she would live vigorously appeared on the scene? If the new developments generated much talk among women, the men of the time contributed their full share as well. You can be certain they didn't maintain any degree of silence.

Chapter 9

Masculine Reaction and More

Whenever the emancipated woman appears in a scene established by the novelist, in just about every instance one finds commentary from male observers, many of whom speak for Gissing himself. We've already heard the tongue-in-cheek opinions of Ross Mallard regarding the education of Cecily Doran. Now we see him expressing concern over her too-frank behavior and how much she dwells upon subjects usually kept under wraps. He is no slave, Gissing tells us, to the out-worn convention that supposes a young girl has no sexual feeling until marriage. Not in the least can he regard her, as does the school of hypocritical idealism, as an innocent child in a woman's body. And yet, though a reasonable man and liberally educated, Mallard remains at heart a Puritan and would like to see more of the old ideal in the girl: *"Secretly, he did not like her outlook upon the world to be so unrestrained."* The sentiment is Gissing's own. In time he rejected most of Ruskin's views on women and their place in the world, and yet the very thought of a girl acting like a man in sexual matters bothered him. Though more than once he called the doubled standard unfair to women, it was strongly in place.

His reaction to the new woman is clearly seen in *Born in Exile* (1892) when Peak, Earwaker, and Malkin exchange views on he subject. Conservative Peak is the first to speak: *"I hate emancipated women with a passion. Women ought to be sexual."* To oppose the harshness of this view, Gissing gives his readers a more considered opinion expressed by Earwaker: *"But the woman who is neither enlightened nor dogmatic is only too common in society. They are fools and troublesome fools. The emancipated woman needn't be a Miss Moxey, nor yet a Mrs. Morton. Marcella Moxey is certainly an incomplete woman. But her mind is of no low order. I had rather talk with her than with one of the imbecile prettinesses."* Later we hear Malkin's liberal opinion of the new woman. When told Marcella is bitterly enlightened, he retorts he can't wait to meet her: *"Really? Magnificent! Oh, I must know her. Nothing like the emancipated woman! How any man can marry the ordinary female passes my understanding."* Not a careful thinker, Malkin is swayed by the influences of the time into being enthusiastic about the new woman. Peak is too emotional to have a balanced judgment. Earwaker represents the mean between the two extremes.

In 1892, though undecided about the outcome of the emancipation movement, Gissing believed that education would eradicate much of the foolishness in women. In 1893, identifying with Everard Barfoot in *The Odd Women*, he shows admiration for such new women as Rhoda Nunn and Mary Barfoot; and yet as Marcella Moxey was said to be incomplete, so is Rhoda Nunn. Becoming a new woman, Gissing believed, didn't happen overnight. Moreover, the conservative viewpoint, present in previous novels but not fully developed, is precisely shown in what Edmund Widdowson believes and says. Devoutly conservative, Widdowson is very much against the new developments. Strongly pro-Ruskin, he thinks of Rhoda Nunn as unwomanly and despises her for wishing to make all women unwomanly. While Micklethwaite is also pro-Ruskin, Everard and Mary Barfoot see Ruskin as standing in the way of the movement toward freedom. Everard tells Micklethwaite that he doesn't have *"anything like the respect for women as women that you have. You belong to the Ruskin school."* He wants to seduce Rhoda Nunn to test her sincerity, but is seduced himself when he falls in love with her.

Gissing's novel of 1894, *In the Year of Jubilee*, puts on display male characters who are conservative in their opinions of women. Stephen Lord gives his foolish son Horace a bit of advice: *"When you are ten years older, you'll know a good deal more about young women as they're turned out in these times. You'll have heard the talk of men who have been fools enough to marry choice specimens. When common sense has a chance of getting in a word with you, you'll understand what I now tell you. Wherever you look nowadays there's sham and rottenness; but the most worthless creature living is one of these trashy, flashy girls, the kind of girl you see everywhere, high and low, calling themselves 'ladies,' thinking themselves too good for any honest, womanly work. Town and country, it's all the same. They're educated; oh yes, they're educated! What sort of wives do they make with their education? What sort of mothers are they? Before long, there'll be no such thing as a home. They don't know what the word means. They'd like to live in hotels and trollop about the streets day and night. Go into the houses of men with small incomes; what do you find but filth and disorder, quarreling and misery?"* By now Gissing's marriage to Edith had fallen into ruin. In this passage his anger comes through so strongly it warps his thinking. Emancipation had taken a turn for the worse. Domestic virtues were being lost.

In the novel of 1890, *The Emancipated*, he could refer contemptuously to Ruskin and sympathize with woman's "slavery to nature." With Cecily Doran's dilemma after she becomes a mother he could indeed sympathize: *"Had she been constrained to occupy herself ceaselessly with the demands of babyhood, something more than impatience would shortly have been roused in her. She would have rebelled against the conditions of her sex. She did not represent that extreme type of woman to whom the bearing of children has become in itself repugnant; but she was very far removed from that older type which the world at large still makes its ideal of the feminine. With what temper would she have heard the lady in her aunt's drawing-room, who was of opinion that she should 'stay at home and mind the baby.'"* He could imply that Cecily's little boy demanded too much of her time, and in *New Grub Street* (1891) he could show Reardon openly disliking his little son. But at that time Gissing was between marriages and had no children of his own. After 1891 he himself had a son, and he expected his wife to love and care for the child with all the energy at her command. His change of mind reveals itself in the tender affection Arthur Peachey (1894) has for his little boy. It further reveals itself in *The*

Whirlpool (1897) when Harvey Rolfe shows intense love for the son his socialite wife has neglected.

In 1894 Gissing was also beginning to question his earlier position concerning woman's absolute equality in all matters. He failed to convince himself that woman in any way was inferior to man, but he now felt that female emancipation was undermining a long-held right and one he had no trouble accepting, the husband's right to rule. In *New Grub Street* (1891) he had already shown that unless the husband is strong enough to dominate his wife, inevitably she will dominate him. In marriage, he was thinking by 1894, there is no such thing as equal status for both partners. And so Lionel Tarrant of *In the Year of Jubilee* makes it clear to Nancy Lord that he, not her, will be the head of the household: *"I am your superior in force of mind and force of body. Don't you like to hear that? Doesn't it do you good when you think of the maudlin humbug generally talked by men to women?"* Learning to accept this injunction, Nancy becomes in marriage an admirable woman educated in nature's university.

In conversation with Mary Woodruff she ponders her destiny: *"It comes to this. Nature doesn't intend a married woman to be anything but a married woman. In the natural state of things, she must either be the slave of husband and children or defy her duty. Who can doubt that it's Nature's law? I should like to revolt against it, yet I feel revolt to be silly. The thought has made me more contented than I was at first. After all, one can put up with a great deal if you feel you're obeying a law of Nature."*

This is a far cry from what Gissing had said of Cecily Doran in 1890. It is in fact just the opposite of what he put in the mouth of Mrs. Wade in 1892. In *Denzil Quarrier* Lilian Northway ventures the opinion that woman's dependence on man is "in the order of nature." Alarmed but controlling her anger, Mrs. Wade replies: *"Very likely. But I am not content with it on that account. I know of a thousand things quite in the order of nature which revolt me."* In 1892 Gissing was in agreement with Mrs. Wade. In 1894 he sided with Nancy Lord.

He is clearly opposed to the wife and mother, as seen in *The Whirlpool* (1897), who neglects her home and family to gad about in society circles. Harvey Rolfe has granted his wife too much freedom, and it brings negative results. Representing a type Gissing thought was becoming all too plentiful, Alma Rolfe abuses the freedom given her while thinking only of pursuing pleasure. She stands in stark contrast to Mrs. Basil Morton, an old-fashioned wife and mother: *"Four children had she borne, and in these little ones she saw the end and reason of her being. Into her pure and healthy mind had never entered a thought at conflict with motherhood. Her breasts were the fountain of life; her babies clung to them and grew large of limb. She would have felt it an impossible thing to abandon her children to the care of servants."* Gissing had reason to believe women of this stamp were rapidly vanishing. On the first day of 1880 he could have read this in a newspaper: *"Governess Wanted. A middle-aged lady to educate and take care of two little children (the mother is delicate and unable to attend to them). The lady must be of good family and qualified for the charge."* Advertisements of this sort were even more common in the 1890's.

Gissing's next publication, *Human Odds and Ends* (1898) concluded with the chronicle of a wife, Mary Claxton, who cheerfully sacrifices herself for husband and children. Entitled "Out of the Fashion," its final paragraph is worth quoting: *"She sits there with thin face, with silent-smiling lips, type of a vanishing virtue. Wife, housewife, mother – shaken by the harsh years but strong and peaceful in her perfect womanhood. An old-fashioned figure out of harmony with the day that rules, and to our so modern eyes perhaps the oddest of the whole series of human odds and ends."* H. G. Wells, happily married to one of his former students, poked fun at the sentimental tone of this sketch. In reply to Wells, Gissing wrote in July of 1898: *"As for 'Out of the Fashion,' why, you and differ to a certain extent on the one great subject. Of course I have bungled what I meant; but the sentiment is ingrained in me, and will outstand every assault of humour."* He believed the simple, self-sacrificing woman of the old ideal had been replaced by a brash, selfish, bicycle-riding new woman who cared little for home and children. The Mary Claxtons were "out of harmony with the day that rules" because the Ada Peacheys had taken over.

What was worse, the change that had produced rather admirable women in the beginning now seemed to be creating extreme specimens. In "At High Pressure" Linda Vassie is a well-dressed bundle of misdirected energy: *"Without the least pretence of preparing herself for any recognised calling, she exhibited an activity which would have taxed the constitution even of a strong man. From morning to night – often, indeed, till past midnight – Linda was engaged at high pressure in a great variety of pursuits."* The least domestic of persons, she uses her liberty to speed about in cabs and trains, to read all the periodicals of the day, to make many new acquaintances, and *"to receive a score of letters by every post."* She belongs to a vast number of clubs and organizations, too many by far, and their names roll off her tongue *"with astounding volubility."* The problem, however, is this: she is silly and half-educated and contributing nothing to society even when most busy. Her type was abundant in London at the end of the century.

In this discussion of the woman question and the movement it generated, I have focused mainly on women of the middle class. The aristocracy had heard about what was going on but paid little attention. In effect they retreated into their own little world to ignore the events swirling around them. But what of the lower classes? Had the clamorous news of female emancipation reached them? In "A Free Woman," one of the stories in *Human Odds and Ends* (1898), Gissing tells us that indeed it had. Charlotte Grub, an independent young woman of the working class, is convinced that *"the first duty of woman was no duty at all."* From an early age she has viewed as intolerable any kind of domestic activity affecting her ability to do as she pleases, and she has certainly become aware of the movements chiefly concerning her welfare: *"It must not be supposed that female emancipation, in the larger sense, is discussed only among educated women; the factory, the work-room, the doss-house, have heard these tidings of great joy. Charlotte Grub could talk with the best on that glorious claim of woman to take her share in the work of the world, and by 'work' she of course understood every form of exertion save the domestic."* For information she reads the Sunday papers and listens to talk in public places.

Charlotte Grub with her pedestrian name belongs to the servant class, but living day and night at the beck and call of another woman is "worse than getting married." Never in her life has she prepared a meal, washed a plate, or sewn a stitch. In good times she earns a precarious living doing menial chores in lodging houses. When times are bad, she takes advantage of the shelters established by charitable organizations. Coming down with an attack of bronchitis, she goes to a free hospital and spends an enjoyable Christmas there. Without charge of any kind she receives food and shelter and even Christmas presents. In a country rapidly becoming a welfare state, Miss Grub has learned to live how to play the system. The propaganda of the women's movement, having sifted down to the lower classes, has been interpreted as meaning that women have open to them all sorts of agencies to look after them as they do whatever they please.

Charlotte is perhaps an extreme example, but she illustrates Gissing's fear that woman's emancipation was producing untoward results. In his commonplace book he recorded an item he had read describing a woman living in a world quite different from Charlotte's and yet much influenced by the times. *"As I woke my husband, the lion – which was then about forty yards off – charged straight towards us, and with my .303 I hit him full in the chest, as we afterwards discovered, tearing his windpipe to pieces and breaking his spine. He charged a second time, and the next shot hit him through the shoulder, tearing his heart to ribbons."* Gissing took the passage from an article on lion hunting, written by a new woman of means and published in *Pearson's Magazine* in May, 1900. He quotes it later, word for word, in *The Private Papers of Henry Ryecroft* (1903) and has Ryecroft (largely Gissing himself) wryly comment: *"It would interest me to look upon this heroine of gun and pen. She would give one a very good idea of the matron of old Rome who had her seat in the amphitheatre. Many of those ladies were connoisseurs in torn windpipes, shattered spines, and viscera rent open. If not so already, this will soon, I dare say, be the typical Englishwoman. Certainly, there is no nonsense about her. Such women should breed a remarkable race."* The commentary came from a man who loved the literature of Rome and Greece and from a man who in childhood hesitated to go fishing for fear of hurting the fish. It came from a man whose son Walter was to die in World War I.

Having once sided with the women's movement as a good thing, by the end of the century Gissing had become wary of female emancipation and had retreated to the ranks of the conservatives. At the beginning of the new century, his position in regard to the woman question was similar to that of Martin Blaydes in *Our Friend the Charlatan* (1901). Two causes, the old man explains, have brought the world to its present condition: the tyranny of finance and the power of women. Of the two the "monstrous regiment of women" is by far the worse. *"Look at the diseases from which we are suffering – materialism and hysteria. The one has been intensified and extended, the other has newly declared itself since women came to the front. No materialist like a woman; give her a voice in the control of things, and goodbye to all our ideals."* But the old man doesn't stop on that note; he has more to say: *"We had our vain illusion; we were generous in our manly way. Open the door! Let the women come forth and breathe fresh air! There's your idle lady with the pretty face. There's your hard-featured woman who thinks that nobody in the world but she has brains. And our homes are tumbling about our heads. Back with them to nursery and kitchen! Back with them or we perish!"*

The charlatan of the book's title, who poses as a strong believer in women's rights, secretly agrees with Blaydes: *"He knew that he himself would have spoken thus had he not been committed to another way of talking."* Later he marries Iris Woolstan, a pretty, freckle-faced womanly woman, and is glad he did. Constance Bride, Gissing's fullest realization of the new woman, might be expected to oppose everything the old man has said. Instead, broadly speaking, she agrees; and so did Gissing though with some reservation. The thoughts of Lord Dymchurch seem more nearly Gissing's own: *"Frankly he said to himself that he knew nothing about women, and that he was just as likely to be wrong as right in any theory he might form about their place in the world, their dues, their possibilities. By temper he leaned to the old way of regarding them; women militant, women in the public eye, were on the whole unpleasing to him. But he was satisfied with an occasional laugh at these extravagances, and heard with patience anyone who pleaded the cause of female emancipation."*

Gabrielle Fleury was a Continental new woman in virtually all respects. Living with her in the last years of his life, Gissing was relatively content. Since he died before he had a chance to immortalize the woman as a leading character in his fiction – although *The Crown of Life* (1899) shows considerable influence – a brief summary of his life with her must take the place of extended treatment. A Frenchwoman of intellectual tastes, Gabrielle wrote to him in June of 1898, asking for the right to translate *New Grub Street* (1891). He later invited her to the home of H. G. Wells, where they would be able to talk with proper chaperonage in a beautiful setting.

On July 6, 1898, Wells and his wife entertained them at a pleasant luncheon. Later they walked in the garden and had much talk and began immediately to bond. Though the woman left Wells unimpressed, her breeding, beauty, musical voice, and intrinsic sympathy captivated Gissing. Wells later described her negatively in his autobiography. Perhaps he didn't like foreign women, or maybe it was just another thing on which the two friends differed. At any rate, after her visit she and Gissing wrote letters to each other almost daily. By October 8, 1898, the two had agreed to live together even though he was still legally married to Edith. On May 7, 1899, in the town of Rouen, they participated in a symbolic wedding ceremony in a hotel. Gissing's diary reads: "In the evening, our ceremony. Dear Maman's emotion, & G's sweet dignity."

After a brief honeymoon in St. Pierre en Port, the couple went to live with "dear Maman" in Paris. For a few months Gissing relished his new life: *"For the first time in my life I am happy! And, if health does not fail me, I shall be happy for many a year."* But he was soon quarreling with Mme. Fleury regarding the kind of food he wanted as daily fare. Dr. Harry Hick wrote that while Gissing wanted bacon and eggs for breakfast, Mme. Fleury considered such a meal disgusting and served him much lighter fare. But we must not suppose she had anything to do with his untimely death. Other factors were at work, emphysema, for example, and weak lungs that could have come from smoking.

As Gissing's health declined, the three moved to Autun and later to St. Jean de Luz, and finally to St. Jean Pied de Port, where Gissing died of double pneumonia at the age of forty-six on December 28, 1903. Responding to a Christmas Eve telegram, H. G. Wells came to be at his friend's side during his last days. Gissing is buried in the English cemetery at Saint-Jean-de-Luz. Though living with Mme. Fleury made him uncomfortable and irascible at times, his four years with Gabrielle were without doubt the happiest of his life. After the unspeakable misery of enduring two failed marriages, she came as if from a realm beyond to comfort him and heal his wounds. She lived on after his death for more than half a century and never remarried.

Chapter 10

Of Marriage and Harlotry

An important issue of the woman question was opening the labor force to women. Each year thousands found themselves unable to marry and were constrained to support themselves. Yet until the last three decades of the century, the work a woman could do consisted mainly of duties in the home. Outside the home the only "respectable" occupation open to women of the middle class was teaching, and the supply was far greater than the demand. It was the aim of the feminists to rectify this situation. They wanted to open more doors for women, allowing them a greater variety of jobs. As so many of his novels powerfully illustrate, Gissing considered the work of women important. It may be seen, then, that a pertinent question confronting many of his female characters is "what shall I do in the world?" These women don't come solely from the middle class but from all classes. His commentary ranges from the prostitutes at the bottom of the social ladder to the fine ladies at the top. Let us begin at the bottom, viewing in some detail Gissing's first marriage and how it influenced his fiction, and work our way upward.

Gissing's portrayal of London's harlots grew out of his own experience. He based his treatment of "them on firsthand knowledge, for as a youth he had known just such a woman who later became his wife. In his own day few people knew about this marriage, but in taking that fatal step in 1879 he seems not to have been alone. With frequency and nonchalance numerous middle and upper-class gentlemen were said to marry beneath them, often uniting with servants or shopgirls but sometimes with harlots, or ladies of the night (the common euphemism then and now). So the wags joked if a gentleman married a lady of the night, it was nothing to be upset about for he married a lady. Yet most of those marriages seldom lasted for long. Economic conditions and the double standard led some young men to prefer a mistress to a wife. Moreover, as we have already seen, thousands of middle-class girls refused to marry men whom they thought had no money. As a young man Gissing had strong physical urges but a sentimental view of women that placed them off limits. Intimacy with a girl of his own class was out of the question, and so while still in college he found himself in a relationship with a girl of the streets. It was a love affair that changed his life.

During his early years in London he lived within a mile of "the Grand Boulevard of London debauchery," the Haymarket. He walked through the neighborhoods where "women of the town" thronged, and his natural curiosity led him to observe them closely. For more than a century the West End had been the center of London prostitution.

Soho, Mayfair, and St. James's had fashionable brothels in the eighteenth century, and in Gissing's day, though fewer in number and not so flagrant, they were still there. Other streets in which the trade flourished were the Strand, Portland Place, Regent Street, Piccadilly, and the streets near Bedford Square, Bryanston Square, and Leicester Square. In Gissing's day attempts were made to clean up the West End but with little progress. Although a lot of work was being done to rescue "fallen women," when one was taken away another took her place and went on plying her trade.

For Gissing the prostitute had none of the glamour that some attributed to her. She might be so well dressed as to be taken for an upper-class woman, but when all was said and done she belonged to "the unclassed," the unfortunate outcasts at the bottom of the social scale. She dragged out her life of forced gaiety on the fringes of a society that used her for a short time before throwing her away. For more than a decade the sordid world of the prostitute was in effect Gissing's own. The death of his first wife finally released him. On Thursday, March 1, 1888, he stood in a squalid little room, wearing his overcoat against the cold, and stared in horror at the body of the woman who had been his first love and his wife. Her maiden name was Marianne Helen Harrison and he called her Nell. He had met her in Manchester in 1876 and had married her in 1879. Now she lay dead at twenty-nine in "a wretched, wretched place," a barren and smelly lodging-house room. All he saw in that room he burned into memory and recorded in his diary.

Hanging on a hook nailed to the door he found a tattered dress and a worn-out overcoat. Under the bed, scuffed and muddy, were the boots she had worn. Any other items of clothing were nowhere to be seen. Half of the bed clothes appeared to be missing; he saw no covering for the bed, only one dirty sheet and a blanket. A number of pawn tickets indicated she had pawned her winter clothes during the summer but couldn't redeem them when the weather turned cold. Any money she received went for drink, and he learned her associates had been so disreputable the landlady banished them from the house. Examining the chest of drawers, one of the few pieces of furniture except the bed, Gissing found a scrap of bread and some rancid butter, the only food in the room. In another drawer he found the letters he had written her during his year in America. She had kept them all, along with an old photograph of him.

Three "pledge cards," promising to stay away from alcohol and signed during the last six months, gave evidence that she had struggled to reclaim herself. Her emaciated body with its signs of disease and dissipation was proof she had failed. Peering into a face that should have been young and yet was very old, Gissing could hardly recognize it. Only her teeth remained the same, as white and perfect as on the first day he met her. He had always seen her teeth as one of her finest features. Perhaps he was thinking of Nell when he described at least nine women in his work as having white, clean, attractive teeth. They come from all classes, but only two of them were created before his wife died. The doctor who attended her during the last hours of her life recorded the immediate cause of death as "acute laryngitis." Though he accepted the diagnosis, Gissing knew the ultimate cause of death was a life of dissolute sexual freedom complicated by excessive drinking and maybe illegal use of drugs.

Once he had taken her to a hospital to be treated for one of her many ailments. When the doctor detected signs of venereal disease and asked her about it, she replied (or insinuated) it had come from her husband. The angry physician turned on Gissing and gave him a tongue lashing. Rather than reveal the true cause of the malady, he endured the rebuke in silence. Later he recounted the incident to Morley Roberts, releasing in a torrent of agonized confession the shock, anguish, and torment he suffered. Now the burden that had clung to his back for a decade was dead, and his response was not revulsion but pity. The sight of his wife in death aroused in him a renewal of the indignation that had drawn him to her at eighteen. He couldn't blame himself for her ruin. He had done his best for her, had surrendered his honor for her sake, but fate or the nature of things had decreed she come to an untimely end.

She and hundreds like her were victims of an uncaring society, of a callous social order that proclaimed a young girl worthless unless she had money. And so, viewing Nell in death, Gissing rededicated himself to his mission as a social novelist: *"As I stood beside that bed, I felt that my life henceforth had a firmer purpose. Henceforth I never cease to bear testimony against the accursed social order that brings about things of this kind. I feel that she will help me more in her death than she hindered me during her life. Poor, poor thing!"* For five tumultuous months, from March until July, he worked in a fever of energy and fury, and the result of his labor was *The Nether World* (1889). It is the only novel by Gissing in which nothing but poverty appears and how it tears the human soul. It is Gissing's purgation of all that reminded him of Nell. The cards, for instance, that showed the futility of Nell's efforts to "take the pledge," and were strewn about the death room, turn up again in the impoverished room of Mrs. Candy, a woman destroyed by drink and deserted by her husband: *"Over the fireplace the stained wall bore certain singular ornaments. These were five coloured cards, such as are signed by one who takes a pledge of total abstinence; each presented the signature Maria Candy, and it was noticeable that at each progressive date the handwriting had become more unsteady."* Gissing's keen eye had seen it all in real life.

Other echoes of Nell in death occur throughout the novel. The death of Margaret Hewett resonates with sentiments expressed in the diary after he left Nell's death room. The wife of Michael Snowdon behaved before she died much as Nell did: *"At last she began to deceive me in all sorts of little things; she got into debt with shop-people, she showed me false accounts, she pawned things without my knowing. Last of all she began to drink."* Sukey Jollop also recalls Nell. She abandoned herself to drink, left her husband, became the mistress of another man, and lost herself in the back streets of Shooter's Gardens: *"Sukey had strayed on to a downward path."* Describing the formative years of Charles Scawthorne, the novelist recollects with a twinge of self pity the pain of his own impressionable years: *"From sixteen to three-and-twenty was the period of young Scawthorne's life which assured his future advancement, and his moral ruin. A grave, gentle, somewhat effeminate boy with a great love of books and a wonderful power of application to study, he suffered so much during those years of early maturity that his nature was corrupted. Pity that some self-made intellectual man of our time has not flung in the world's teeth a truthful autobiography."* In many respects *The Nether World* (1889) is autobiographical. Mainly, however, it's about the hopeless poverty of buried lives in wretched slums seldom seen by the upper classes. It is the best of Gissing's proletarian novels.

It brings to mind the Manchester episode in his life. When he first encountered Nell on the streets of Manchester as a college student of eighteen, he knew of prostitutes only from imaginative literature and the pictures of William Hogarth. Even as a boy the eighteenth-century painter and satirist fascinated Gissing. In a caricature drawn when he was fourteen, he depicted himself as a round-backed scholar, bending over a large book entitled "Ossian." He must have known even then something of the literary falsehood perpetrated by James Macpherson in the eighteenth century. On the floor nearby is a pile of books with a large tome at the bottom labeled "Hogarth." The volume had belonged to his father, and the boy prized it. His initial interest in London street life and the lives of the poor may well have been stimulated by Hogarth's art. Yet there were other influences that shaped more directly his behavior on meeting the Manchester girl. He grew up with a sensitive attitude toward suffering, and certainly the spectacle of afflicted womanhood aroused his sympathy. He was outraged to learn that women in Russia were forced to sell their hair in times of hardship.

At sixteen, he enrolled at Owens College in Manchester and tasted the freedom of college life for the first time. Years later he confided to Morley Roberts that he should never have been turned loose at that age in a big city to live alone in lodgings. He was able to confide in Roberts, a friend and fellow student, and began to tell him of having met a girl: *"On day he showed me a photograph. It was that of a young girl, aged perhaps seventeen, he at the time being very little more. She was not beautiful, but had a certain prettiness, the mere prettiness of youth, and she was undoubtedly not a lady. After some interrogation on my part he told me that she was a young prostitute whom he knew."* Roberts tells us he didn't approve of the affair and wanted Gissing to break it off as soon as possible but with no success. The girl was not only young and attractive but seemed to idealistic Gissing the very picture of abused innocence. To his eye she was a fair maiden in distress, a lady in need of a knight, an unfortunate person sorely in need of rescue. In William Lecky's memorable phrase from his *History of European Morals* (1869), the student thought of Nell as *"the eternal priestess of humanity, blasted for the sins of the people,"* and he resolved to help her as much as he could.

She seems to have told him that she became a prostitute as the only way of staying the bite of poverty. If he alleviated her economic distress, she could leave the streets and that way of life and become respectable. With this in mind he sacrificed to buy her a sewing machine to help her support herself. It was another example of undiluted idealism. The girl was not about to labor as a needlewoman for thirteen hours a day at very low wages. It was much easier to use her womanly wiles to get money from him, and as the months passed she took most of the small income he got from his scholarships. We know he gave her gifts and money, even selling a cherished watch left him by his father, but he soon found it wasn't enough to meet her needs. Perhaps by the time he met her she had already taken to drink and was prostituting herself to get money for it, though probably the craving for alcohol came later. It is likely she went on the streets at fifteen or sixteen because she was destitute and unwilling to work at honest labor to support herself.

We know she demanded more and more money from Gissing, and to keep her from reverting to her old habits, he gave her whatever he could. When that was gone, he turned in despair to stealing books, money, and coats from the common room and locker room at Owens College. A detective hired by the college caught the desperate student in the act of rifling a locker. Gissing was summarily jailed and expelled from the college. His resolve to rescue Nell had ended in tragedy. For the sake of a young girl who impressed him with her prettiness, he had thrown away honor and academic talent and the whole course of his life was changed. Gissing met Nell perhaps at the beginning of 1876 and was later caught stealing *"some marked money from an overcoat in the cloakroom of the college."* He was sentenced to one month in prison at hard labor. Shortly after serving his prison term he departed for America with hopes of starting a new life. While his crime can't easily be explain in terms of cause and effect, perhaps it isn't too much to say it was an act of love.

He was experiencing a strong sexual impulse, a feeling he chose to call love, and the object of this love was in danger of slipping away from him. Under the circumstances, as he considered the situation, the rules of a hypocritical society seemed unimportant. He could justify stealing from a system he didn't respect for the sake of a maiden that system had wronged, particularly if he saw her as a victim of a plutocratic society that cared little whether she lived or died. But the crux of the matter is that Gissing stole for Nell because he loved her. We have much evidence to support this view. In August of 1876, as he prepared to sail for America, his thoughts turned inevitably to the girl he was leaving behind. They were thoughts riding on tender emotion, and they found expression in a poem he wrote called "A Farewell." At about the same time, perhaps while crossing the sea, he wrote two conventional sonnets in praise of womanly virtue. Though addressed to fictional ladies, it's easy to see Nell as their inspiration. Also he jotted down some weak little verses entitled "The Two Gardens." In them the young man, waxing sentimental, expresses his love for the girl left behind in tones of saccharine sweetness. She is a "dear little flower" that blooms summer and winter without fading in the garden of his heart.

In the autumn of 1877, after little more than a year in America, Gissing returned to England. An itinerary on the flyleaf of the cheap notebook he kept at the time shows he went directly home, not to Germany as some have supposed. He left Boston near the middle of September and arrived in Liverpool on October 3, 1877. From there he went home to Wakefield for a few days and then to London. On October 18, his brother William (who was to die in 1880) sent him a letter expressing concern about employment in London. At that time Gissing was living alone in the neighborhood of Tottenham Court Road at 22 Colville Place. Later Nell came to live with him in other lodgings, and after a few months they married in October, 1879. In *The Crown of Life* (1899), a novel written late in his career, he recollects his feelings of 1879 and sadly reflects on them: *"Love-anguish of one-and-twenty; we smile at it, but it is anguish all the same, and may break or mould a life."* He had married Marianne Helen Harrison because he loved her. When she became his wife he was twenty-one.

There is evidence also that he was motivated by a sense of guilt. Mr. Tollady in Gissing's first novel, *Workers in the Dawn* (1880), leaves an ailing mother to gratify a selfish desire to travel. Disgraced and punished for having committed a crime, young Gissing left Nell to fend for herself in Manchester while he sought a better life in America. Using Mr. Tollady's words to rebuke himself, he writes: *"I think it would be impossible for any youth to be more selfish than I was during these years. I had no thought but for my own annoyances, my own wishes and plans. I hate myself when I look back at these years."* Tollady found on returning to England that his mother had died; Gissing found the eager girl he had plucked from the streets the year before had perhaps returned to the streets. Also by then she was perhaps an alcoholic. She was the victim of her own bad habits, but such a thought seems never to have entered the young man's mind. He blamed himself for her relapse, for when she needed him most (he reasoned) he wasn't there to help her; he had run away. To expiate his sin, to resolve this guilt, he decided to do all he could to retrieve her. As a first step he would make an honest woman of her. His proposal of marriage was the deepest avowal of faith that he could show her.

During the early years of their marriage they were troubled by poverty but enjoyed a precarious happiness such as we find in the novels of Henri Murger. Gissing's grisette made a brave attempt to mend her ways and manage with economy the little household. Both resorted to vegetarianism for a time in order to save money. In later years Gissing disliked vegetarianism very much. From *Henry Ryecroft* (1903) comes this indictment: *"There comes before me a vision of certain vegetarian restaurants, where at a minimum outlay I have often made believe to satisfy my craving stomach. One place do I recall where you had a complete dinner for sixpence; I dare not try to remember the items. But well indeed do I see the faces of the guests – poor clerks and shop-boys, bloodless girls and women of many sorts – all endeavouring to find a relish in lentil soup and haricot something-or-other. It was a grotesquely heart-breaking sight."* At times he and Nell ate bread soaked in grease to stave off hunger. She was on cordial terms with Algernon but not with his mother, and to the sheltered girls in Wakefield, the two sisters, she was unknown.

In less than a year her health seemed to be breaking, and her husband, to establish himself as a novelist, was spending more and more time away from her. But poverty, unreliable health, and half-acceptance by Gissing's family couldn't spoil at first the bitter-sweet happiness both enjoyed. Then came the years that were sordid. After 1880 Nell declined rapidly, tormented by almost continual ailments. Never very bright, she began to appear almost foolish and annoyed Gissing by the stupidity of her sentiments or the vulgarity of her speech. The victim of a "weak and unstable constitution," she found temptation hard to resist, and she began to drink more heavily than ever. Fired by drink she made herself objectionable to her husband, to the landlady, and to the other lodgers. Her behavior caused them to move from one lodging house to another frequently. Then after a persistent debauch she would make vain and pitiful efforts to reform. Morley Roberts in his roman à clef, *The Private Life of Henry Maitland* (1912), described these phases of the marriage: *"The fact remains that they were turned out of one lodging after another, for even the poorest places, it seems, could hardly stand a woman of her character in the house. I fear it was not only that she drank but that at intervals she deserted him and went back for the sake of more drink and for the sake of money, which he was unable to supply her, to her old melancholy trade. And yet she returned again with tears, and he took her in, doing his best for her."*

Roberts tells us he never met the woman. This refusal on the part of her husband to introduce her even to his closest friend was an insult she couldn't ignore. It must have intensified her feelings of unworthiness, and this in turn could have accelerated her decline. Gissing's friend was invited into the sitting room while Nell remained in the bedroom, *"usually unfit to be seen because she was intoxicated."* On one occasion Roberts was invited to the apartment in Tottenham Court Road and expected to meet Nell, but again she was drunk and with some embarrassment Gissing had to ask him to leave. He described Gissing's home this way: *"The front room in which he received me was both mean and dirty. The servant who took me upstairs was a poor foul slut, and I do not think the room had been properly cleaned or dusted for a very long time. The whole of the furniture in it was certainly not worth seven and sixpence from the point of view of the ordinary furniture dealer. There were signs in it that it had been occupied by a woman, and one without the common elements of decency and cleanliness. Under a miserable and broken sofa lay a pair of dirty feminine boots."*

Some of the time Nell wasn't drunk when Roberts called but painfully sick. At different times she suffered from neuralgia, rheumatic disorders, swollen arms and legs, an eyesight condition for which she had an operation, and convulsions that brought on comas. In April of 1881, she had a fit in a chemist's shop and had to be carried home through the streets. The incident deeply disturbed her husband, but he retreated from immediate reality by working harder than ever on his second novel, "Mrs. Grundy's Enemies." On March 13, 1881, he wrote to his brother Algernon: *"I hope now to get some steady work at my book. My plan is to lock my door every evening from 5 to 9 and peg away."* The new novel progressed steadily through 1881 but was not finished until September, 1882. In the first week of that month he said: *"Novel is completed; tomorrow I send it to Smith & Elder, though with the usual doubts."* Another novel was already begun, *The Unclassed*; it was published as his second novel in 1884. Smith & Elder brusquely turned down "Mrs. Grundy's Enemies," claiming it would never have an audience because Mudie's Lending Library would never accept it. Another publisher picked up the book and requested revision. Subsequently the manuscript was either destroyed or lost. The novel is the best example of Gissing's abortive fiction.

In 1882, writing to Algernon, he began to speak more openly about his life with Nell. In the middle of January of that year she was hospitalized for one of her many disorders but came home sooner than expected. The next day she went shopping but had a fit in a chandler's shop and fainted in the street while on her way home. In the hospital again, the doctors couldn't understand the causes of the convulsions usually followed by unconsciousness. She was by then an alcoholic and was often overcome in public places, creating scenes that humiliated her husband. Even though she begged him not to send her there, he put her in an invalids' home in Battersea for rest and removal from the alcohol she craved. In June she escaped her captivity and went to live with friends who sent abusive letters, accusing Gissing of mistreating her. By October he had taken her home again, but her stay was only temporary. He lived alone during most of 1883, and in September a policeman called to tell him she had become involved again in a disturbance at one-thirty in the morning. After that Gissing didn't live with Nell again and didn't see her again for more than three years. Then in 1888 he went to her death bed.

Chapter 11

Of Harlots and Harlotry

Inevitably bittersweet remembrance of Nell came into Gissing's fiction. In *Workers in the Dawn* (1880) she is the inspiration for Carrie Mitchell, who slowly falls apart after being seduced by a clergyman's son. In a moment of indecision the author suggests *"the girl herself might possibly be to blame,"* but then quickly asserts that a "heartless brute" robbed her of virtue. Accusing the man of casting her off *"when she most needed his help,"* he may be recalling his own behavior years earlier. When Carrie has a baby out of wedlock, her aunt berates her and orders her out of the house. Later, in a classic scene of Victorian melodrama, she begs to be admitted but is cruelly rejected. A "fallen woman," she must fend for herself in a world that scorns her. In the bitter cold of the streets her infant dies in her arms of starvation and exposure. A parallel situation is that of Lotty Starr in Gissing's second novel, *The Unclassed* (1884). Her seducer supports her for a year, during which time her child is born, and then abandons her. *"The familiar choice lay before her – home again, the streets, or starvation."* With the child in her arms she goes meekly for help to an unforgiving father who turns her away. Prostitution becomes the only way to survive, "and the little one lived."

As Gissing had gone to the aid of Nell after returning to England from America, Arthur Golding goes out to rescue Carrie. He puts her up in comfortable quarters, nurses her back to health, and eventually marries her. But aid comes too late. Her time on the streets has broken her: *"Carrie's experience had been that of the numberless girls in a similar destitute condition whom London nightly pillows in her hard corners, the only peculiarity being that she had found a way out of her misery without having recourse either to the workhouse or the river. Of one thing, however, Arthur felt certain, and it was that the period of wretched vagabondage had done Carrie considerable moral harm."* At a time when society has labeled her superfluous and cast her aside to die, nature demands that Carrie bring into the world an innocent child. When the child dies, the last vestige of her inner strength goes with it. Blaming herself, at least in part, for the death of her child, she spirals downward.

Soon after her marriage to Arthur, reflecting Nell's behavior, Carrie begins to drink and becomes an alcoholic. At that point her degeneration gathers momentum: *"Arthur fancied that he could observe her features growing coarser, and he felt convinced that her voice had no longer the clearness of tone which had once marked it. Yet of none of these signs did she herself appear conscious."* To get money for cheap gin she falsifies household accounts, pawns any object that will bring a few pence, and finally turns to prostitution. Arthur learns she is receiving visitors, tawdry young women, whom the landlady considers suspect. When they quarrel, she leaves her benefactor to take up again with the man who seduced her. Before long she is on the streets, a common whore sought after by middle-class gentlemen. Admittedly, the wives of those men would have called her "common," but in her heyday Carrie cut a fine figure: *"A tall girl showily dressed with features of considerable beauty, but spoiled by thick daubs of paint applied to conceal the pallor of the cheeks. Her face wore a devil-may-care expression; her eyes had that bleared, indistinct appearance so common in girls of the town; her features afforded numerous indications of the ruin she was bringing upon her constitution by excessive drinking. By her air and dress she appeared to belong to the aristocracy of the demimonde."*

It isn't long before Carrie becomes sick, and that alone allows Gissing to indict Victorian society for turning its back on women who desperately need help. The fear-ridden despair of the sick prostitute, attempting to survive in a city totally indifferent, fed the maw of melodrama. She could support herself in a fair degree of comfort only so long as health and good looks remained unimpaired. When she became sick, she resorted to begging or stealing, went to the detestable workhouse or a charitable shelter, died in the streets, or drowned in the river. In *The Unclassed* (1884) a young prostitute sinks to begging when she can no longer sell her sick body: *"He felt his elbow touched and met the kind of greeting for which he was prepared. He shook his head and did not reply; then the sham gaiety of the voice all at once turned to a very real misery, and the girl began to beg instead of trying to entice him in the ordinary way. He looked at her again and was shocked at the ghastly wretchedness of her daubed face. She was ill, she said, and could scarcely walk about but must get money somehow; if she didn't, her landlady wouldn't let her sleep in the house again, and she had no where else to go to. There could be no mistake about the genuineness of her story, at all events as far as bodily suffering went."* Carrie, fallen sick, must also find a way to survive.

Combing London for her, Arthur finds her in a vice den "situated in a very shabby back street," posing ostensibly in the nude for five shillings a week. At the risk of having thirty or forty men beat him to a pulp, he takes her out of the place and again tries to rehabilitate her. Soon afterwards she dies of syphilis, remaining unreclaimable to the end. Prophetically Gissing has traced in Carrie Mitchell's deterioration what will happen to Nell eight years later. Carrie's behavior seems at first glance to be based act for act on Nell's. However, Nell did not return to the streets until well after *Workers in the Dawn* was published in 1880. The pattern of deterioration set forth in the novel has to be described as remarkable prediction even though Gissing must have felt she would eventually come to such an end. A plot outline in the American notebook reads: *"Two young people marry and live in poor lodging house. Man becomes dissipated and leaves his wife, who through strange circumstances rises high in society and has good offers of marriage. Husband returns. Live together again, and husband by his dissipation brings wife to suicide."* To veil his true thoughts, perhaps even from himself, the gender of the two principals is reversed. Even so, the passage is almost a circumstantial account of the course his own marriage would take years later. It also suggests the plot of *Workers in the Dawn* (1880), for Carrie Mitchell's unassailable depravity ultimately brings her long-suffering husband to suicide.

Another woman similar to Carrie is Harriet Casti (née Smales) in Gissing's second novel, *The Unclasssed* (1884). She too is modeled after Nell, and so we may expect to find resemblances between her and Carrie. But if Carrie is Gissing's depiction of Nell in the early years of their marriage, Harriet is the way he saw her after he had come to loathe her. With Harriet Smales we have a representation of Nell in a far more cynical interpretation. At this point Gissing's disillusionment is dark indeed. He has given up the idea that Nell and her kind can be saved, for they are the victims not of society but of their own bad habits. We have redeeming traits in Carrie but few in Harriet; she is by far the more despicable of the two. In appearance the two women are similar, and so their physical traits help us sketch a picture of Nell. Adding to the picture and helping to support the view that Nell was the model for both Carrie and Harriet is the physical appearance of Laura Lindon, the idealized Nell in Gissing's first story, "The Sins of the Fathers." He had Nell in mind when he described Laura this way: *"The dark, flashing eyes, the long black hair all unkempt and streaming over the girl's shoulders, the face, lovely in its outlines."* Laura is also said to be tall and shapely.

Both Carrie and Harriet are tall, shapely, and graceful in movement. They have dark hair, dark eyes, a dark complexion, and sensual lips. Carrie is "very pretty" before she becomes dissolute and sick, but deepening cynicism regarding Nell led Gissing to describe Harriet as having an unattractive face of "sickly hue." The personal traits of the two women are also suggestive of Nell. Both have a propensity for the low life, for what is base. To the dismay of their respectable husbands, they take low and vulgar people as friends and accept as confidantes coarse women older than themselves. Carrie becomes the friend of Mrs. Pole, and Harriet of Mrs. Sprawl. On at least one occasion Carrie and Mrs. Pole fight like animals in the street, clawing each other and pulling hair. Harriet in a seizure induced by a violent quarrel with Mrs. Sprowl, plunges down a flight of stairs to lie unconscious at the bottom. Both are visited by flashy young women who are obviously prostitutes, and both get into trouble with husbands when the landlady complains. Neither knows how to occupy her time constructively, complains of boredom, complains of living too much alone, and accuses the respectable husband of failing to provide her with acquaintances.

Both are restless, self-willed, discontented, querulous, jealous of other women, and ill-natured; but Carrie shows a temper only when goaded while sour temper is a way of life with Harriet. Carrie is pathetic in weakness, but Harriet is harshly drawn. She is ill-natured, malevolent, selfish, hateful, peevish, stupid, surly, basically evil, and strangely detestable. Yet Harriet drinks only for sport while Carrie, a confirmed alcoholic, guzzles alcohol in earnest. Carrie has a deep sense of personal unworthiness and seeks oblivion in drink; she has a conscience which Harriet does not have. Both crave the gay life, and the fate of both is much the same. They take up with low people, become harlots, sink to utter depravity, become sick, and die. Carrie dies of dissipation and a dread disease; Harriet has an epileptic fit and breaks her neck in a fall. Both are dead before thirty. The close resemblance to Nell (who died at 29) is at once apparent. Again I should note that Nell's death didn't occur until 1888.

If the two women share many personal traits in common, there is one outstanding difference: Carrie is dissolute merely while Harriet is depraved. Carrie is betrayed by natural impulses and is morally tainted by the hardships of life, but Harriet's moral depravity is traceable to hereditary factors. Gissing had studied heredity and was intensely interested in the subject, an interest that increased after he had children of his own. Arthur Peachey of *In the Year of Jubilee* (1894) is worried over the possibility that his little boy has inherited Ada's despicable traits. Assuming that Harriet's many faults were inherited the moment she was born, Gissing never says she is evil. Unwilling to pass judgment, he prefers to call her weak. Waymark in the novel describes her as *"miserably weak in body and mind."* She is weak to such a degree that she becomes dangerous to those around her, for she has no moral sense. Her sense of right and wrong is warped because of *"a scrofulous tendency in her constitution"* that she inherited. This inherited flaw in her character, and perhaps in her body as well, leads Harriet to ruin: "*The scrofulous taint in her constitution was declaring itself in many ways. The most serious symptoms took the form of convulsive fits. On Julian's return home one evening, he had found her stretched upon the floor, unconscious, foaming at the mouth, and struggling horribly.*" While Carrie is a study of gradual deterioration, Harriet is unregenerate from the moment of conception.

Gissing also used heredity to explain the weak moral nature of another prostitute, Lotty Starr of *The Unclassed* (1884). "*Lotty, as she grew up, gradually developed an unfortunate combination of her parents' qualities; she had her mother's weakness of mind without her mother's moral sense, and from her father she derived an ingrained stubbornness, which had nothing in common with strength of character.*" Concepts of heredity became for Gissing useful tools for explaining the character and fate of these women, but all the time he was thinking of Nell. Harriet is the monstrous perception he had formed of Nell after he failed to save her from a sordid life. Beginning with the belief that she was an innocent victim of society, he came full circle to the conclusion that Nell was naturally depraved and therefore irretrievable. There was little anyone could do to save her because her course was directed by natural law, by the chemistry of her own body.

In a novel he published exactly ten years later, *In the Year of Jubilee* (1894), Mrs. Damerel explains to her son Horace that Fanny French, the girl he wants to marry, is morally unacceptable. When Horace protests in anger, suggesting some villain must have corrupted the girl, his mother replies: *"How can anyone drive a girl into a life of scandalous immorality? It was in herself, dear. She took to it naturally, as so many women do."* Despite his mother's strong resistance, Horace makes plans to wed Fanny French, viewing her as very desirable. On the eve of the wedding Mrs. Damerel reiterates her opinion of the girl: *"You haven't seen her. She looks what she is, the vilest of the vile. As if anyone can be held responsible for that! She was born to be what she is. And if I had the power, I would crush out her hateful life to save poor Horace!"* The irony here is plain. While Horace has trouble seeing the faults in Fanny that his mother clearly sees, the latter is incapable of seeing that her beloved son is drawn to Fanny because he too is naturally depraved.

Perhaps Gissing's first wife "took to it naturally," and yet we have him declaring in 1888 that "the accursed social order" was really to blame for her untimely and miserable death. He had reached the conclusion in 1884 that constitutional factors were involved, but the emotional shock of seeing Nell in death moved him again to curse the nature of things. Perhaps at that moment Nell became a symbol of all the oppressed females throughout the world, or certainly in London. In any event, if Gissing at one time regarded her as a victim of society and later as a victim of heredity, conflicts more serious than this appear frequently in his thought. He was no single-minded reformer intent on achieving a goal with a single project, but a man of highly personal and often contradictory ideas. On many of the important issues of the day, including the woman question, his intelligent opinion turned from a liberal to a conservative bias, from sharp and steady decision to wavering indecision.

For all that, Gissing would have been the first to admit that if some women take to prostitution naturally, most who begin to practice that profession are forced into it by circumstances mainly economic in nature. A prostitute named Ida Starr, prominent in *The Unclassed* (1884) and admired by Gissing, is a good example. When Osmond Waymark meets Ida at midnight on the streets of the West End, he looks into her fresh, bright face and tells her he would like to remember it as it is, not as it will be soon with marks of suffering and degradation upon it. Ida retorts what while her face may show suffering it will never display signs of degradation. *"Why should I be degraded?"* she asks. Waymark replies it's because of the life she has chosen. Suddenly indignant and angry, amazed that he thinks she had a choice in the matter, she explains the only choice she had was one of life or death and she chose to live. Later with incisive word-pictures, she describes the conditions of her early life and the events that plunged her into the cesspool of London's unclassed.

She tells Waymark that when her mother died, she was thrown on her own at the age of eleven. Weak or non-existent child-labor laws permitted her to work as a scullery maid in a restaurant from early morning until late at night. She received no wages, only left-over food and a place to sleep in the kitchen. From this sordid existence she soon ran away, fleeing a lecherous employer, the cruelty of his wife, and the unremitting toil beyond her strength. With not a single person in all of London willing to help her, the girl's luck suddenly turned and she was befriended by a lonely old lady. She lived in the woman's spare little house for six years as her companion. When her benefactor died, at the age of seventeen Ida found herself once more alone in a hostile world. For six months she worked in a laundry and then became a lady's maid in the home of a pretentious family with two grown-up daughters and a son. The wages were criminal, the food inadequate, and the toil endless. *"The slavery left me every night worn out with exhaustion."*

To escape that dreary existence she became the mistress of the son in the family. After six months he abandoned her, and again she was alone in the world. Unable to find a job of any kind, she drifted into harlotry and now on meeting Waymark has been a whore for four months. She falls in love with this man who has taken an interest in her, and to make herself worthy of him she performs a symbolic ceremony of cleansing and rebirth. Morley Roberts writes that George Meredith objected to the passage and wanted it expunged. In our time the passage is critically acclaimed as one of the highlights of the novel: *"Ida dipped her hands in the water and sprinkled it upon her forehead. Then she took off her boots and stockings and walked with her feet in the ripples. A moment later she stopped and looked all around, as if hesitating at some thought, and wishing to see that her solitude was secure. Just then the sound of a clock came very faintly across the still air, striking the hour of one. She stepped from the water a few paces and began hastily to put off her clothing; in a moment her feet were again in the ripples, and she was walking out from the beach till her gleaming body was hidden. Then she bathed, breasting the full flow with delight, making the sundered and broken water flash myriad reflections of the moon and stars."* The vivid symbolic bathing in the sea has washed away Ida's sins. She has transcended the glare of the gas-lamps and the commerce of the pavement through the power of love.

Though a prostitute and the daughter of a prostitute, Ida Starr is one of Gissing's angel-women. Other women who merit that title are Helen Norman (1880), Isabel Clarendon (1886), Adela Waltham (1886), Thyrza Trent (1887), Emily Hood (1888), Jane Snowdon (1889), and Irene Derwent (1899). They are women idealized in the manner of Ruskin and placed on a pedestal. Any reader of Gissing's novels can't help but see many bad-seed types that suggest a negative, even vindictive evaluation of women. The perceptive reader will see as well this sentimental over-evaluation of women. Ida Starr is a prime example. She is the author's vision of Nell not as she was, but as she might have been. As a young woman forced into prostitution by necessity, she hangs on to her sense of worth, her dignity, and is spoken of as one of "the high and haughty lot." Her mother, Lotty Starr, though weaker, also didn't associate with the rank and file: *"In the profession Lotty had chosen there are, as in all professions, grades and differences. She was by no means a vicious girl, she had no love of riot for its own sake."* And so she lived away from the red-light district and went there to ply her trade only when necessary.

Her daughter, Ida, can be seen as an angel-woman, and yet she not so idealistically conceived as to be unbelievable. She rises from poverty and prostitution to become a strong, well-balanced, virtuous woman of practical mind always willing to help others. Osmond Waymark quickly returns her love to make her even stronger. *"You can't call her educated,"* he says of her, *"but she speaks purely and has a remarkably good intelligence. She is strong in character, admirably clear-headed, mild, gentle, womanly."* Revealing substance and moral strength in all she does, she exemplifies the woman of rare type who escapes prostitution with soul intact. Of similar type is Sally Fisher in the same novel. A famous print from Hogarth's *The Harlot's Progress* (1732), a print surely known to Gissing even as a boy, shows an innocent young girl, fresh from the country, falling into the clutches of pimps in the city. The strait-laced nineteenth century, insistent upon strict moral attitudes, required artists to pay homage to Mrs. Grundy. In the many novels that poured from the presses, the girl was usually portrayed as becoming a servant. However, at the risk of having his books rejected by the powerful founder of Mudie's Lending Library, Gissing wanted to show what really happened to many of these girls.

Sally Fisher, a fresh young girl looking about seventeen, came to the city to seek her fortune and have fun doing it. Quickly she finds she must work very hard to make a living. In the daytime she toils in a city workroom. We see her in conversation with another girl:

"And how much do you think I earn a week?" she asked.

"Fifteen shillings or so, I suppose?"

"Ah, that's all you know about it! Now, last week was the best I've had yet, and I made seven shillings."

"What do you do?"

"Machine work, makin' ulsters. How much do you think we get, now, for makin' a ulster – one like this?"

"Have no idea."

"Well, fourpence! There now!"

"And how many can you make in a day?"

"I can make no more than two. Some make three but it's blessed hard work. But I get a little job now and then to do at home."

"But you can't live on seven shillings a week!"

"I sh'd think not! We have to make up the rest as best we can."

"But your employers must know that?"

"In course. What's the odds? All us girls are the same. We have to keep on the two jobs at the same time. But I'll give up the day work before long. I feel all eyes, as the sayin' is. And it's hard to have to go out into the Strand when you're like that."

Back-breaking labor many hours each day and only seven shillings a week! At the time the action of the novel is taking place it was impossible to live decently in London on less than a pound, or twenty shillings, a week. So at night Sally must supplement her meager earnings by turning to prostitution. Her employers know she is not receiving a living wage, but they know also that if she quits, another girl will eagerly take her place. Sally's predicament is a striking example of how the unscrupulous, laissez-faire employer exploited the surplus of young women in the labor market. Such marginal living among workgirls, Gissing noted, was not uncommon: *"A girl who says that she is occupied in a work-room is never presumed to be able to afford the luxury of strict virtue."*

That same statement with little modification could apply to shopgirls. Though slightly higher in the social scale, their weekly pay wasn't much higher. Many appear to have supplemented their earnings in the shop by moonlighting in the Strand. We have evidence in *The Odd Women* (1893). The scene is the girls' dormitory of Scotcher's and Company, a large drapery firm: *"Just before one o'clock there entered the last occupant of the bedroom. She was a young woman with a morally unenviable reputation, though some of her colleagues certainly envied her. Money came to her with remarkable readiness whenever she had need of it. As usual, she began to talk very loud with innocent vulgarity, and then she became very scandalous. When the candle was out she still had her richest story to relate – so Rabelaisian that one or two voices made themselves heard in serious protest."* The girl confesses she rather likes her night job.

Greedy, money-mad employers were forcing girls into prostitution when they might have prevented it. Yet the problem was not so simple as this. Economic laws of supply and demand sometimes left even a well-intentioned employer powerless to keep his girls from the streets. In the short story "Phoebe" (1884), which Bertz thought good enough to translate into German, Gissing says of Phoebe, an unemployed flower-maker: *"It was no fault of her own that she had lost her work some weeks ago. The season had been a bad one; the powers and principalities who rule in such matters had decreed that it should be fashionable to wear feathers, and for flowers there was proportionately little demand. Hence trouble in the work-rooms here in Hoxton, where most of the flower makers live."* In spite of hard times, Phoebe doesn't go the way of the flesh. Instead she manages to scrape a meager living from odd jobs: *"A little needlework, a little cleaning of door-steps, some running of errands, minding of children now and then, washing vegetables for sale."*

All of that work she must do simply to pay the rent. Girls like her, without help from a charitable organization, turned in desperation to prostitution. The brutal choice of the streets or starvation faced many girls of the day, and what appalled Gissing was that no one seemed to care. Nor was this the lot only of the working girl. In the shop-keeping world of the lower-middle class, girls were often faced with the same bleak choice. The shopgirl who couldn't endure the interminable hours of the shop, who couldn't find a husband, who had no relatives to help her and shuddered at the thought of being carted off to the workhouse, inevitably went on the streets. In *New Grub Street* (1891) Edwin Reardon, who is working temporarily as a clerk in a hospital, speaks of *"a tall, good-looking, very quiet girl"* who has come to the hospital for help. When he asks her to name her occupation, she replies, "I'm unfortunate, sir." He had looked her over and taken her for a milliner or dressmaker. The incident could be a recollection of something that really happened when Gissing himself worked as a temporary clerk at St. John's Hospital, London in September of 1878.

In *The Odd Women* (1893) the plaintive and pathetic Miss Eade, knowing the shop is undermining her health, tries desperately to snare the attentions of a nondescript clerk named Bullivant. But unlike Sally Fisher, who was able to marry a genial Irishman and live happily with him, Miss Eade is forced by overwork to leave the shop for a brothel. Near the end of the novel, though lost and on the brink of being lost forever, Miss Eade still hopes a Mr. Bullivant will save her. She is the sort of woman who could be reclaimed if anyone cared enough to take the trouble. Unless she is reclaimed (as were Ida Starr and Sally Fisher), she will suffer misery, become sick, and die before her time. As late as 1894, when *In the Year of Jubilee* was published, Gissing was still wrestling with the issue of what makes a woman go bad. With Fanny French of that novel he again blamed hereditary factors, but he also felt that women of her kind were victims of immoral predators, who roamed through all classes, unheeded by an apathetic society. His opinions fluctuated and at times seem contradictory, and yet his proletarian novels in particular lodge an enduring protest. As he composed these early novels, he was hoping some person of influence might read his pungent words, see the sordid pictures of lives being wasted, and do something about it.

Chapter 12

Female Servants

In Gissing's day, with only a few exceptions, the prostitute was an outcast living at the bottom of the social ladder among the criminals. Slightly above her and on the lowest rung was the female domestic servant. In the eyes of the typical mistress she was little more than a piece of property. *"Yes, she is our creature,"* says Adela Waltham in *Demos* (1886). *"We pay her and she must remember her station."* Yet the times were rapidly changing, and many feared that servants were not remembering their station. Guardians of the status quo complained that female domestics were becoming insolent and independent. Feeding on the newly established democratic doctrines of equality and recognizing no superiors, they sometimes deliberately offended the people who tried to buy their services, particularly the nouveau riche whom they despised. Before the century was over the cry for equal rights for women had sifted down to the working class, and like Charlotte Grub in "A Free Woman," many working-class women thought the new freedom meant doing exactly as they pleased, obeying impulse only. The result was much discontent among servants and mistresses and a gravely serious servant problem. Though attempts were made to improve the lot of servants, changes in their economic and social position were slow in coming.

As in most occupations, especially in middle-class England, one could find a scale among domestic servants that ran from the lowest scullery maid to the respected housekeeper. The girls who did the roughest work of a household were usually quite young and the daughters of day laborers. They came from homes the reverse of clean or tidy, and they served in homes that were not much better, usually those of artisans or skilled craftsmen. Though sometimes treated with kindness, they were often looked upon as almost sub-human and given more work than they could reasonably do. Charles Booth, author of a monumental work in seventeen volumes entitled *Life and Labour of the People in London* (1889 and later), said the worst situations were those in lodging houses. There the servants were on duty during all their waking hours. It wasn't unusual for a girl to labor seventeen or eighteen hours a day at very low wages. In 1894 the Metropolitan Association for Befriending Young Servants (mainly an employment agency) estimated the average yearly wage for a girl of sixteen at about seven pounds. Actual wages with room and board sometimes began as low as one shilling a week, or less than three pounds a year. As the girl grew older and more experienced her wages increased, but it was rare for girls in lodging houses to earn as much as seventeen pounds a year at any time.

Next in the scale of servants were the children of artisans. They came often from homes that were well kept. Usually they had some rudimentary education and good references. They found places in the homes of clerks or people in business and sometimes received training that allowed them to go on to something better. It was not uncommon for them to work from seven in the morning until midnight for wages that seldom went above ten pounds a year. On occasion they were given a Sunday off or an evening out, but in most cases they had only one day off each month. Some girls entered domestic service only temporarily when work in the factories was slack, or when they thought a change would be pleasant. Because they valued their independence, they usually returned to the comparative freedom of factory life as soon as they could. Servant girls who had the alternative of factory work were far too independent to kowtow to bosses, especially to a woman. When provoked they were known to quit even a good job on the spur of the moment without giving notice. Mrs. Denyer of *The Emancipated* (1890) complains: *"I paid Charlotte her wages, and the very first thing she did was to pack and go!"*

In a middle-class family where three or four servants were employed, the best position was that of housekeeper. Her duties were not overwhelming, and her annual wage could be as much as twenty-two pounds. A lady's maid received only two pounds more, though a good cook often earned as much as twenty-five pounds. The age of the average housekeeper was said to be about forty-three; servants under her supervision were younger. She was often tall and stately, for tallness of stature and thinness of build were considered desirable in superior servants. Most of the time a woman reached the position of housekeeper through hard work and slow advancement. To have intelligence, a calm personality, and leadership also helped. In not a few cases a widow or spinster who had seen better days became the housekeeper of a relative or close friend. Two examples are Mrs. Cumberbatch of *Workers in the Dawn* (1880), a poor widow, and Miss Harrow, an ex-governess, of *New Grub Street* (1891). An example of a gentlewoman reduced to a charwoman is Mrs. Handover in Gissing's *The Whirlpool* (1897). When Rolfe's charwoman falls ill and can no longer hold the job, his friend offers to take it. The proposal startles Rolf, for he has always seen Handover as an equal.

Female servants of all these ranks have their place in Gissing's work. Those on the lowest level he called domestic slaves, and once more social investigators confirmed the accuracy and realism of his representation. The term is just barely figurative, for the girls receiving that label lived and worked on the premises and were required to labor from early morning till late at night, and sometimes in the middle of the night. For their labor they got nothing more than a place to sleep and a plate of coarse food, some complaining they got too little food. They were abused by all around them (because of their low status), and their work was hard, rough, and nasty. They were usually found in lodging-houses, inns, and restaurants. In *The Unclassed* (1889), Ida Starr as a child of eleven toils long hours in the kitchen of a restaurant. In *The Nether World* (1889) Jane Snowdon is held in virtual bondage by a lodging-house keeper claiming to be a relative. Neither girl receives pay of any kind.

Another drudge scarcely better off than a slave is Moggie in *The Town Traveller* (1898). A lowly fixture of Mrs. Bubb's boarding house, the lodgers abuse her almost as a matter of principle. As the novel opens, Polly Sparkes, a girl of the shop-keeping class, is venting her temper on the hapless servant: *"If it wasn't too much trouble, I'd come out and smack your face for you, you dirty little wretch!"* Blaming her faulty memory on the fact that at birth her "'ead had never closed at the top," Moggie can't remember the simplest of orders. Though something of a humorous figure, she is similar to many servants in real life. In the spring of 1901 Gabrielle Fleury Gissing, living away from England, complained to Catherine Wells: *"Our servant is a very honest girl, in every respect, and cooks well, but she has no memory whatever and you have to repeat her twenty times a thing and even to see her doing it, if you will be sure of its being done."* At the age of sixteen, Moggie works a seventeen-hour day, sleeps a few hour on rags in a corner, eats for breakfast a crust of black bread with strong coffee, is given a few minutes to wash her face and comb her hair, and is back at work again. For an entire year she will earn fewer than seven pounds.

Servants in Gissing's novels who work in the homes of the middle class are seen at times to be not much better off than Moggie. People such as Reardon in *New Grub Street* (1892), though struggling to make ends meet, somehow manage to employ a servant. In a foolish attempt to "keep up appearances" even when insolvent and owing money, a surprising number manage to keep more than one servant. It is said of Mrs. Edmund Yule, Amy Reardon's mother: *"Like the majority of London people, she occupied a house of which the rent absurdly exceeded the due proportion of her income. She kept only two servants, who were so ill paid and so relentlessly overworked that it was seldom they remained with her for more than three months."* Other women of this stamp are Mrs. Morgan of *In the Year of Jubilee* (1894) and Mrs. Cross of *Will Warburton* (1905). Of Mrs. Morgan, Gissing writes: *"All her married life had been spent in a cheerless struggle to maintain the externals of gentility. For close upon thirty years the family had lived in houses of which the rent was out of all reasonable proportion to their means; of course they kept a servant, her wages nine pounds a year."*

Invariably a woman of the servant class resented working for a family that struggled just to support itself, and the outcome in most cases was a conflict that resulted in dismissal. In his posthumous novel *Will Warburton* (1905), Gissing treats this problem fully as he focuses on Mrs. Cross. A mean-minded widow of the lower-middle class, she must have a servant not only to keep up appearances, but also to bait. She lives with her daughter Bertha in a tidy little house on an income that barely sustains them, and yet she employs a servant. *"To say that she 'kept' one would come near to a verbal impropriety, seeing that no servant ever remained in the house for more than a few months."* Underpaid, underfed, and overworked, her servants are incompetent, peevish, rebellious, and under seige in continual warfare. Their employer is acrid of temper, impatient, parsimonious, and incapable of supervising another woman. The servants come and go, and the interior of the little house is forever in a muddle. When it appears that she may never find another servant, Mrs. Cross discovers one who seems the perfect domestic. Though it requires a bit of sacrifice, she hires Martha at fifteen pounds a year.

It is more than former servants have received, and for a time Martha is content. But as time passes Mrs. Cross exacts more and more work from her, some of it unnecessary, and feeds her less. Under the brunt of mistreatment the girl, quite docile in the beginning, rapidly becomes rebellious. When Mrs. Cross reproaches her for accidently ruining a towel, Martha flies into a rage. Fortified by secret drinking on the job, she dashes the crockery piece by piece to the floor: *"You think you'll make me pay for them? Not me, not me! It's you as owes me money – money for all the work I've done as wasn't in my wages, and for the food I haven't had when I'd ought to. You want to make a walkin' skeleton of me, do you? But I'll have it out of you, I will. There goes another dish! And there goes a sugar-basin! And here goes your teapot!"* Uttering shrieks of dismay and alarm, Mrs. Cross springs forward to save the cherished teapot. With the sudden movement comes more alarming behavior. Martha seizes a poker and chases her employer about the house, yelling threats and abuse, until exertion and love of the bottle bring collapse.

The scene is too vivid not to have come at least in part from personal experience. Gissing's second wife Edith is the model for Mrs. Cross and her servant troubles. At the end of 1895 he wrote to his younger sister Ellen: *"Our last three servants (wages 20-25 pounds) have stayed one month each, and all declare there is work for three strong women and a boy! We are now going to have back a loutish creature who was here a year ago; the only one who ever did her work (however badly) without grumbling or insult. Her tart crust had to be broken with hammers, but we can't help that."* Edith was uniquely ineffectual when it came to supervising servants. She was too familiar with them or too hostile, and they left on a regular schedule after getting a taste of her temper. To get away from the incessant quarreling in his home, Gissing thought of giving up housekeeping altogether and perhaps finding a way to live in hotels. It would be an escape from the servant question that plagued him, but of course Edith would have none of that.

Even on the southern-most tip of Italy he couldn't get away from wrangling of the kind that jarred his nerves at home. While on his Calabrian journey, an embattled servant accosted him to complain woefully of unjust treatment. His sensitive description of her tells us that as late as November of 1897 he could be moved by the suffering of women in another country: *"Picture a woman of middle age, wrapped at all times in dirty rags (not to be called clothing), obese, grimy, with dishevelled black hair, and hands so scarred, so deformed by labour and neglect, as to be scarcely human. She had the darkest and fiercest eyes I ever saw. Between her and her mistress went on an unceasing quarrel; they quarrelled in my room, in the corridor, and in places remote; yet I am sure they did not dislike each other. Unexpectedly one evening this woman entered, stood by the bedside, and began to talk with such fierce energy, with such flashing of her black eyes and such distortion of her features, that I could only suppose that she was attacking me for the trouble I caused her. In fact she was appealing for my sympathy, not abusing me at all."* All he could say, responding in broken Italian, that her life might soon be better. She wanted only to unburden herself.

The servant in revolt was common enough near the end of the century. Yet for one servant in England who rebelled, more than half a hundred suffered in silence. A prudent servant knew only too well that one supreme moment of satisfaction could bring endless pain. In Gissing's work middle-class women often complain of their servants, and yet the servants themselves are given good reason to complain. The conflict is usually between servant and mistress. Men without meddling wives have little difficulty with servants because they are capable of exerting the necessary authority. Often one finds mutual respect between master and servant, resulting in a calm and close relationship. *"Mrs. Jenkins isn't as refined as she might be,"* says Dagworthy in *A Life's Morning* (1888), *"but she's been with us here for more than twelve years, and I should be sorry to replace her with any other servant."* Though he tends to view his servant as more mechanical than human, he is able nonetheless to appreciate her value. In *The Whirlpool* (1897) Harvey Rolfe's cook-housekeeper has become indispensable. When she gives notice she must leave, Rolfe is thrown into consternation. He knows finding someone to replace Ruth will be very difficult if not impossible.

Similar to Ruth is Ryecroft's servant in *The Private Papers of Henry Ryecroft* (1903). He sees her as a superlative woman, hesitates to call her a servant, for she has dedicated herself to the task of taking excellent care of him and his house. She is there to make his life comfortable, not merely for money but because she believes it her duty. He praises her as the best of women: *"From the first I thought her an unusually good servant; after three years of acquaintance, I find her one of the few women I have known who merit the term of excellent. She can read and write – that is all. More instruction would, I am sure have harmed her. She is fulfilling the offices for which she was born, and that with grace and contentment."* Ryecroft believes his nameless housekeeper was born to serve and would be immensely unhappy were she educated and attempting to do something else. In 1898, while living alone at Dorking, Gissing himself had such a housekeeper. She was the model for Ryecroft's faithful, dedicated, unobtrusive servant.

While the two share a common sympathy in Ryecroft's household, the housekeeper is fully aware she can never cross a severe line of class distinction. On occasion, and yet almost never, a master in Gissing's work ignores class prejudice and either marries his servant or promotes her to equal status with his family. Stephen Lord of *In the Year of Jubilee* (1894) makes Mary Woodruff an equal and a friend: *"You shall sit at our table with us and live with us."* After her promotion Mary remains humble, loyal, and sensible; and Stephen's daughter Nancy readily accepts her as a social equal. In real life, however, such an arrangement often brought conflict, especially when the head of the household married his servant. This aspect of the servant problem Gissing presented in "A Yorkshire Lass" (1896). Kate Kirby can't believe her father has married the housekeeper and refuses even to acknowledge the marriage: *"Do you think it right to put a servant over my head in this house without as much as asking me if I should like it?"* Highly class-conscious, Kate worries about how people in the town will react, believing they will laugh at her as she walks down the street, believing they will sneer at her behind her back.

Surely the most irksome aspect of "the servant question" was finding and keeping a good servant. Gissing's later novels in particular comment on this problem, for after 1890 he was increasingly caught up in servant difficulties. His second wife, Edith, was incapable of supervising a servant, and Gabrielle, his third, irked him by turning her "executive power" over to her mother. In November of 1895 he wrote to his German friend, Bertz: *"Of course the whole question of domestic service is one of the gravest of our time, and I hope to write a book about it. I have immense material."* Although he never wrote a book specifically on the servant question, he used the material nonetheless, having characters in his novels express his thoughts. Even before 1895 he had published pungent commentary on the problem. Lionel Tarrant of *In the Year of Jubilee* (1894) asks Nancy Lord: *"Do you give much thought to the great servant question? I have my own modest view of the matter."* Tarrant's "modest view" is worth considering.

Even though Tarrant is more liberal in attitude than Gissing, his opinions are the same: *"We must begin,"* he tells Nancy, *"by admitting that the ordinary woman hates nothing so much as to have another woman set in authority over her. Now before the triumph of glorious Democracy, only those women kept servants who were capable of rule, who had by birth the instinct of authority. They knew themselves the natural superiors of their domestics, and went through an education fitting them to rule. Things worked very well; no servant difficulty existed. Nowadays every woman who can afford it must have another woman to wait upon her, no matter how silly or vulgar or depraved she may be; the result of course is a spirit of rebellion in the kitchen."* Women in the democratic milieu of the 1890's marvel that servants have the nerve to revolt against them, but what could be more natural? The women who are attempting to exercise authority over them are utterly incompetent when trying to supervise others. They bungle the job miserably every time they attempt it, and that actually encourages revolt. The incompetents are so vast a majority, Tarrant in the guise of Gissing asserts with conviction, that sooner or later they will spoil all the servants in the entire country.

In his commonplace book Gissing noted it was rare to see a woman of his day smoothly exercising power of rule, for the "doctrines of equality" had made the servant class more troublesome than ever. In the old days servants were taught from childhood to know their station, and so it wasn't hard to keep them in order, but in the 1890's with talk of equality in the air servants were finding it difficult to take orders from people they looked upon as their equals. In *The Whirlpool* (1897) Harvey Rolfe complains: *"There isn't a servant to be had unless you're a Duke and breed them on your own estate. All ordinary housekeepers are at the mercy of the filth and insolence of a draggle-tailed, novelette-reading feminine democracy. Before long we shall train an army of men-servants, and send the women to the devil."* Later, when Alma Rolfe suffers insolence from democratic servants, Gissing intrudes to comment: *"No one could better have illustrated the crucial difficulty of the servant-question, which lies in the fact that women seldom can rule, and all but invariably dislike to be ruled by their own sex; a difficulty which increases with the breaking up of social distinctions."*

Gissing believed only the rarest of women could maintain harmonious relations with a domestic over an extended period of time. He believed that a fundamental cause of the servant problem was the inability of most women to demand and receive respect from their domestic help. The women of the new prosperity simply cannot rule, he repeatedly proclaims; the idea appears again in *Our Friend the Charlatan* (1901): *"She could not brook a semblance of disregard for her authority, yet like women in general, had no idea of how to rule."* In the same novel, by way of contrast, he presents a woman who can rule: *"Rarely had Lady Ogram any trouble with her domestics; she chose them carefully and kept them for a long time; they feared her, but respected her power of ruling, the rarest gift in women of whatever rank."* Lady Ogram represents a type that was rapidly vanishing. In her place came an army of incompetents, females incapable of exercising fair, firm authority over other females. They upset the delicate balance that had always existed between mistress and maid, but democracy was also to blame.

In several places Gissing seriously suggested a solution to the servant problem. He wasn't so radical as Harvey Rolfe, who would forget the women and train only men-servants; yet the solution he proposed must have set his contemporaries grumbling. He said the girls of the laboring class should be taught from infancy that domestic service is no shame, and above all they should be taught how to cook. Rolfe wants to train Minnie Wager, abandoned by her widowed father, to become a cook. Her guardian, speaking for Gissing, thinks the idea a good one: *"I would rather see her a good cook in a lady's kitchen, if it came to that, than leading a foolish life at some so-called genteel occupation."* The problem could be solved, at least in part, by establishing special schools to train young women to become servants. It would certainly be better for them to work in private homes than in mills or workrooms. Other schools would teach cooking and baking to girls of higher rank. Such training would allow many women, particularly the daughters of the lower-middle class, to live without servants. In others it would instill a sense of authority that comes only with having mastered the work done by subordinates. Knowing how to cook, she could advise and supervise without giving offense.

Gissing also set forth the idea, causing consternation in some quarters, that young women of "a higher sort" should also become servants, especially if they had no prospect of marriage. In that way the superfluous women infesting London would find useful places in society. In "Miss Rodney's Leisure" (1903), a busy-body schoolteacher admired by Gissing makes it her project to send the idle, parasitic daughters of her landlady into service. The mother indignantly cries out, *"We're not so poor, miss, that we need send our daughters into service."* But that is precisely why the Turpin girls with their refinement would suit a lady of the leisure class, the teacher retorts. In another story, "The Foolish Virgin" (1896), Rosamund Jewell, one of those odd women portrayed so well by Gissing, finds security and peace of mind as a domestic. She has been living for eight years in boarding houses, trying desperately to snag a husband. When her relatives tell her they can no longer support her, she becomes a servant in a good family. The story concludes with her mistress saying: *"It's no small thing to find your vocation, is it? Thousands of such women, all meant by nature to scrub and cook, live and die miserably because they think themselves too good for it."* Again Gissing has chosen a mouthpiece to express exactly his own sentiments.

When taken as a whole, his remarks on servants and the servant question, scattered through several novels, show unequivocally that he was worried about what he thought was a serious decline in the quality of domestic life in England. He had seen it in his own household, in those of his friends, and in the many articles that poured from the presses of the day. The women's movement with its cry of emancipation and equality was turning women away from their natural calling, leaving them restless and unhappy. He wanted them back in the home. He wanted those who couldn't find jobs in a very competitive society to work in the homes of other women and take pride in their work. No woman who became a servant had to feel ashamed or feel she had fallen downward in life. Girls should be taught in childhood that it's an honorable pursuit to serve others.

Gissing portrayed female servants near the end of the nineteenth century in circumstances corroborated by the work of Charles Booth, one of the most prominent social investigators of the time. Often he depicted hapless servants as grossly mistreated, and then he showed them in revolt against overwork, low wages, and poor working conditions. However, he didn't champion the servant; his treatment was impersonal rather than sympathetic. In his early novels he could work himself into a rage over social iniquities, but his later work struck a note of mater-of-fact reporting. In the novels of the eighties he had little to say about servants, but in those of the nineties he recognized a servant problem, tried to get at its roots, and offered solutions that some of his readers saw as radical.

Chapter 13

Women With Needles

The servant and the working woman came generally from the same class, for they were the daughters of laboring men. The woman who worked in a mill or factory, however, considered the servant a social inferior and became a servant herself only for the sake of variety or when times were hard. Ida Starr became a lady's maid as a welcomed change from working in a laundry, and Lotty Simpson went into service when the bad times began. Pennyloaf Candy, a girl of the laboring class, was proud that she had never toiled as a domestic: *"She herself had never been a servant – never,"* Gissing tells us in *The Nether World* (1889). *"She had never sunk below working with the needle for sixteen hours a day for a payment of ninepence. The work-girl regards a domestic slave as very distinctly inferior."* If the working girl snubbed the servant as a creature beneath her, she looked upon shopgirls, even those who worked in restaurants, as her superiors: *"She* [a flower-maker named Phoebe in the short story by the same name] *was hungry, keenly hungry, but it was beyond all possibility to think of walking up to such a counter as that and addressing that superb young lady who stood behind it."*

As with servants, one found subtle class distinctions within the ranks of working women. The wages of needlewomen were much the same in all branches of the industry, but the workers didn't always come from the same social level. Sewing was often done at home by destitute women of the middle class who kept aloof from those beneath them by not working with them. Similarly, the daughters of clerks, skilled artisans, and laborers worked together in the factories but remained apart socially. Numerous young women in factories were seen by Booth as *"very respectable, not at all like factory girls."* They didn't frequent the haunts of the typical factory girl, and whenever possible kept to themselves. So it may be seen that the term "factory girl" didn't include all girls in factories. It was applicable mainly to the unskilled factory worker, who lived on a low social level at low wages. Girls in factories earned eleven shillings a week and upwards, but the factory girl earned only seven to eleven shillings and rarely more. It was not unusual for a whole factory to regard itself as socially superior to another. The girls in a jam factory, for instance, didn't associate with those in a match factory because they prided themselves on being sweeter and cleaner. A girl who made caps and head gear could earn more in a jam or match factory, but the loss of social status made the change unthinkable.

Generally the women in workrooms earned less than those in factories. The lowest wages among needlewomen, according to Charles Booth, were paid by the furriers. A good worker averaged from ten to twelve shillings a week, but often fell below the average. Unskilled "hands" and those doing the commonest work never got more than nine shillings, and then only in season. For several months of the year the fur-sewers had no work at all, or only enough to earn about three or four shillings a week. These were indeed starvation wages, and those doing work of this kind invariably received a small income from other sources. A main source of extra income, as we've already seen, was prostitution. A young and healthy harlot could earn more in a single night than she could as a needlewoman in a month. Intensely ironical was the fact that some working women envied "the swell women" who accosted johns in the West End every evening.

In the trouser-making trade the lowest-paid workers were married women who took up the work under pressure of want. They started as learners at two shillings, sixpence a week, at most a token wage. The pay rose to a maximum of ten shillings for ordinary hands and thirteen for superior ones, but even then it was below the standard of living. Yet employers had little difficulty obtaining women to do the work. Booth said an employer in this trade once found it necessary to advertise for additional workers and was surprised to see the next day more than eighty women of all ages standing in line in the cold, waiting patiently in fond hope of getting a job. Most of the work was done at home where the women could sew, boil potatoes, and care for their children at the same time.

Slightly above the trouser-maker on the economic scale was the shirt-finisher. She was generally an older woman, infirm, penniless, and a widow. She never expected to have to labor for a living, and when obliged to do so, worked at whatever she could, usually some kind of sewing. She took the work at whatever price it was offered and earned very little. One woman could finish a dozen shirts a day, making button holes and putting on buttons, and earned fivepence. From this twopence had to go for tram fare, and *"if she went to prayer meeting,"* according to Booth, *"she had to work till 11 o'clock to do the dozen."* Whether she got fivepence a dozen or threepence, it was equally impossible for her to live on earnings so meager, and even as an old woman she had no subsidy from the government and no pension of any kind. An over supply of workers and sub-contracting were said to be the two main causes of the low wages paid for shirt-making. Another was the consumer's indifference to the quality of the shirt he bought. Years earlier Charles Kingsley had complained about that in *Cheap Clothes and Nasty* (1850).

The wages of collar-makers were said to be considerably higher, from eleven to seventeen shillings, because collars were worn to be seen. The same was true of cravats, but work in this area was erratic. When orders came they had to be filled immediately, and the tie-stitcher sometimes worked all night to have an order ready by nine in the morning. Then for several days there would be nothing to do, but even so the wages remained higher than that of shirt-making. Workers on articles worn to be seen invariably made more money, but wages were sometimes cut when factories competed with one another. Such was particularly true of the fancy-trimmings factories. In that industry child labor was exploited by home workers who took as much work as they could get from various factories and paid children about two shillings a week to do simple parts of it. The children were known to work very long hours, beginning sometimes at eight in the morning and going on till after nine or even eleven at night. "Working for a friend at her own house" was labor that harmed the children, but their parents thought it preferable to having them do menial chores in public.

The lowest wages among female factory workers, as opposed to the women in workrooms who did some kind of sewing, were earned by those who made match boxes at home. These boxes could be made by children of nine or ten year of age, for the job required no previous training and very little skill. Match-box making, therefore, was the last resource of the destitute or the first occupation of little girls. A child with nimble fingers could earn a penny an hour, and the women who made the boxes couldn't do much better. If a girl worked hard for very long hours every day (often getting no more than six hours sleep), she could earn eight or nine shillings a week. Some of the more crafty women, knowing the wages were too low for subsistence, took the work, investigators reported, to qualify for assistance from charitable organizations.

Women working in the match factories making matches rather than boxes for matches earned slightly more. The average was ten to twelve shillings a week, though a rapid worker could earn as much as fifteen. The match-girls were required to stand in one place all day, ten hours or more, as they put smelly chemicals on little sticks. It was not an easy task and at times they came down with phosphorus poisoning. But when the day was over, Booth recorded, they displayed an energy in striking contrast to the listlessness of workers in other trades. From June to August the match industry was slack and the girls were laid off. However, the jam factories were running full steam and often hired the match-girls. The jam-makers looked down on the match-girls, causing conflict, but also bringing about a strong esprit de corps among the latter. The match-girls were fond of each other and generally withdrew from women they couldn't associate with on equal terms. Against external forces they instinctively organized and in the 1880's instituted a series of strikes. A prolonged strike in the summer of 1888 – Gissing attended two of their meetings – brought about the formation of the largest labor union in England composed entirely of women.

A trade similar in many respects to the match industry was the making of artificial flowers. It attracted girls of similar type and had a similar wage scale. Good workers could earn from ten to sixteen shillings, but the majority earned from eight to ten and didn't have constant work. The trade was seasonal, and even in season it was extremely irregular owing to changes in fashion. During these periods of unemployment the flower-makers found work in other industries, were assisted by relatives or charitable institutions, starved, or went on the streets. While the annual wage was below the standard of living, most flower-makers lived at home and were partly supported by fathers or brothers. As the century ended and England moved into a new century, the maker of artificial flowers became a symbol of the oppressed worker in all British factories. She even inspired ballads that exaggerated her plight and were sung in music halls.

In the confectionery factories the girls earned less as a rule than match-girls, but the work was considered far more desirable. The women had very little to do with the actual making of jam, preserves, pickles, or even sweets. All work requiring anything beyond manual dexterity was done by men. Girls and women washed bottles, filled them, put on labels and wrappers, poured syrups into cans, packed raisins, peeled oranges, squeezed lemons, and filled packing crates. Some of these factories employed no girl under eighteen, refusing absolutely to resort to child labor, and paid all workers ten to twelve shillings a week. As in the other trades, forewomen earned more, sometimes as much as twenty shillings a week. For ordinary workers in any of the factories the maximum wage per week, regardless of skill or time employed, was twenty shillings or one pound.

The novels of George Gissing present girls and women at work in almost all the industrial trades. It is rare to find in his fiction a girl of the working class who has never worked. In London he had ample opportunity to observe working women, and they caught his eye even when he traveled abroad. From Venice he wrote to Bertz in February, 1889: *"Heaven!*

The beautiful faces that I pass every hour. They are magnificent, these Venetian work-girls! And for the most part in robust health with red cheeks and bright eyes. They walk with much dignity; I never see them frisking about or laughing noisily. In figure and motion they correspond to the gondoliers, who are often splendid fellows." In *The Emancipated* (1890), the novel that came out of the Italian trip, Reuben Elgar describes Venetian girls in similar terms: *"You know them, how they walk about the Piazza; their tall, lithe forms, the counterpart of the gondolier; their splendid black hair, elaborately braided and pierced with large ornaments; their noble, aristocratic, grave features; their long shawls! What natural dignity!"* From Florence, Gissing wrote: *"This morning I was in the Uffizi Gallery and noticed with much interest the numbers of low-class girls. They are fat-faced and ruddy-cheeked, cheerful but never noisy, and they come to the gallery because they really find pleasure in looking at the pictures. It was the same in Rome."* Gissing was obviously impressed by the women he saw in the streets of Italy. He didn't like their counterparts in France.

Observing the girls in the streets of London and looking into their working conditions, he sometimes made their poverty worse than it really was. Such may be seen when we compare the wages of Pennyloaf Candy with those of the needlewoman in actual life. Gissing tells us Pennyloaf worked with the needle "sixteen hours a day for a payment of ninepence." At that rate she made less than one shilling a day, and with no Sunday work only 4s/6d for an entire week. Booth's researchers, including Clara Collet, showed that only at irregular work during the winter months did needlewomen earn wages so low. Even those doing the commonest work got at least seven shillings a week, and often as much as nine. Similarly, Gissing minimized the wages of Sally Fisher. She made overcoats at fourpence each and during a very good week could earn only seven shillings to meet the cost of living by half. In actual life the sewer of overcoats earned more, and yet payment was extremely low and allowed the worker only marginal living at best. By calling attention to low wages and making them even lower, Gissing dramatized the dolorous predicament of hundreds of women who barely kept themselves alive while working themselves to death.

A striking example of Gissing's veering toward melodrama when emphasizing the hard existence of poor women is the case of Mrs. Hewett in *The Nether World* (1889). Before her marriage at nineteen she had been a needle slave for several years at four shillings a week. On this incredibly low sum she managed to eke out a bare existence but lived in utmost penury. When work was slack and when she could no longer buy even the crudest of food, she was driven by want to steal from her employer. Caught immediately, she was tried for her crime, found guilty, and sentenced to prison. Recalling the court-room scene, Gissing dramatizes the need for immediate and sweeping changes in the garment-making industry. His technique is to reproduce a realistic newspaper account of the trial. In method and matter the report is similar to the way both John Ruskin and Matthew Arnold highlighted the misery of the poor. In "Of Kings' Treasuries" (1864)

Ruskin cited a newspaper account that recorded the death by starvation of a "translator of boots." In "The Function of Criticism at the Present Time" (1864) Arnold quoted from a newspaper account that coldly described the misery of a girl driven to kill her illegitimate child. The account ended with "Wragg is in custody."

Gissing's trial account, though fictional, shows the influence of both Ruskin and Arnold and seems intimately based on a real event: *"On Friday, Margaret Barnes, nineteen, a single woman, was indicted for stealing six jackets, value 5 pounds, the property of Mary Oaks, her mistress. The prisoner, who cried bitterly during the proceedings, pleaded guilty. The prosecutrix is a single woman, and gets her living by mantle-making. She engaged the prisoner to do what is termed 'finishing off,' that is, making the button holes and sewing on the buttons. The prisoner was also employed to fetch the work from the warehouse and deliver it when finished. On September 7th her mistress sent her with the six jackets, and she never returned. Sergeant Smith, a detective who apprehended the prisoner, said he had made inquiries in the case and found that up to this time the prisoner had borne a good character as an honest, hard-working girl. She had quitted her former lodgings, which had no furniture but a small table and a few rags in a corner, and he discovered her in a room which was perfectly bare. The prisoner, when called upon, said she had had nothing to eat for three days, and so gave way to temptation. The Judge said it could not be allowed that distress should justify dishonesty and sentenced the prisoner to six weeks' imprisonment."* On being released from prison Margaret Barnes is rescued by John Hewett, a generous and kind-hearted workman, who later marries her.

If not for Hewett, negative forces in the life of the young woman would have sent her to a brothel, or resisting she would have died in the streets. While charitable organizations could provide temporary refuge, the workhouse would have shunned her as a convict. In actual life the trap Margaret fell into wasn't so complete, nor the outlook so gloomy, but throwing a bit of sunlight on her condition would have gone counter to the writer's purpose. An indifferent society destroys this young woman hardly before her life has begun, and Gissing tells us how. Even before she goes to prison overwork and too little food have damaged her health, and so the security of marriage has come too late. *"There's such hard things in a woman's life,"* she exclaims on her deathbed. *"What would have become of me if John hadn't took pity on me! The world's a hard place; I should be glad to leave it."* Her husband, fully aware that "things are wrong somehow," speaks her epitaph: *"She's had nothing but pain and poverty all her life, and now they'll pitch her out of the way in a parish box. Do you remember what hopes I used to have when we were first married? See the end of 'em! Look at this underground hole, look at this bed as she lays on! Is it my fault?"* Writing this, Gissing was again purging his system of Nell who died in similar surroundings. The sentiments uttered by John Hewett, even the momentary guilt, were those of Gissing on the morning of March 1, 1888. And like Nell, Margaret Hewett dies before reaching thirty.

At least the woman was able to marry a man who was kind to her, but Emma Vine in love with the hero of *Demos* (1886) is denied even that. She lives in two grubby little rooms with four other persons and can't look forward to a better home even as her story ends. In two small rooms she lives with her sister Kate, recently become a widow, their sister Jane, a victim of rheumatic fever, and Kate's two sickly children. All exist without assistance from anyone. In time Emma believes she'll be able to marry Richard Mutimer who will choose to support her and her sisters in some degree of comfort. In the meantime she supports herself and the others by constantly plying the needle. One afternoon he pays the family a visit: *"Richard entered an uncarpeted room which had to serve too many distinct purposes to allow of its being orderly in appearance. In one corner was a bed, where two little children lay asleep; before the window stood a sewing-machine, about which was heaped a quantity of linen; a table in the midst was half covered with a cloth on which was placed a loaf and butter, the other half being piled with several dresses requiring the needle. Two black patches on the ceiling showed in what positions the lamp stood by turns."* Since the room has no fireplace, Mutimer wonders how the girls get their meals. *"We can boil a potato now and then, and that's about all we can do nowadays."*

Jane is too ill to work and Kate is too much a slattern to work regularly. So the responsibility of keeping five people alive falls on Emma who knows only how to sew. She is fortunate enough to own a sewing machine, and she makes it hum all day and well into the evening. Nor does she rest on Sunday. To make ends meet, she must toil every day of the week. Even then she doesn't make enough to support life and must supplement ten shillings a week by working on bank holidays as a charwoman. Although the cleaning job means a loss of social status, it represents a triumph over those forces that would have her starve, sink into degradation, or be consigned to the workhouse. Carefully developed as an admirable person despite her poverty, Emma endures the hardships of her lot without complaint.

She is not a machine, however; her strength eventually fails her, sending her to the hospital. When she returns to the cluttered two rooms, sick and only slightly rested, she has to work harder than ever to restore order to the wretched home. After toiling in a workroom fifteen hours in a single day, she does more work on Kate's idle machine at home. She might have married Mutimer had she been willing to abandon her sisters. He marries Adela Waltham, a girl of the middle class, and Emma the workgirl is left to work without hope. As the novel concludes, dramatic events have swirled around her, but all she does is use the sewing machine beside the window. She will continue until she dies. No other future seems possible.

Similar to Emma's predicament is that of two nameless sisters in *The Nether World* (1889): *"On the floor below dwelt at present two sisters who kept themselves alive (it is quite inaccurate to use any other phrase in such instances) by doing all manner of skillful needlework; they were middle-aged women, gentle-natured, and so thoroughly subdued to the hopelessness of their lot that scarcely ever could even their footfall be heard as they went up and down stairs; their voices were always sunk to a soft murmur.*"They seem defeated but like Emma Vine, they have the will to endure. Emma's sister Kate, however, goes under as another "silent victim of industrialism." Intense competition in the daily struggle to earn a living has made Kate Clay sour. Never graced with much sweetness of disposition, she exhibits under hardship a violent temper which she can't control. In time she becomes a bitter termagant, inpatient with Emma and often scolding and slapping the children. As things grow worse, she turns to heavy drinking that triggers a process of emotional and physical decay: *"She was more slovenly in appearance than ever, and showed all the signs of extreme poverty. Her face was not merely harsh and sour, it indicated a process of degradation."*

Craving the companionship of people like herself, she begins to spend her evenings away from home, at first loitering in the streets and then in taverns. While she enjoys the warmth and comfort of the public house, her hungry children cry themselves to sleep. For a time it appears that Kate turns to prostitution to buy money for drink. When her sisters beseech her to mend her ways, she promises she will in time. We know from the example of Carrie Mitchell that women in Kate's predicament were incapable of saving themselves, but again (as with Margaret Barnes Hewett) luck intervenes. Middle-class women find the sisters better living quarters at a distance from Kate's undesirable companions, and her slow descent into degradation is arrested. Bringing forward social workers to rehabilitate Kate, Gissing is remaining true to his conviction that many unfortunate women could be saved with just a little help from society. Depicting the young woman's slow but steady deterioration, he is thinking of his first wife whom he lost sight of at about the time this novel, *Demos* (1886), was being written.

In *Thyrza* (1887) Gissing again considered the plight of needlewomen, focusing this time on working conditions. Thyrza Trent and her sister Lydia work as "trimmers" in a hat factory. They finish hats by sewing in the lining and putting on the bands. In the busy season their wages when combined average about a pound a week. At dull times they earn even less and occasionally have to support themselves for a week or two without employment. Mrs. Ormonde, the book's "woman of the world" (a special type developed in the novels of the nineties), remarks that the work Thyrza is compelled to do is "the consumer of all youth and joy." Seeing that Thyrza is in poor health, Mrs. Ormonde finds her sewing that requires only six hours a day while her sister Lydia remains in the workroom. Gissing's vivid description of Lydia's fellow workers has all the earmarks of firsthand observation: *"All belonged to the class of needlewomen who preserve appearances; many of them were becomingly dressed, and none betrayed extreme poverty. Probably a fourth came from homes in which they were not the only wage earners, and would not starve if work slackened now and then, having fathers or brothers to help them."* The description is quite accurate. Throughout *Thyrza* (1887) Gissing viewed the girls in workroom and factory with less distortion than in other novels. In the books that came before this novel and later in *The Nether World* (1889), he was savage in his fierce condemnation of those forces that brought misery to working girls. To drive home what he considered to be an important point, he sometimes exaggerated their condition, showing it as much worse than in real life. Yet on the whole, the accuracy of his presentation of needlewomen was corroborated by Charles Booth and Clara Collet who as leading social scientists made careful studies of working women in the industrial trades of London.

Chapter 14

Factory Girls and Landladies

Young women who work in factories in Gissing's novels are given plenty of room to express themselves and are treated most of the time with gentle amusement. He presents factory girls as earthy, sarcastic, boisterous, outspoken, warm-hearted, laughing, singing, and seldom overworked. In striking contrast is the portrayal of needlewomen: *"See how worn-out the poor girls are becoming, how they gape, what listless eyes most of them have! The stoop in the shoulders so universal among them merely means over-toil in the workroom."* Even so, on occasion he can throw into sharp focus the misery of a factory girl. In a tavern in Lambeth a girl of the slums sings a ballad of springtime in the country and new love: *"The girl had a drunken mother and spent a month or two of every year in the hospital, for her day's work overtaxed her strength. She was one of those fated toilers, fated to struggle on as long as anyone would employ her, then to fall among the forgotten wretched. And she sang of May in bloom and love; of love that had never come near her and that she would never know."* Though she may never know love, she has something Gissing admires.

Lacking physical strength, she has strength of will. Even so, most factory girls in Gissing's fiction fare better.

In the same novel Totty Nancarrow likes her life as a factory girl so well that she refuses to give it up for a more comfortable existence. Her uncle would like to take her into his house and make a lady of her, but Totty laughs, *"he'll wait a long time till he gets the chance!"* To Thyrza who wonders why she doesn't jump at the chance to live free of daily work in a factory, she explains: *"I'd sooner live in my own way, thank you. Fancy me havin' to sit proper at a table, afraid to eat an' drink! What's the use of livin' if you don't enjoy yourself?"* Convinced that her independent way of life is better, she is happy and wholesome and eager to accept each day as it comes so long as she has some control. Possessing a lithe, shapely figure, she has no trouble attracting men but ignores them while laughing or humming a tune or walking sprightly "with her usual independence." She is a lover of crowds, enjoys being jostled on the sidewalk, enjoys packing her room with people, and delights in scenes of revelry that gather momentum until they reach a crescendo of merry-making.

In a tavern where Totty and her friends have gathered for the evening, her laughter rings above the din and brings laughter from others. *"The girls who sat with glasses of beer before them, and carried on primitive flirtations with their neighbors, were honest wage-earners of factory and workshop, well able to make themselves respected. If they lacked refinement, natural or acquired, it was not their fault; toil was behind them and before, the hours of rest were few; suffering and lack of bread might any moment come upon them, but now they enjoyed themselves."* The laughing, joking, singing, flirting, dancing, and drinking recall certain features of the opera *Carmen* (1875), but more likely Gissing was thinking of the bohemian life portrayed in the dramas of Henri Murger and Alfred de Musset. It is easy to say that Gissing's portrayal of factory girls is more romantic than realistic. Yet in actual life the girls seem to have been much the same as he depicts them. His representation of the typical factory girl is quite similar to Clara Collet's factual account in Booth's *Life and Labour of the People in London* (1889+). Miss Collet wrote that the factory girl could be recognized *"by the freedom of her walk, the numbers of her friends, and the shrillness of her laugh."* She could be seen on Sunday afternoons, decked out in her finest apparel, *"promenading up and down the Bow Road, arm in arm with two or three other girls."* Later one could find her with a young man drinking in one of the many taverns of the East End. The description exactly fits fun-loving Totty Nancarrow; so once again the social scientist supports the accuracy of Gissing's realism.

Clara Collet was sketching a composite picture of those girls who worked mainly in jam, match, and artificial-flower factories. Of the flower-makers Gissing has much to say, but he never got around to bringing the jam-makers or the match-girls into his fiction. It appears, however, that he thought of introducing the match-girls into a novel, for in July of 1888, just two weeks before completing *The Nether World*

(1889), he was present at two of their strike meetings. These meetings were part of a prolonged strike that resulted in the formation of a labor union. An entry in Gissing's diary indicates a sympathetic interest in their activities: *"Sunday, July 8. In morning to Mile End Waste for a strike meeting of Bryant & May's match-girls. Very few of the girls themselves present. Speeches by middle-class leaders. Gave 1/s at collection. Evening, into Regents Park where I again attended the strike meeting, and again gave a donation because I was ashamed to give nothing in my bourgeois costume."* At the time he was gathering this material, he was bringing to completion his last novel in which the poorer classes play a dominant role. After *The Nether World*, except for random short stories, he turned to subjects closer to the middle class.

Though he said little about the jam-makers and match-girls, he used the notes he took on the flower-makers in a number of places. In the short story, "Phoebe" (1884), the central character is a flower-maker: *"Phoebe's sister had been a flower-maker, and Phoebe herself, having gone through her period of apprenticeship to the same handicraft, had now attained the position of 'improver.' When things went well, she could earn perhaps eight shillings a week; in time she might hope to become a 'hand' and then, if lucky, might receive as much as fifteen. Unless her health broke down, she might very well keep out of the workhouse to a tolerably advanced age."* Again Gissing stresses low wages and the incessant struggle for existence. The work was often irregular, depending on fashion, and frequently the girls were unemployed. He places emphasis on the fact that during these intervals many girls went hungry. He was never able to resist the pathos around him, and there was something pathetic about a girl hired to make flowers having to go hungry.

In *The Nether World* (1889) Jane Snowdon, Bessie Byass, and Clem Peckover are flower-makers. Unlike Phoebe, none of these girls will go hungry when work is slack. Both Jane and Clem are relatively well off, and Bessie supplements the income of her husband by making flowers: *"On the side-table were some open cardboard boxes containing artificial flowers and leaves, for Bessie had now and then a little 'mounting' to do, and in that way aided the income of the family."* Some other working wives in various novels are Hilda Castledine, Mrs. Christopherson, Louisa Clover, Maggie Dunn, Mrs. Ellerton, Mrs. Emerson, Mrs. Lanyon, Nancy Lord, and Dora Milvain. The middle class thought it scandalous for a man to allow his wife to go out to work, and yet some did it anyway. The lower classes, according to Booth, were also reluctant to see a man *"willingly let the mother of his children go out to a factory."* Yet working wives of the working class were commonplace. Their children when old enough sometimes worked with them. In a factory described in *The Nether World* sixty women and girls work side by side. They range in age from *"the child who had newly left school"* to *"the woman of uncertain age who had spent long years of long days in the workroom, and showed the result in her parchmenty cheek and lack-lustre eye."* Mixing children with adults on the same job was not a good policy, said Clara Collet who spoke out against it.

She said, moreover, that too many of the girls fell victim to unscrupulous foremen who took advantage of them. On a daily basis they were confronted with ugliness, temptation, and imminent ruin. For a struggling girl it was not a pretty life, but most adjusted well enough and found at least a modicum of happiness. Those who couldn't adjust reaped a bitter harvest of frustration, despair, semi-madness, and early death. Clara Hewett of *The Nether World* (1889) exemplifies the rebellious workgirl who cannot or will not adjust to living her life in her own class. When we first see Clara she is seventeen and in revolt against her father. Of the opinion that she is too young to know her own mind, he objects to her desire to become a waitress. Sidney Kirkwood, wishing to mend the rift between father and daughter, urges the man to be more flexible: *"Let her go to Mrs. Tubbs for a month's trial. The girl can't put up with the workroom any longer. It's ruining her health, for one thing, anybody can see that, and it's making her so discontented she'll soon get reckless."* When John Hewett remains adamant, Kirkwood reminds him that *"we're the lower orders; our girls have to go out and get their livings."*

At this moment Clara enters the room. She is slim, erect, graceful in movement, and attractive. He face is stamped with youthful sensuality competing with intellectual vigor. Her eyes betray *"an unconscious appeal against some injustice,"* and her lips are defiant. For years she has harbored "an inheritance of revolt," and now in her teens it begins to express itself. Hewett tries once again to assert his authority, but the girl is determined to have her way and displays an insolence he hasn't seen before: *"She had never faced him like this before, saying more plainly than with words that she defied him to control her."* Parental resistance has succeeded only in making her more determined than ever: *"Already there was a plan in her mind for quitting home, regardless of all the misery she would cause."* Then to her surprise her antagonist submits, and she is "moved to warmest gratitude." In revolt she has "a defect of tenderness," but can afford to be generous in triumph.

Clara becomes a waitress in Mrs. Tubbs's "Imperial Restaurant and Luncheon Bar." The hours are unbearably long, more than one hundred a week, and from early morning till midnight she is on her feet shuttling heavy trays of food from kitchen to table. Her weekly wage, room and board included, is five shillings for seven days. She gets one Sunday off and one week day per month. The unchanging odors of the poorly ventilated eating place make her sick and rob her of appetite. By nine o'clock in the evening, though she can hardly stand on numb feet, she must go on somehow until midnight. In *Thyrza* (1887) the lead character also becomes a waitress for a short time. The establishment of Sarah Gandle, her employer, is located in one of the most noisome slums of London. Unlike Mrs. Tubbs, Sarah Gandle makes no attempt to decorate her eatery or make it pretentious. Because it caters to the same social class, it is similar to Mrs. Tubbs's restaurant though worse. The kitchen, for example, *"was a room of some ten feet square, insufferably hot, very dirty, a factory for the production of human fodder."* Two sweating cooks take up all the room.

While waitressing Clara meets Charles Scawthorne, the kind of man her father had feared she would meet as soon as she began to serve the public. His fears were not unwarranted, for Charles Booth observed that London waitresses had become known for suspect morality and were therefore preyed upon by men who led them astray. *"A questionable morality,"* he wrote, *"largely prevails amongst young women in the hotel and restaurant business."* Scawthorne revives in Clara an old love of the stage and sets her to thinking of a career in the theatre. A girlhood friend, Grace Rudd, is already on the stage and Clara begins to believe she can follow a similar course. For a time she can't bring herself to quit her job: *"She wished to break free of her slavery but had not the force to do so."* Then without giving notice and on the spur of the moment, as if driven by a power other than her own will, she quits the restaurant. In search of other work, she hears from time to time the angry voice of Mrs. Tubbs beating a tattoo in her ears.

In a futile effort to find work, she trudges from place to place for several days, her emotions barely under control. The experience degrades her, for in every place of business she is given to understand that she is altogether superfluous. Rapidly she learns that whether she lives or dies is of no consequence to anyone; London and the entire world seem totally indifferent to her existence. Kirkwood pleads with her to return home, but adamantly she refuses. To go home would be to admit defeat, and that she is unwilling to accept. It is then that she enters deliberately into "a feud with Fate." Once her position is made clear, unseen forces, mindless but seeming to act with direction, strike out against her. Returning to her rented room, exhausted and fevered, she flings open the window for air, breaks the cracked window pane, and cuts her hand. For a moment she is spellbound by the sight of her own blood gushing to the floor. Then in temporary defeat she gives way to uncontrollable sobbing.

The following morning, after a fitful night of sleeplessness, she decides to submit to the stresses that torture her. She reaches the conclusion that an unfriendly fate has brought her to this pass and struggling against it is foolish: *"Fate was busy in all that had happened during the last two days. Why had she quitted her situation at a moment's notice? Why on this occasion rather than fifty times previously? It was not her own doing; something impelled her, and the same force – call it chance or destiny – would direct the issue once more."* The decision made and her mind relieved from "the stress of conflict," she gives way to an amorality that makes her laugh at strict conventional law. She has discovered that the law of the jungle is the only law she must obey. Let her family talk about her. They wanted to keep her on the low level to which she was born, but she would prove herself worthy of something better. Having made up her mind, she rejects her family and friends and isn't heard from for three years. Gissing enjoins his readers to make a special effort to understand Clara, *"this girl of the people with brains."* To do so, we must examine specific influences upon her.

From her mother she inherited intelligence and ambition, and from her father came her rebellious nature. John Hewett had always been defiant of social injustice, and "Clara inherited his temperament." Her father also helped develop in her the notion that she was meant for better things. When she was eleven he came into an inheritance of 400 pounds, and one of the first things he did was to rent a piano for his daughter so that she could learn to play music. He wouldn't see her robbed of opportunity simply because her birth wasn't that of a young lady. He would help her every way he could, and she would become a schoolteacher. A favorite teacher, Miss Harrop, encouraged the idea and set Clara to thinking she would become a teacher but only as preparation for something better. Busy in the same fatal work was her school friend Grace Rudd, who also flattered Clara. Then as the nature of things would have it, Miss Harrop left London, Grace disappeared, and John Hewett lost his money. Clara found herself out of school and working in a factory stamping crests on stationery at less than ten shillings a week.

As a workgirl she was maladjusted and bitterly dissatisfied. She was also rankled by the poverty she had to endure. Instead of having a room to herself she had to share a grubby little bedroom with three children. Two little girls slept with her in the same bed, and a little boy lay on a dirty mattress placed on the floor. Her one desire quite early was to climb above her station in life. Maybe she could throw off the bondage of class and become an actress. When Scawthorne meets her toiling from early morning to midnight in a steaming restaurant, she is ripe for any suggestion: *"The disease inherent in her being developed day by day, blighting her heart, corrupting her moral sense, even setting marks of evil upon the beauty of her countenance. Like a creature that is beset by unrelenting forces, she summoned and surveyed all the crafty faculties luring in the dark places of her nature."* To come to terms with the forces that have backed her into a corner, she must use every device at her command. Though intelligent and sensitive, she is willing now to barter away even her "woman's honor," if necessary, to achieve her ends. Scawthorne is willing to help her but only for a price.

After a lapse of three years we see Clara Hewett once again. In return for his help, she became Scawthorne's mistress but soon left him to be on her own. Eventually she became an actress, but her career after three years at best is precarious. Her new life has brought her no peace of mind and no satisfaction: *"This life is no better than what I used to lead years ago; I'm no nearer to getting a good part than I was when I first began acting."* As miserable as she has ever been, *"not many women breathed who knew more of suffering."* Even so, her fierce ambition to become something more than a workgirl remains undaunted. She is struggling against severe competition in the theatre, and the world at large is still her enemy.

She does her acting with ill-humor, despising her audience for their acceptance of the playwright's claptrap, certain that she can do better than the actresses with leading roles. She is now in the company of her schoolgirl friend, Grace Rudd, but because Grace is now her rival she shows no pity for the young woman when she becomes a victim of tuberculosis. Despite poor health, Grace is given the lead role in the company's one play. When she muffs her lines, Clara is offered the part and accepts without a moment's hesitation. Horrified by Clara's betrayal, Grace tries to reason with her but is told the world is a jungle where only the strongest survive: *"We have to fight, to fight for everything, and the weak get beaten."*

In a delirium Clara walks to the theatre to prepare for her first performance as leading lady. At long last she appears to be on the eve on triumph. As a famous actress she will move in a world where class barriers are non-existent. Near the entrance a veiled woman steps in front of her. *"That you, Grace?"* she asks almost kindly. *"The answer was something dashed violently into her face – something fluid and fiery – something that ate into her flesh, that frenzied her with pain, that drove her shrieking she knew not whither."* Broken and defeated, her face horribly burnt with acid, Clara permits her father to take her home. She had aimed at becoming a famous actress but only as a way to enter the world of wealth and leisure. She might have realized her dream, but she was selfish and flawed and saw the world as her enemy. Fate had flung her to the ground and decreed she live out the rest of her life in a darkened room, brooding on what might have been: *"Oh, I had hope once! It might have been so different with me. The thought burns and burns and burns, till I am frantic!"*

Doomed to spend the rest of her life in poverty, at twenty-three she will live until death frees her.

This chapter wouldn't be complete without some mention of Gissing's nemesis, the London landlady. When he arrived in London in the autumn of 1877, it was a city of four million with numerous slums in many neighborhoods. Facing the need to live as economically as possible, he settled in a shabby neighborhood near Tottenham Court Road, and for the next eleven years lived in one mean lodging after another. The keepers of these lodging-houses were cut from the same cloth and the same pattern. They were so much alike that in later years Gissing found it difficult to distinguish one from the other. On average they were past middle age and hardened in the ways of their trade. Ugly, sloven, selfish, meddling in the lives of their tenants and feeding off the poverty around them, they irritated him and made him dislike them. So in his fiction, particularly the early novels, he depicted them as garrulous, coarse, clamorous, suspicious, greedy, callous, sometimes vicious, and often dishonest.

The first of his fictional landladies, and one of the most repulsive, is Mrs. Blaltherwick of *Workers in the Dawn* (1880). Gissing etches her in acid, describing her as an aging harpy and hag, presenting her as vicious, degraded, hideous, cruel, remorseless, and motivated by a grasping self-interest. Grimy with untold layers of dirt and wearing clothes equally dirty, she talks in a loud, raspy voice with breath that would stun a horse. She cheats poverty of its last pence, and yet she seems no worse than the redoubtable Mrs. Pole of the same novel. *"Arthur had never much liked her appearance. At present she was slatternly in the extreme, and had the look about the eyes which distinguishes persons who have but lately slept off a debauch. He noticed that her hands trembled, and that her voice was rather hoarse."* She drinks heavily, consorts, with prostitutes, brawls with other bawds in public, and uses "the language of a Billingsgate fishwife."

Mrs. Pettindund, another landlady in the novel, is on a slightly higher social plane even though her instincts for unabashed cruelty are highly developed. She is perpetually having a bad day and can be a terror when crossed. She has *"the inimitable ferocity of the true London lodging-house keeper"* and screeches at the top of her lungs when irritated. Her loud metallic voice is coarse, gin-thickened, over-fed, and her tongue is a purveyor of lies and calumny. Never graced with a very good temper, too much of *"the brave, thick, medicated draught"* makes her a savage. At times her behavior brands her as more animal than human, and she is feared by most of her lodgers.

A landlady who lives almost entirely on the beast level is Mrs. Peckover of *The Nether World* (1889). In a jungle where only the fittest survive, she and her daughter Clem have reverted to a more primitive strain. Viewing with interest her strength, agility, and raw beauty, Gissing reluctantly admires Clem: *"The girl is now in the very prime of her ferocious beauty. She has grown taller and somewhat stouter; her shoulders spread like those of a caryatid* [he couldn't resist the classical allusion];

the arm with which she props her head is as strong as a carter's and magnificently moulded. The head itself looks immense with its pile of glossy hair. Reddened by the rays of the fire, her features had a splendid savagery which seemed strangely at discord with the paltry surroundings amid which she sat; her eyes just now were flaming with a crafty and cruel speculation which would have become those of a barbarian in ambush. I wonder how it came about that her strain, after passing through the basest conditions of modern life, had thus reverted to a type of ancestral exuberance."

The girl has become the embodiment of fierce life independent of morality: *"That Clem's no better than a wild-beast tiger."* She and her mother both have acquired the strength, cunning, ferocity, and amorality of the tiger. The surname implies they have become aristocrats in the pecking order, but because they are ruled solely by instinct and perverse inducement, they frequently battle each other. Their brawling isn't anything at all like that of drunken women in the street. They tear and claw one another like two superb cats in a jungle clearing. They bite, scratch, kick, slap, pull hair, and punctuate their screams with raw profanity and animal growling. Some other landladies not so splendid as Mrs. Peckover are Mmes. Blogs, Bolt, Bubb, Budge, Conisbee, Elderfield, Ladds, Ledward, Oaks, Turpin, and Wick. They live in a colorful, interesting world filled with people coming and going and with the problems that people cause.

In the Peckover lodging-house lived Clara Hewett, a girl of the people but also a girl of intelligence and talent. As we have seen, she tried desperately to escape the world of Mrs. Peckover but failed in the end. In the same sordid surroundings lived Jane Snowdon, a *belle fleur* on a dunghill, who was eventually rescued by a rich relative. In similar houses Gissing himself lived and worked, and like Clara he dreamed of something better. Though naturalistic by definition and therefore somewhat bolder than life, his portraits of the London landlady were drawn directly from his own experience. The subject matter of his proletarian novels he knew intimately, and even the social scientists of the day respected the realism of his art. Charles Booth seems to have read *Demos* shortly after its publication in 1886, and singled it out as one of the few novels of the time that gave trustworthy information about the lives of the poor in London. Clara Collet, a researcher for Booth and one of Gissing's closest friends after 1893, published books on the work of women which also prove the accuracy of Gissing's fictional presentation.

Chapter 15

Shops and Shopgirls

The shopgirls of Gissing's time belonged to the lower-middle class and considered themselves superior in social status to working girls. They were an aggressive new breed, as Gissing called them, partly the result of the emancipation movement, and he viewed them with a certain dismay. Discussing Fanny Dorrit, created by Dickens at about the time the type was emerging, Gissing wrote perceptively though negatively about her counterpart in his own time. *"In the London of today there is a very familiar female type known as the shop-girl. Her sphere of action is extensive, for we meet her not only in shops, strictly speaking, but at liquor-bars, in workrooms, and unfortunately, sometimes in the post-office, to say nothing of fifty other forms of employment open to the underbred and more or less aggressive young woman. Dickens saw nothing like so much of her, but he has drawn her portrait with unerring hand in Fanny Dorrit."* He went on to say that some basic characteristics of the shopgirl in his day are misguided ambition, vanity, selfishness, ignorance, candor, and a vulgar good nature. She expects certain privileges and doesn't mind asserting herself to gain them, and yet she is untaught on the whole and rather incompetent in the work place.

Gissing is somewhat unfair in his estimate of the London shopgirl, but one should remember that he wrote in the aftermath of the bitter separation from his second wife, Edith. He considered her a member of the shop-keeping class, and viewing shopgirls through her, he despised them all. Yet his portrayal of this very familiar female type in most of his novels is largely dispassionate. As with the working-class girls, he is concerned mainly with their conditions of work, their station in life, and their struggle to survive in a harshly competitive world. On occasion he can show compassion, as with Sally Fisher and Martha Pimm who were being exploited. Both girls are employed in shops but combine their sales work with domestic duties. Sally formerly worked in a sweat shop (workroom to Gissing) but gave that up for a job in a chandler's shop. The hours are from early morning till late at night, *"and there's a baby to look after when I'm not in the shop."* Unscrupulous predators have taken advantage of these two, but in the end they fare better than most of their counterparts in actual life. Sally marries a laughing Irishman who treats her well, and Martha inherits 2,000 pounds for a better life.

Monica Madden of *The Odd Women* (1893) represents Gissing's most careful treatment of the shopgirl's suffering, even though she isn't typically of that class. As the daughter of a middle-class physician who has just died, leaving no fortune and no insurance, she enters the shop-keeping world out of necessity: *"To serve behind a counter would not have been Monica's choice if any more liberal employment had seemed within her reach. Certainly it might be deemed a pity that such a girl could not be introduced to one of the higher walks of life; but the time had come when she must 'do something,' and the people to whose guidance she looked had but narrow experience of life."* The time is 1882 and she is fifteen. Her surviving sisters – three others are dead – have taken genteel positions as governess and companion, but in so doing have forfeited the hope of marriage. In a shop Monica, young and pretty, will perhaps have a chance to meet a compatible young man. The sisters hope that before long she will *"find herself relieved of the necessity of working for a livelihood."* She marries and leaves the shop in 1888.

At twenty-one she has worked in a draper's shop for six years, but because of her upbringing in a refined home she has never acquired the tastes and habits of the typical shopgirl. Her birth and breeding prevent her from accepting these girls on an equal footing: *"Monica always felt too tired to walk after ten o'clock; moreover, the usual conversation in the dormitory which she shared with five other young women was so little to her taste that she wished to be asleep when the talkers came to bed."* She despises the life but is unwilling to marry Mr. Bullivant, an impecunious young clerk who has fallen in love with her. If she is to escape the shop through marriage, it must be to a man of means, a man who can support her in style. She comes across such a man in the person of Edmund Widdowson: *"All days and times were the same to him, he said. And he drove about the country for his pleasure. A man of means."* He isn't the perfect man, however, and far from it. Monica is fully aware that he is *"an oldish man with grizzled whiskers and a rather stern visage."* Their May-December marriage is doomed to failure.

As he traces the course of Monica's life as a shopgirl, Gissing presents a vivid picture of the conditions under which these girls work and live. At Scotcher and Company where Monica is employed the girls stand on their feet behind counters from eight in the morning till half-past nine in the evening. They are given Sunday off and one evening a week, but on Saturday they must work till half-past eleven or midnight. Some girls in factories and even servants worked fewer hours and earned more. But only as a last resort did a shopgirl go into a factory or become a servant. One girl, whose health was breaking under long hours, left the shop to become a lady's maid. She suffered a loss of social status but found the new job more pleasant and less strenuous than the shop. At Scotcher's she was making fifteen pounds a year with room and board. As a servant she earned twenty-five with room and board and was able to sit down now and then. Also she had her own room nicely furnished.

Since the young women spent almost all their waking hours in the shop, it was thought a good idea to provide them with meals and sleeping quarters on the premises. Under this arrangement it could never be said that the girls were subject to starvation, and so the management was not obliged to pay them a living wage. The food was plain but served in substantial portions so that no girl went hungry. The living quarters were crowded and uncomfortable. Resident girls were housed six to a room, their beds placed side by side as in a barracks. They had scant space for personal belongings and no privacy. The room was alternately too hot or too cold, too drafty or too stuffy. It was noisy till the early hours of the morning, for the girls had their own latch-keys and were free to come and go as they chose. With scathing irony Gissing found fault with that: *"Messrs. Scotcher and Co. were large-minded men. Not only did they insist that the Sunday ought to be used for bodily recreation, but they had no objection whatever to their young friends taking a stroll after closing time each evening."* It was late at night and London's streets were dangerous.

Though the company ministers to the material needs of the employees, it is oblivious to their moral and spiritual welfare. The girls never go to church, are free to walk the streets at night, and may spend their Sundays any way they choose. Gissing thought the practice somewhat less than wholesome and spoke out against it. In a long conversation between Monica Madden and Rhoda Nunn, his purpose is clearly revealed. A militant feminist assisting in the operation of a school where girls learn typing, Rhoda invites Monica to come in for an interview. The young woman looks exhausted, hollow-eyed, and haggard. She tells Rhoda that her work is very hard but feels she can't leave it at the present time. Asked how long is given her for meals, she replies: *"Twenty minutes for each meal, but at dinner and tea one is very likely to be called into the shop before finishing. If you are long away you find the table cleared."* And there is no sitting down on the job: *"We suffer a great deal from that. Some of us get diseases. A girl has just gone to the hospital with varicose veins as well as others. Sometimes on Saturday night I lose all feeling in my feet; I have to stamp on the floor to be sure it's still under me."* Christmas is the worst time in the shop.

During the holidays for more than a week the girls work till one o'clock in the morning and are often carried out in a faint from sheer exhaustion. At the end of the week if a shopgirl's "book of takings" doesn't measure up to what is expected of her, she loses her job because she has shown herself too weak to work harder. Since the employers know any girl can be easily replaced, the job has no security and a girl can be fired at a moment's notice for the slightest offense. Though Monica would like to leave the shop, she's hesitant to try something new. She is fearful of change. Rhoda tells her that good jobs are available for women who can use a typewriter. She shows the girl one of the machines and explains its use. *"One must practise until one can do fifty words a minute at least. I know one or two people who have reached almost twice that speed."* After much indecision Monica quits her job at the shop and enrolls in the school.

The newfangled typewriter was a beacon inviting many women into the world of business. The first commercially successful typewriter was an American invention dating from 1868. It was put on the market as the Sholes and Glidden typewriter. In 1873 the rights were sold to the Remington Arms Company, which brought out lower-case letters in 1877. The Remington, as it came to be known, soon became popular world-wide. The typewriter shown to Monica was a Remington: *"They went to a room downstairs, a bare little room by the library. Here were two Remingtons, and Rhoda patiently explained their use."* An efficient operator could achieve excellent results on one of these early machines, but the remark by Rhoda that one or two girls had attained speeds of almost one hundred words a minute is surely an exaggeration. Many years later competent typists on the new electric machines seldom reached a hundred words a minute. Although Gissing tediously wrote his books by hand in a tiny gnarled script, he had some of his later books set in type. By the 1890's publishers were asking that manuscripts submitted to them be typed.

A week passes and we see Monica Madden working away *"without enthusiasm but seemingly contented"* at learning to type. Glad to be out of the shop and doing something better, she experiences a growth in self respect that's beneficial to her health. Then after several weeks of steady application she enters an emotional slump and becomes "dull, remiss, unhappy." Violent headaches attack her and she becomes ill. Upset by what she interprets as weakness in the young woman, Rhoda Nunn speaks her mind: *"Her guardians dealt with her absurdly; they made her half a lady and half a shop-girl. I don't think she'll ever be good for much."* Her thoughts are exactly those of Gissing, who is careful to emphasize the point that Monica's upbringing has made her useless and superfluous in a competitive society. Soon after becoming sick, Monica leaves the school and marries Edmund Widdowson, an eccentric, much older man. Having failed to become a typist to prepare for a good job, she fails in marriage too. In less than a year the young woman, daughter of a doctor, is dead.

Another woman forced by necessity to work in a shop is Mrs. Christopherson of the short story "Christopherson" (1902). A *"pale, thin, slightly made woman,"* she had once been a governess but is now married to book-lover without a job. Times are hard and they require her to support not only herself but also her husband.

"She works for her living, then?"

"Ay, and for his too. No, not teaching; she's in a shop in Tottenham Court Road; has what they call a good place, and earns thirty shillings a week. It's all they have, but Christopherson buys books out of it."

Christopherson, something of a comical character, is a bibliophile with a mania for collecting books. While his wife slaves in the shop, he saunters into the streets to visit all the book sales, taking his time "sniffing about the second-hand shops." Even in poverty he has managed to acquire a roomful of books: *"One wall had completely disappeared behind volumes, and the bookishness of the air made it a disgusting thought that two persons occupied this chamber every night."* For years he has lived on the earnings of her labor, has starved and stinted her to buy books, and she has never complained. She is "just about ready to drop" from overwork in the shop and would like to take a job as the housekeeper of a wealthy relative, but the woman won't have the books in her house: *"How could you dream for a moment that I would let you fill my house with musty old books?"* That quenches Mrs. Christopherson's hope of getting away from the shop. It's interesting to note that the relative, though wealthy, is quarter educated at best, has no use for books, and probably doesn't read at all.

Day after day Christopherson works long hours, spinning the thread of her life a little thinner. Her husband wanders the streets in search of books he never quite finds the time to read. When she begins to have fainting spells, he sells his beloved books and they move to the country. Like Monica Madden, this woman escapes the drudgery of the shop but unlike Monica, who went from one form of bondage to another, she is favored by fate and finds contentment. We never learn what kind of shop Mrs. Christopherson was employed in, only that it was in Tottenham Court Road. It is doubtful that the shop was a fashionable or expensive place, even though her wages were quite good. In Gissing's day Tottenham Court Road, less than a mile from the British Museum, was the main thoroughfare of a slum district where many poverty-bitten intellectuals lived to be near the museum. It was the habitat of writers, artists, philosophers, tutors, and bohemians who were usually too poor for the ordinary comforts of modern life. In his early years in London, Gissing spent many days at the museum. Others used the men's room to bathe themselves, causing the library to erect a sign: *"Readers are requested to bear in mind that these basins are to be used only for casual ablutions."*

Another shopgirl somewhat superior to the average girl is Nancy Lord of *In the Year of Jubilee* (1894). The daughter of a petty tradesman in Camberwell, she has some education and talks "rather above her station." Until the year of jubilee (1887) she has never worked. Her mother is irritated that she should have to take a place in "a house of business," but later agrees it's a good thing, a sign of progress. However, when Nancy begins to look for employment, she realizes that in spite of her education she has no training whatever for a suitable job: *"What was there she could do? Teach children perhaps, but as a visiting governess she could hope for nothing more than the paltriest remuneration. Be somebody's secretary? She had not the training. In an office, in a shop, who would dream of giving her an engagement? In the battle of life every girl who could work a sewing-machine or make a match-box was of more account than she. If she entered a shop to make purchases, the young women at the counter seemed to smile superiority. Of what avail her education, her culture?"* In a bookshop she comes across a little volume on "employments for women," but its contents only deepen her discouragement.

In the book are many occupations that she might learn, but like so many girls of her time she is incapable of choosing one and taking the necessary steps to train for it. She faces the same dilemma that confronted Monica Madden, and try as she might she can't make up her mind to decide on anything. The result is to shrink back into her suburban home and make excuses: *"The word 'home' grew very sweet to her ears. A man, she said to herself, may go forth and find his work, his pleasure, in the highways; but is not a woman's place under the sheltering roof?"* Brought up in the old tradition of lady-like idleness and feminine helplessness, Nancy Lord yields to that tradition even when pretending emancipation. At home and idle she reads of a young woman who became overnight a successful novelist with many readers and a fat income. Then a splendid thought occurs to her: *"Why shouldn't she earn a little money by writing stories? Numbers of women took to it; not a few succeeded. It was a pursuit demanding no apprenticeship, that could be followed in the privacy of home, a pursuit wherein her education would be of service."* She begins immediately to write a novel, drawing her material from her own experience, but self-doubt defeats the project and she puts away the few pages of the manuscript never to see them again.

Later Nancy gets employment in a dress-supply business run by Beatrice French. Though Beatrice has known her for years, the young woman is hired mainly because of her good looks. She becomes "a walking fashion-plate," a living mannequin to display the product, as she advises ignorant women with money on the latest fashion. The job requires no mental effort and only enough education for one to speak without a Cockney accent. The salary is ten shillings a week, and the hours are from ten to five with Saturday afternoons off. The work is easy, the pay is low but competitive, the hours too are reasonable; and the business has the distinction of being a "dress-supply association" rather than a mere shop. Nancy's duties are to answer the questions of female customers and to look ladylike at all times even when tired. She doesn't like her customers, doesn't like her job much at all, but lacking anything better she does it anyway.

A shopgirl meeting all the characteristics ascribed by Gissing is Polly Sparkes of *The Town Traveller* (1898). Polly is rather proud of the fact that she has all the vulgarities and pretensions of the lower-middle class. She is a saucy young woman with high self-esteem, and like Dickens' Fanny Dorrit, is fond of merry-making and a good time. She also has a fiery temper and likes nothing better than a good quarrel. The novel opens with Polly abusing the put-upon servant Moggie. Later she prepares herself for a fray with her worthy landlady: *"Meaning to pass an hour or two in quarrelling with Mrs. Bubb, she had arrayed herself thus early with more care than usual that her colours and perfumes might throw contempt upon the draggle-tailed landlady."* Polly's resemblance to Louise Derrick in *The Paying Guest* (1895) is at once apparent. Both girls represent the epitome of the shopgirl as Gissing viewed her, and yet in several ways they differ.

Polly has a smattering of education and doesn't drop her H's as most workgirls were known to do. Louise also manages to sound her H's in conversation and has good enunciation. Both come from the same background, though Louise is better off financially. Her stepfather, Mr. Higgins, is a well-known businessman, and at twenty-two Louise has never worked: *"I haven't learnt to do anything, and I suppose I shall never need to."* Polly, on the other hand, is the daughter of a waiter and earns her living by *"selling programmes at a fashionable theatre."* It is evening work, pleasant and lucrative, but a change in the management puts an end to the job, forcing Polly to look in vain for similar employment elsewhere. Although Louise has no need to look for work, her mother's marriage to a vulgar man with new money damages her ability to make and keep friends: *"I've had lots of friends, but I never keep them for long. I don't know whether it's their fault or mine. My oldest friends are Amy Baker and Muriel Featherstone. Amy does typewriting in the city and Muriel is at a photographer's. They're awfully nice girls but haven't got enough money to live in a nice way."* Relying on her stepfather's money, Louise is able to live in "a nice way" and wants to be friends with "nice people," but they see her as vulgar and shun her.

Though economically secure, Louise Derrick is chastened by insecurities involving her social life. Polly Sparkes, however, doesn't worry about people and what they may think of her; she worries only but about finding a way to support herself in bad times. Yet both girls accept life as they find it and with fiery tempers enjoy a good quarrel. Though more refined than Polly, Louise notably vents her temper on her mother, stepsister, and current friends. Polly's temper by comparison is fiercer. When Christopher Parish follows her in the street, she turns upon him in a rage, eyes flashing. After roundly abusing him, she threatens to report his conduct not to the police but to his employers: *"Then you'll have plenty of time to go taking walks and chasing women."* Not in the least an innocent damsel, she knows his employers can do him worse harm than the police. In time she marries Christopher because she knows he will submit to her. Another factor is the young man's sudden wealth; he has just won £550 in a "missing word" contest. In all respects Louise Derrick and Polly Sparkes are "a very familiar female type."

Before concluding this discussion of shopgirls, some mention should be made of Patty Ringrose who tends to enhance the qualities of Eve Madeley in *Eve's Ransom* (1895). Patty is a "thin-faced but rather pretty girl" who belongs also to the shop-keeping class. It is not a class admired by Gissing, but she redeems herself by displaying a pleasant personality and "a certain vivacity of feature." She earns her living by working in the shop of her uncle. Often when a girl went out to work in a shop, she chose one owned and run by a friend or relative. Then her family could say she wasn't really working because she had to work, but because she generously wanted to help those related to her. So Patty works for her uncle in a music shop where she sells the latest popular music, and where she plays on the piano the sheet music of any tune a customer may wish to buy. She is a typical shopgirl, but the ease with which she is able to find a job is not typical. She can find employment with no trouble at all because she has a skill that many girls have not acquired. Yet more and more of her class (as opposed to the upper classes where the piano for young women was common), are learning to read music and play various instruments. Louise Derrick plays the piano; and when Eleanor Cartwright in *A Life's Morning* (1888) is required to teach the instrument, "a first pupil was speedily found."

Chapter 16

Shops and Shopkeepers

Toward the end of the century, besides the girls employed in shops, more and more women were becoming managers and even owners of the shops in which they worked. Many strong-minded women operated successful retail businesses that catered to a variety of consumers and earned a good living doing it. Shops in the poorer districts near Tottenham Court Road were less modern, less chic than those in more fashionable areas, but since they belonged to an older period of time, they and the people who ran them were certainly more colorful. The concept of the department store was coming into vogue at this time, and some of these stores were large and elegant. The smaller and poorer shops, aside from the time-tested general store, restricted their merchandise and services mainly to one line. In *The Unclassed* (1884) Sally O'Gree (née Fisher) worked at one time in a chandler's shop, but after her marriage she and her husband opened a small grocery store, an old-time store simple and unassuming.

The store, in fact, is a mirror of the people who run it, reflecting in particular Sally's passion for order and cleanliness.

On a Sunday afternoon in October, Osmond Waymark and Julian Casti pay a visit to the O'Gree Grocery. The shop is new, clean, and bright. The proprietor's name gleams in golden letters above the door. An assortment of good and tasty food is displayed in its window: *"There was half a large cheese, marked by the incisions of the tasting-knife; a boiled ham garlanded; a cone of brawn; a truncated pyramid of spiced beef released from its American tin; also German sausage and other dainties of the kind. Then there were canisters of tea and coffee, tins of mustard, a basket of eggs, some onions, boxes of baking-powder and blacking; all arranged so as to make an impression on the passersby."* The vividness of detail suggests a longing for good and wholesome food which Gissing in his poverty was unable to buy. In 1883 when this passage was written, he was struggling against overwhelming odds to write his second novel, and the pleasure he took in a well-laid table was largely vicarious.

Standing outside before entering the shop, the two friends could see and agree that the grocers inside, Philip and Sally O'Gree, are capable, clean, energetic, affable, and in business not only to make a profit, but to serve the neighborhood. When they go inside, we get a vivid description of the place: *"The shop was very small and did not contain much stock. The new shelves showed a row of biscuit-tins, but little else, and from the ceiling hung balls of string. On the counter lay an inviting round of boiled beef. Odours of provisions and of fresh paint were strong in the air. Everything gleamed from recent scrubbing and polishing. On the walls the enterprising tradesman had hung gorgeous advertising cards."* The shop is open seven days a week for many hours each day. Though trade is picking up, only small amounts of money have crossed the counter: *"Roaring trade, Waymark! Done two shillings and threepence three farthings this Sunday morning,"* O'Gree is speaking to get a laugh.

The two shillings represent half a day's work, but since their living quarters are in the rear, they don't have to be in the shop all the time, and certainly don't have to spend the whole day standing. Once a schoolteacher, O'Gree can hardly believe the shop is his: *"He drew out the till behind the counter and jingled his hand in coppers. Then he rushed about in the wildest fervour, making passes at the beef and the ham with a formidable carving-knife, demonstrating the use of a sugar-chopper and a coffee-grinder, and lastly calling attention with infinite glee to a bad halfpenny which he had detected on the previous afternoon and had nailed down to the counter. Then he lifted a hinged portion of the counter and requested his visitors to pass into the back-parlour."* Though the furniture is scant and simple, the visitors find in the parlor the same perfect cleanliness as in the shop. The table is laid for tea with a spotless cloth and with knives and forks that sparkle.

Then Sally, *"one of the most remarkable women it was ever your lot to meet,"* emerges from the tiny kitchen: *"Sally was charming. Her trim little body attired in the trimmest of homely dresses, her sharp little face shining and just a little red with excitement, her quick movements, her laughing eyes, her restless hands graced with the new wedding-ring – all made up a picture of which her husband might well be proud. He stood and gazed at her in frank admiration; only when she sprang forward to shake hands with Waymark did he recover himself sufficiently to go through the ceremony of introducing Julian."* At one time in her life, shortly after coming to London from the country, Sally Fisher toiled each day in a city workroom at starvation wages. To make enough money to stay alive after working all day, she was forced to prostitute her body at night. Later she and O'Gree fall in love and marry. O'Gree's exuberant adoration of his young wife makes her the most joyful woman in all of Gissing's work.

A shop similar to the O'Gree establishment, though dilapidated rather than new, is that of Mrs. Bower in *Thyrza* (1887). It is located in Lambeth, a district with many slums, and operated by a woman whose husband works in a factory. Her daughter Mary, *"A girl of nineteen, sparely made, and rather plain-featured,"* helps out as a clerk in "The Little Shop with the Large Heart," but its presiding genius is Mrs. Bower. The store is situated in a neighborhood of small houses, with factories and workshops among them, but few commercial shops. Since there is little competition, the Bower business is solid, prosperous, and stagnant. On a warm summer's afternoon in 1880 Luke Ackroyd, a central character in *Thyrza*, pays a visit to the shop: *"Over the door stood the name of the proprietor – Bower – and on the woodwork in characters of faded red: 'The Little Shop with the Large Heart.' Little it certainly was and large of heart if the term could be made to signify an abundant stock. The interior was so packed with an indescribable variety of merchandise that there was scarcely space for more than two customers."* The Bower Grocery has become a general store, selling merchandise of all kinds, but too small to contain it.

The shop's slogan suggests that at one time the owners were an energetic lot, but its faded characters show any original plan to run a vigorous, competitive business also has faded. Showing signs of decay, the shop is the opposite of bright and clean. On entering Ackroyd is confronted with an awesome disarray that gives way to a strange blend of odors: *"Every article in the shop – groceries of all kinds, pastry, cooked meat, bloaters, newspapers, petty haberdashery, firewood, fruit, soap – seemed to exhale its essence distressfully under the heat; impossible that anything sold here should preserve its native savour. The air swarmed with flies. On the counter, among other things, was a perspiring yellow mass, retailed under the name of butter. Advertisements hung around proclaimed themselves in many-coloured letters."* The shop reflects the woman who runs it – fat, middle-aged, given to laughter, but growing tired. Chatting with Ackroyd, she mentions the sultry weather and says if it continues *"there won't be much left o' me. I'm a'goin' like the butter."* She will take with her when she departs, an era that was rapidly passing.

A shopkeeper of the new era is Louisa Clover in *The Town Traveller* (1898), a novel dedicated almost entirely to shop people. In the absence of an errant husband, she rents finely made cups and saucers to people who want to impress their friends at tea or dinner. Mr. Gammon, the town traveler, pauses outside the shop: *"In the window hung a card with an inscription in bold letters – 'Glass, china, and every kind of fashionable ornament for the table for hire on moderate terms.'"* Inside Mrs. Clover tells him business is good: *"Two teas and a supper yesterday. A wedding breakfast this morning."* Already this "neat, comely, and active woman" has "a young lady" as shop assistant and a boy to do the heavy work. The shop is flourishing because its proprietor, with the aid of her friend Gammon, has understood correctly the tenor of the times. As they talk, a customer drives up in a low-slung hansom cab, the driver perched on the sprung seat behind the vehicle.

A loudly dressed woman enters the shop and converses with the owner "in the lowest possible voice." Presently she returns to the vehicle that has waited for her, glancing uneasily from left to right, and disappears down the street. The woman lives in an eight-room house in an upscale neighborhood and must keep up appearances when throwing a party by having her guests admire her expensive tableware. She won't tell them the silver, china, and crystal are items she rented. The shop's main source of revenue is from people like this woman, people who can't afford to buy tableware of quality and thus resort to renting it. They can afford to hire hansoms and invite scores of people to their teas, weddings, and suppers, but not invest in proper tableware and silverware for such occasions. Of the shop-keeping class, Mrs. Clover despises her customers even though their hypocrisy and snobbery provide her with a good living.

The shopkeeper has taken advantage of the new mercantilism that was invading the retail world, replacing the old, time-worn system based on Puritan ethics. On the coat-tails of the new system, promoted by unbridled capitalism, came a new brand of advertising. Florio in *The Crown of Life* (1899) is one of the new advertising men. He views the whole world as a potential billboard, and has no use for human dignity whatever: *"I was thinking what a pity they do not use the back of the bus driver to display advertisements. It is a loss of space. Those men are so beautifully broad, and one looks at their backs, and there is nothing, nothing to see but an ugly coat."* With a good deal of anger Gissing opposed Florio's point of view, but there was little he could do about it. Commercialism was in the air and in full control. Gaudy advertising would be painted on slabs of wood and hung on hungry men to walk the crowded streets and be noticed as "sandwich men."

Most of the shops run by women were concerned with "fashion" and were in business to sell ready-to-wear clothing to female customers. Mrs. Damerel of *In the Year of Jubilee* (1894) observed that even women of quality were opening shops of this kind: *"Now we have women of title starting as milliners and modistes, and soon it will be quite a common thing to see one's friends behind the counter."* Mrs. Damerel is characterized as a pretender, and so her statement has to be taken with a grain of salt, and yet an increasing number of middle-class women were becoming shopkeepers even when their friends raised eyebrows in disapproval. The aunt of Constance Bride in *Our Friend the Charlatan* (1901) begins to keep a bakery when her funds run low. Miss Bride, though a wholesome new woman in command of the new ideas, is irritated at first and ashamed: *"I don't mind telling you that, when I first knew about it, I wished Mrs. Shufflebotham and her shop at the bottom of the sea, but I soon got over that."* Later without shame or hesitation she discloses her aunt's occupation to the ladies of the town: *"Mrs. Shufflebotham keeps a little shop and sells cakes and sweetmeats. Does it distress you?"* Some of the more snobbish are indeed distressed, though most accept the widow's shop.

While Constance Bride of the upper middle class pays little attention to one's rank in life, Emily Cadman of *Born in Exile* (1892) is keenly aware of class distinctions. She keeps a millinery shop in the town of Twybridge and doesn't see herself an ordinary tradeswoman. Circumstances have allowed her to gain a better education than most women of her standing, and in spite of becoming a shopkeeper she manages to retain the friendship of certain ladies who were at one time her classmates. Overly sensitive about her social position in the town, the milliner worries about the children of Mrs. Peak, her widowed sister. She has been told they run through the town as errand boys, and that horrifies her. She renders financial aid to allow the boys to spend their time playing sports. By doing that she frees them of "degradation" and regains social respect.

Charlotte Peak, her pretty niece of sixteen, goes to work in Emily's shop. At the time she becomes engaged to Mr.

Cusse, a draper's assistant, Charlotte has been living and working as a shopgirl for six years and is fully adjusted to her surroundings. Unlike her brother, Godwin Peak, she has never shared his ambition to rise to a higher station in life. Having accepted the shop-keeping community, she has found a life of usefulness to other people. At the end of the novel she is happy in her husband, her children, and a flourishing business. Her brother, bitten by idealistic ambition that has caused him to spend his life chasing rainbows, dies in lonely exile. Another woman who has made the most of her shop-keeping background is Beatrice French of *In the Year of Jubilee* (1894). Capable and intelligent, she is representative of those women in real life who were extending their activities beyond the shop into more complex business.

Until the time of her father's death Beatrice supported herself as a clerk in the postal service. Dying, the Camberwell builder left her and her two sisters enough to live on without having to work. While her sisters squander their income, Beatrice with an eye for business manages to save most of hers so as to open a dress-supply shop. She tries to get her younger sister to come in as a partner, but Fanny is afraid of the risk. Beatrice argues that the business of selling clothes at a discount would appeal to thousands of suburban women more interested in appearance than quality: "*We should make out that a dress we sold them for five guineas was worth ten in the shops, and the real cost would be two. See? The thing is to persuade them that they're getting an article cheap.*" Joining forces with an enterprising speculator named Luckworth

Crewe, Beatrice creates a flourishing discount house (called a "slopshop" by those in the know), and before Christmas of the year of jubilee (1887) a handsome shop with a club room is in operation.

Behind the façade is an ingenious, rapacious establishment that feeds on woman's vanity and operates just within the law. It is called the South London Fashionable Dress Supply Association and masquerades as a social club rather than a business. *"It was an undertaking shrewdly conceived, skillfully planned, and energetically set going. Beatrice knew the public to which her advertisements appealed; she understood exactly the baits that would prove irresistible to its folly and greed."* The customer would save money, getting fine dresses for almost nothing and could be persuaded she was buying garments of high fashion of supreme quality. Beatrice knows the women who patronize her shop – servant-keeping females in Brixton, Camberwell, and Peckham – are ignorant of quality, have little taste in clothes, and will buy anything at what they think is a good price. She knows too that they have a very difficult time making up their minds even when buying a pair of stockings. When it comes to visible garments, they are lost.

To solve the problem Beatrice hires Nancy Lord to advise female customers, but then she learns Nancy herself knows very little about fashion. Unfazed, she asserts: *"You can learn all you need to know in an hour. It's the ladylike appearance and talk more than anything else. You are good looking and well-dressed, and that is very much to your advantage."* Middle-aged women looking at a pretty shopgirl see themselves all young and pretty in the clothes they plan to buy. Luckworth Crewe is the advertising manager of the business and expends a great deal of energy to make it known to the public the amazing advantages of belonging to the South London Fashionable Dress Supply Association. All over the southern part of London he distributes hand-bills, leaflets, nicely printed pamphlets, and "gorgeously designed placards" to drum up business. He knows the value of advertising in the new era of commerce, and before the year is out the place is booming with countless customers. Some other female shopkeepers are Hannah Clinkscales, Mrs. Mayhew, Mrs. Ogle, and Mrs. Wilcox.

In the novels Gissing wrote during the 1880's, with the exception of *Isabel Clarendon* (1886) and *A Life's Morning* (1888), he is primarily concerned with the laboring classes. In the 1890's he wrote novels peopled mainly by men and women of the English middle class. The wide-ranging middle class was composed of sub-classes with shopkeepers at the lower end of the scale and wealthy industrialists at the top. Gissing's fullest consideration of the class is found in six novels of the nineties: *Born in Exile* (1892), *The Odd Women* (1893), *In the Year of Jubilee* (1894), *Eve's Ransom* (1895), *The Paying Guest* (1895), and *The Town Traveller* (1898). In *Charles Dickens: A Critical Study* (1898), he also had something to say of the shopgirl and gave his readers a bitter summary of her outstanding characteristics. Those characteristics are to be found in their purest form in Polly Sparkes of *The Town Traveller* and Louise Derrick of *The Paying Guest*.

Toward the end of the century, besides the girls employed in shops, increasing numbers of women were operating shops of their own. These shops ranged from the humble grocery and general store of the laboring class to the glittering salon catering to ladies of fashion and to the first of the department stores. There also appeared at this time a class of capable, intelligent women who extended their activities beyond the shop into higher finance and complicated business. Beatrice French was typical of this new kind of businesswoman. Shrewd and calculating, she went into business not merely to make a living but to become wealthy. Concerned mainly with profits, her business catered to women more interested in show than quality. It found a market of hundreds of women eager to spend their money on frippery. For only a few shillings more they could have had the best, but most of them preferred two costumes that looked good to one that was good. Beatrice and her partner also knew the value of advertising, and so do others in Gissing's novels. At the turn of the century rampant commercialism and capitalism were swiftly running hand in hand. Those inimitable forces were to run even faster and with more power in the new century.

Chapter 17

Governesses

As Gissing published his first book and began his career as a novelist, hoping to win acclaim by offering workable solutions to some of the problems of the time, an extensive number of unemployed governesses advertised for work. In the first week of 1880, through the classified columns of London's leading newspaper, more than three hundred young women sought employment. Governesses belonged to a social rank higher than shopkeepers, but it was well known that many of these women earned less in a year than superior servants. On January 6, 1880, in the classified section of the London *Times*, subscribers read this advertisement: *"Resident Governess. A young lady will teach English, fluent French and German, Italian, Spanish, good music, singing, drawing, Latin. £15 with use of piano."* Governesses in 1880 were asking more than fifteen pounds a year, and employers were paying more, but the salary required by this young lady of many languages revealed the hidden desperation of many. A "good, plain cook," with room and board and a daily ration of beer, could earn as much as twenty-five pounds annually.

As late as the first of January in 1889 "a small ladies' school in Yorkshire" wanted a young governess to teach music and Latin for a cook's salary of twenty-two pounds. Even Mrs. Sarah Stickney Ellis, the voice of conservative womanhood in England for more than half a century, complained in stiff and high-brow language of the low pay and scandalous treatment suffered by governesses: *"Nothing can more clearly indicate a low state of public morals than the vulgar disrespect and parsimonious remuneration with which the agents employed in education are sometimes requited."* The difference between "Situations Wanted" and "Situations Vacant" was salary. Most of the governesses wanted salaries higher than employers were willing to pay, some asking as much as 80 to 120 pounds a year. Yet at the same time, an "experienced, highly recommended, certificated" governess was asking only thirty pounds. Other women, whether "certificated" or not, required forty to seventy pounds. Employment agencies advertised salaries ranging from thirty to eighty pounds in one instance and twenty to fifty in another: *"English, German, and French governesses wanted for immediate vacancies in schools and families. Salaries £20 to £50."* The salary settled upon would be, in most instances, no more than thirty pounds.

Some employers were willing to pay a good governess as much as forty pounds, but many wanted the best for the least: *"A good, industrious Churchwoman able to teach English, vocal and instrumental Music, and develop the common sense of four children, six to twelve, can find a comfortable Home in a roomy house with large Garden in a Northern suburb. Salary £30 per annum. Rudimentary Latin and French required."* A number of desperate women thought a home was salary enough: *"A Lady, willing to undertake the tuition of three small children, wishing to find a comfortable home with laundress in return for her services."* One young woman, a "lady by birth," desired a position where she would be treated as one of the family, "a greater consideration than salary." The best salaries went to those with many certificates: *"A young lady, well associated, about 20 years of age, who has just finished her education and holds a first-class certificate from the College of Preceptors and two from the London Academy of Music would be glad to meet with a position as governess at a moderate salary."* French and German governesses were in high demand.

One could reasonably expect a foreign governess to know at least one language other than English, and some knew more. But the English girl claiming knowledge of Latin and Greek and fluency in five modern languages was viewed with cold suspicion. Many a householder had discovered that a governess hired to teach several languages – as well as singing, music, mathematics, and drawing – could just barely speak and write English without glaring solecisms. A reader of the advertisements receives the impression that English womanhood in 1880 was superbly educated. In reality, even when "certificated," governesses were sometimes dismally ignorant. By 1900 the picture was changing. Writing in May of 1901, Mary Maxse, the governess-keeping wife of a member of Parliament, declared that the education of women "during the last 50 years" (she might have said 20), had altered for the better: *"And the governesses have kept pace with the times. It is now considered essential that they should be educated women."* Mrs. Maxe preferred and hired foreign governesses.

As the new century got under way, the supply of governesses had diminished and salaries were much higher than twenty years earlier because English girls were turning to other pursuits. New jobs had opened in business, industry, and the professions. Those who would have become governesses in 1880 were now becoming bookkeepers, secretaries, stenographers, typists, journalists, nurses, and even doctors. On January 1, 1900 a school advertised for sixty-five student governesses to fill vacancies in it training program. It was something unheard of just a few years earlier when schools for lack of space were turning applicants away. The new commercial schools, the colleges, and the universities now admitting women had no need to advertise. Like the Milvain sisters in *New Grub Street* (1891), many English girls were no longer interested in becoming governesses. The pay had always been notoriously small, the hours dreadfully long, and the working conditions awkward or strained. Moreover, they had to compete with foreign governesses who were paid more. While Englishwomen sought better jobs elsewhere, many foreign women – French, Belgian, Swiss, German, Italian – remained in the profession.

Any casual reader of Gissing's work may find without difficulty at least sixteen governesses presented with sensitivity and sympathy in considerable detail. Three of them (Isabel Clarendon, Emily Hood, and Lilian Northway) are central characters in long novels. One (Miss Hurst) is the main figure of a short story. Several (Zillah Denyer, Maud Enderby, Alice Madden, and Jessica Morgan) play roles of unequivocal importance in their respective novels. All but two leave the profession before their stories are told. Mrs. Christopherson goes into a shop; Isabel Clarendon marries wealth after being trained to become a governess; Zillah Denyer returns home to nurse her invalid sister; Maud Enderby goes into religious seclusion; Miss Harrow becomes a housekeeper; Emily Hood moves upward to become a schoolteacher; and Miss Hurst becomes a social worker.

Another Miss Hurst – Gissing had no computer to tell him he had already used this name – quits her governess job in old age and retires. Alice Madden becomes the guardian of her deceased sister's child; Dora Milvain becomes a writer of children's books; Jessica Morgan joins the Salvation Army; and Lilian Northway, to escape her dreary life as a governess, becomes the mistress of a politician. May Rockett enters the movement for female emancipation to be supremely humiliated by two haughty women of the upper class; and Pauline Smith, through no fault of her own, is asked to resign her position. Miss Pope remains a governess in the home of Tobias Liversedge; and Winifred Elvan continues her governessing in France. These two, in order to support themselves and still retain a remnant of gentility in a world that places high value on social rank, have entered upon "a lifetime of governessing" and will do it until they die, or until encroaching old age forces them to resign.

It was preferable, of course, for gently bred women to concern themselves with things of the home and not have to worry about earning money. In *Isabel Clarendon* (1886) Rhoda Meres tells a friend, *"I shall have to earn a living somehow."* Astonished, the man replies, *"A living? Women don't make a living; that's all done for them."* The girl would like to believe this but knows better. The general view of the situation was that women of the middle class were not expected to become wage earners. It was thought they should not have economic obligations at all, but the facts of life were different. When a father died, leaving his family not well provided for, his daughters had to support themselves. Nearly always the occupation that middle-class girls chose was governessing. When the father of Isabel Clarendon died, it was decided she would be trained to become a governess. When Dr. Madden of *The Odd Women* (1893) died, two of his six daughters became governesses and the other four perished.

The school that Isabel Clarendon attended was the equivalent of one that advertised in *The Times* on January 4, 1889: *"Eagle College. Refined home school for young ladies; seven professors weekly; resident English, French, and German governesses. Music, languages, and decorative art specialities. One moderate, strictly inclusive fee for everything."* Isabel remained in school for a year and a half and was "finished off" with the usual accomplishments. If we may judge from the advertisements, these accomplishments were a smattering of English grammar, basic French and German, arithmetic, music, singing, and drawing. On leaving the school, Isabel received a certificate proving she had passed unspecified examinations. In *The Odd Women* (1893) Alice Madden laments that the younger governesses with whom she must compete have *"certificates and even degrees."* Since Jessica Morgan of *In the Year of Jubilee* (1894) is *"armed with certificates of examinational prowess,"* she has little difficulty finding work as a governess.

As for the wages governesses received, Isabel was ready to take a salary of twenty-six pounds a year. Miss Hurst in "An Old Maid's Triumph"(1895), served thirty years as a governess and earned at the peak of her career a salary of twenty-nine pounds. Alice Madden became a nursery governess at sixteen pounds a year. Sixteen years later and no longer young, she accepted a similar position that paid only twelve pounds. Since nursery governesses received less than those who taught older children, sixteen pounds was about average for 1872 when Alice began teaching. But for 1888 twelve pounds was far below the average. For girls just out of school and with a certificate, the salary offered Isabel Clarendon was near the average. That of Miss Hurst, however, should have risen at least to forty pounds a year but reached only twenty-nine, "the wages of a middling cook." She earned in her best years slightly more than most cooks, and yet was paid a pittance for performing with competence the important task of training young minds.

Those attempting to reform the system repeatedly singled out governesses as making too little money for doing an important job. But numerous mothers were known to treat governesses with so little respect that their pupils were unruly and even abusive. In *The Unclassed* (1884) Maud Enderby, a gentle, retiring, delicate girl, is hired to teach three "unlicked cubs" in the Tootle household. She is one of many governesses who have come and gone, unable to endure the bossy Mrs. Tootle and her undisciplined children. In the classroom to sit in on a lesson so as to judge Maud's effectiveness, she interrupts the young woman to make it plain that her children must not be punished for anything they do: *"My children are high-spirited and must be discreetly managed. This must be done without the help of punishment in any shape; I disapprove of those methods altogether. Now let me hear you give them a lesson in geography."* Finding the new governess mild and submissive, mother and children tyrannize over her and devise inventive ways to make her life miserable.

When young Felix Tootle throws his copybook at the head of his teacher and hits her on the cheek, she lets it be known that she will give up her position at the end of the quarter. Another girl with more gumption would have blistered the buttocks of the little savage and quit on the spot, but Maud is too gentle and too civilized to do more than give notice. She has been a governess for only a few weeks. Her first engagement convinces her that she is pitifully unfit for the job, but what else can she do? She takes another position at low pay: *"There are only two children, quite young. I think I'll succeed better with them, I hope so."* Later she tells Osmond Waymark that her new employers are kind to her, but their attempts at conversation bore her silly: *"The family I am with consists of very worthy but commonplace people. They treat me with more consideration than I imagine governesses usually get, and I am grateful to them for this, but their conversation, especially that of Mrs. Epping, I find rather wearisome. It deals with very trivial concerns of everyday life, in which I vainly endeavour to interest myself."* She lives with the Eppings as one of the family, dining with them, going to church with them, and otherwise fitting in with their social life.

While this social equality would have delighted another governess, Maud Enderby is burdened by the religious formalism of the Eppings and their friends: *"They are High Church. They discuss with astonishing vigour and at dreadful length what seems to me the most immaterial points in the Church service, and of course I have to feign a becoming interest in all this and take part in their religious ceremonies."* After six months she returns to London. Vainly seeking to understand herself, she remains at home for a time before announcing she will become a governess again. She accepts a situation with a French family and goes off to live with them in Paris. After a brief time events at home bring her back to London. Her father's trouble with the police, her mother's madness, and her own mysticism becoming heavier by the day have made her a tormented young woman. Breaking her engagement with Waymark, she withdraws from the world to practice a life of asceticism. Later we learn that she and her maiden aunt, Miss Bygrave, have become members of "the true Church," a quasi-religious cult in a midland town. Her term as a governess has lasted ten months.

Maud Enderby was never meant to be a governess. At nineteen her brief, unpleasant career is over, but Emily Hood in *A Life's Morning* (1888) is ideally suited for the position. She enters the profession at nineteen, determined to excel in the performance of her duties, and develops a positive attitude that sustains her. When we first see her she has been a governess for three years in Liverpool, years of importance, for during that time she moved from girlhood to womanhood. She has a good job as the governess of Edith Rossall's twin daughters in the wealthy Athel household: *"Few governesses had so pleasant a life. Mrs. Rossall imposed on her children a minimum of brain work. Bodily health was after all the first thing, especially in the case of girls. A couple of hours' school in the morning, one hour given to preparation of lessons after tea – this for the present was deemed quite enough."* The twins are not remarkably fond of their lessons, but in Emily's hands they are docile and eager to please. She knows how to win the affection of children without losing control, and her pupils regard her with reverence.

Thankful that she is quiet, unassuming, and polite, the adults in the well-appointed house also accord Emily respect: *"It is such a good thing to have a governess who really seems well-bred; it does make it so much easier to treat her with consideration."* And yet her position in the Athel household isn't so cozy as it first appears. To the casual observer she is fully accepted as one of the family, yet there are hidden rules that remind her repeatedly to remember her place. She's allowed to eat breakfast with the family, for example, but doesn't dine with them or mingle with guests. *"Though Mrs. Rossall said it was a distinct advantage to have in the house a governess whom one could in many respects treat as an equal, yet there was naturally a limit in this as in all other matters. We have not yet, either in fact or in sentiment, quite outgrown the social stage in which personal hiring sets on the hired the stigma of servitude."* The very idea of living in servitude stung most governesses to the quick.

Every young governess wanted to be known as educated and professional. Any inference that her position was similar to that of a servant was not to be tolerated. Her sensitivity on this issue was troublesome to employers, yet they agreed it was not entirely without cause. *"At present her condition too much resembles that of a trusted servant,"* said a contemporary. *"And it is the consciousness of this and the dread of being so considered that poisons her mind and causes her to snatch at straws and brew teapot tempests in vindication of her rights. Her place at the table, her seat in the carriage, her precedence through doorways are questions which shake her to her foundations."* Emily Hood is not in rebellion and therefore accepts without protest the dreary indignity of not being permitted to dine with the family, or to meet them evenings in the drawing-room or library. However, she is hurt when scatter-brained Jessie Cartwright says to her: *"Can you imagine me teaching? I always hated school and I hate the thought of being a governess. Why I should be thought no more of than a servant, I suppose I should have to make friends with the milkman and the butcher's boy. And how's a girl to get married if she spends all her time in a nursery teaching children grammar*?" Emily is hurt, too, when the father of the man she will marry is astonished that his high-born son would even think of marrying a governess. *"It is, in a very pronounced sense, marrying beneath you."*

Though it sometimes happened that a gentleman fell in love with a governess, more often she merely whetted the sexual appetite. A traditional tableau in the fiction of the period is that of the lustful son or lecherous employer pursuing a fleet-footed governess with intentions other than honorable. Yet with not one of his governesses does Gissing make use of this theme. The young men who pursue Emily Hood, Maud Enderby, and Lilian Northway have only marriage in mind. Even the violent Dagworthy who chases after Emily Hood as though she were fair prey in a jungle is willing to marry her; and wealthy Wilfrid Athel has only the purest love for her. Osmond Waymark, a sometime teacher, writer, and rent collector, isn't really in love with Maud Enderby but rather than break their engagement is willing to marry her. Denzil Quarrier proposes to Lilian Northway only to learn she is married to a man who was arrested and sent to prison as soon as they left the church. Eventually, because she finds it impossible to obtain a divorce, they live out of wedlock.

This is the one unconventional relationship in the restricted lives of Gissing's governesses. Lilian goes against the stern moral code of the time and for a brief interval is happy. Later, however, her behavior comes back to haunt her and she commits suicide. She lost but at least she loved, and that is more than can be said for most of these governesses in Gissing's fiction. Too many are plain and bloodless creatures, who must find a way to support themselves because they have no power to attract men. Lady Kent of *Isabel Clarendon* (1886) is opposed to training Isabel to become a governess because the girl is the opposite of plain and mousy: *"She is far too good-looking, has too much blood, doesn't at all belong to the governess breed."* That may be true of Isabel but not of Zillah Denyer of *The Emancipated* (1890). Denied the hope of love and marriage, she is *"a tall, awkward, plain girl with a fixed expression of trouble."* Nervous and unsure of herself, she twists her fingers together while talking, speaks in quick, short, abortive sentences, and breaks off looking downward in embarrassment.

Zillah had once pretended to be advanced in thought and feeling. But when as a governess she comes under the influence of conservative people, gradually she ceases to deceive herself, and one by one the characteristics of the emancipated woman fall away from her. She is similar in some respects to Maud Enderby, for in the home of her pupils the parents confront her with tedious religious questions she prefers to avoid. However, while Maud resisted the religion of her employers, Zillah slowly undergoes a spiritual awakening that brings her exactly in line with the way the family thinks: *"Living with a perfectly conventional family, she adopted not only the forms of their faith – in which she had, of course, no choice – but at length the habit of their minds; with a profound sense of solace, she avowed her self-deceptions and became what nature willed her to be – a daughter of the Church."* Reverting to a conservative position, Zillah is comparable to Mrs. Peak in *Born in Exile* (1892): *"For several years she had nourished a secret antagonism to her husband's spirit of political, social, and religious rebellion, and in her widowhood she speedily became a pattern of the conservative female."* Both women, living honestly and without pretense, find some degree of happiness.

While Zillah Denyer gained solace in religion, Alice Madden of *The Odd Women* (1893) seeks relief from "the barrenness and bitterness of life" by performing a private ritual. Each night for half an hour she reads the Bible. Then she cups her hands over her eyes and against her face and prays fervently but silently. She is another governess who must endure a life of celibacy and insecurity because of her plainness. We see Alice first in the summer of 1872 at the age of nineteen, and she is *"a plain, gentle-mannered girl, short of stature, and in movement something less than graceful."* When we see her again it's the spring of 1888, and her age is thirty-five. Though she speaks with good enunciation, her voice has "an unpleasant hoarseness," and she speaks with a "stiffness and pedantry of phrase" from the years of teaching. Her sedentary life as a governess has made her round-shouldered and flabby. Poor food has spoiled her complexion: *"Her face would not have been disagreeable but for its spoilt complexion; the homely features, if health had but rounded and coloured them, would have expressed pleasantly enough the sincerity of her character."* Her sister Virginia, faring worse, has taken to the bottle and become an incorrigible alcoholic.

Jessica Morgan of *In the Year of Jubilee* (1894) is another bloodless governess with few personal attractions: *"She looked over-wrought and low-spirited; a very plain and slightly made supper gown exhibited her meagre frame with undue frankness; her face might have been pretty if health had filled and coloured the flesh, but as it was she looked a ghost of girlhood, a dolorous image of frustrate sex."* Like the poignant Miss Eade, who desperately wanted Mr. Bullivant, the self-important clerk in *The Odd Women* (1893), Jessica is fiercely in love with Samuel Barmby, a little man with a high opinion of himself. Like Mr. Bullivant, who ignored Miss Eade, the quarter-educated Barmby – a disciple of culture – can't be bothered even to recognize her existence. Winifred Elvan in *Will Warburton* (1905) is also shy, unattractive, and insecure. Though her becoming a governess "involved a social decline," she is content to remain a governess for the rest of her life: *"Winnie has a terror of finding herself destitute. She jumped for joy when she was offered that work, and I'm sure she'd be content to live there in the same way for years."* She knows that as she grows older her services will be in less demand, and her salary will gradually decrease. But what can she do?

That is what happened to the salary of Alice Madden in *The Odd Women* (1893). When Alice found herself out of a job at thirty-five, the possibility of securing another at the same salary was slight. She was aware that she would have to take a position at perhaps a lower salary, but she was shocked when the parents of five children wanted her services for "not a penny of salary." They had the gall to offer no money whatever, only a room to sleep in and her food. Yet in real life, as we have seen, some women were asking only for room and board for round-the-clock service to several children. Alice and her sister Virginia agree that the proposal was shameless, but they know anything better could be very difficult to find. By 1888 people who could afford it were looking for young governesses better prepared than in earlier years, and that Alice knows: *"There is so little choice for people like myself. Certificates, and even degrees, are asked for on every hand. With nothing but references to past employers, what can one expect? I know it will end in my taking a place without salary."* It's possible, she says, wringing her hands, that the time will come when no one will offer even room and board for her services. Then what will she do?

After several months of searching, growing leaner on spare food all the time, she finds a place at a salary of twelve pounds a year. She doesn't earn the twelve pounds, however, because in less than a year she has to quit. The family has taken shameful advantage of her, expecting her to do several jobs instead of one: *"The situation she was about to quit had proved more laborious than any in her experience. At first merely a governess, she had gradually become the children's nurse as well, and for the past three months had been expected to add the tendence of a chronic invalid to her other duties."* Out of work and with little hope for the future, Alice concludes that her career as a governess is over, and yet somehow she must go on living. Her experience deftly illustrates what was being said by any number of would-be reformers: *"It is a career without a future. When too old to teach, the poor lady loses her comforts at the time when she needs them most, and retires upon savings which barely serve to keep body and soul together."* With a little help from others – a concept Gissing was constantly pushing – Alice manages to live comfortabley and also care for her dead sister's child.

In the story "An Old Maid's Triumph" (1895), Gissing wrote about this same problem. Miss Hurst at fifty-eight (not to be confused with another governess with the same name who becomes a social worker) is about to lose her present engagement, the last she can expect to have: *"What will the poor old thing do? Impossible, I fear, that she can have saved anything. I wish we could do something but you know we can't."* Her friends, Mrs. and Mrs. Fletcher, don't know that Miss Hurst with unusual frugality has managed to save enough to insure her security for the rest of her life. After thirty years of governessing, she is able to face the future with serenity and dignity. From an average pittance of twenty-nine pounds, she has put aside fifteen each year. For thirty years she has never spent a shilling without much consideration, and now she will be able to live out the rest of her life on a pound a week or more: *"The long fight was over, and she had triumphed."* In the absence of social security, or "national insurance" that came much later, governesses too old to work and not as frugal as Miss Hurst ended their days either in abject poverty or in special homes provided by welfare organizations.

A picture darkly tinted emerges from any study of governesses and their situation during the nineteenth century in England. Advertisements in newspapers, articles by social scientists, and writers of fiction all agreed that most of these women were destined to lead dreary lives, suffer poverty in old age, and die penniless. Those who tried to improve the lot of poor governesses used terms like "down-trodden" to describe them, and images of abused governesses predominate in the fiction of the time. As the century was coming to an end, however, their situation was slowly improving. Newspaper advertising reflected the trend as well as firsthand observation. Yet some astute observers doubted their lives were really better.

Chapter 18

Female Teachers

Provision for "superannuation" (a fat word coined by someone liking Latinate construction) was also a problem of schoolteachers. As early as 1847 the Education Department began to give retirement allowances to elementary teachers in the amount of one-third of their salaries, but in 1862 the program ceased. From then till the end of the century no adequate provision for old age was settled upon, and teachers – in a predicament similar to that of governesses – had to live after retirement as best they could. On the job, however, things were improving. Changes in the educational system brought increased demand for good teachers, and training was available even at major universities. New opportunities were open to young women who viewed becoming a governess as anathema in their lives. Also the new demand brought higher salaries to teachers. In the first week of 1900, when newspaper advertisements displayed only one vacancy for a governess, employment agencies were seeking schoolteachers to fill numerous positions. One agency "urgently needed" 340 qualified applicants to teach in public and private schools.

Another agency, calling itself the "Central Registry for Teachers," boasted that it could recommend assistant schoolmistresses who were university graduates. In its files were the records of fully qualified high-school teachers, foreign teachers, and kindergarten teachers. The qualifying certificate once earned, teachers had little trouble obtaining a situation. Charles Booth noted that *"in no other calling is demand and supply so nicely balanced, but if anything the supply is deficient."* So schools offering low salaries were finding it difficult to hire competent teachers, who fell into two main groups: those in elementary education and those in secondary education. Women who wanted to become elementary teachers, according to Booth, had to undergo long and rigorous preparation.

After receiving their basic education, they began a four years' apprenticeship as student teachers. Then came the Queen's scholarship examination, feared and highly respected for its toughness. Those who passed with high grades were eligible for college training. After two years of college they had to pass the "certificate examination" and practice-teach for eighteen months. Following this, they obtained the coveted "parchment certificate" and after eight years of preparation emerged as qualified teachers. These were the cream of the crop; other programs dedicated to training teachers were less rigorous. Secondary training was completed in shorter time, though near the end of the century many secondary teachers held university degrees. At the bottom of the scale was the girl of sixteen with feeble qualifications assigned to a private school at low pay.

The board schools were open five days a week from 9:00 to 4:30 with one and a half hours off for lunch. The hours were frequently extended in order to coach backward students, and teachers as well as students had homework. Elementary teachers were given six or seven weeks vacation each year, and secondary teachers had three months during the summer. Salaries for elementary teachers began at eighty-five pounds a year and rose to ninety after two years. Annual increments could result eventually in a salary of 125 pounds, the top figure for all teachers. Head mistresses received 120 to 250 pounds or more, depending on the size of the school. In the best schools some were known to receive as much as 700 pounds per year. Inferior schools, most of them private institutions, paid female teachers as little as 35 to 50 pounds without extras. In schools throughout the nation women were paid less than men.

Female teachers in Gissing's fiction range from a poor woman who gives piano lessons at sixpence an hour to a university graduate teaching in a high school. In "A Song of Sixpence" (1895), a "professional lady" named Miss Withers is willing to accept any child who will pay her the meager sum she requires. Once comparatively well off, she now struggles against all sorts of forces to keep herself alive. A widow left unprovided for and alone in the world, she must somehow support herself by teaching. With no friends or relatives to help her, she is compelled to work for anyone willing to pay for music lessons. Though not more than forty, she is rapidly aging and to complicate matters has lost a leg. Plagued by a yearning for alcohol to escape her misery, she worries about becoming sick, growing old, and having a pupil come for a lesson to find her drunk.

Belonging to a higher class than her patrons, she must also worry about treating them with condescension. She finds it hard to swallow her pride and accept the advice of ignorant parents who know nothing about music. Once she made the mistake of attempting to teach music the way it should be taught, beginning with notes and scales. After the third lesson the mother complained: *"My child don't seem to be gettin' on very much. When are you goin' to teach her a toon, Miss Withers? Her father says that kind o' plyin' mikes his 'ead ache."* The teacher curtly replies the little girl will learn tunes at once, and within a few days she's hammering out a familiar melody. Detecting "a toon," however badly played, the parents applaud Miss Withers and recommend her to their friends. It is a living but little else.

Another music teacher is Mrs. Emerson in *Thyrza* (1887). Instead of working merely to support herself, she must work to supplement the small income of a never-do-well husband. A vigorous woman determined to survive in a world of hardship, she often walks for many city blocks in cold weather (as Gissing did in his early years in London) to meet with her pupils. Still another teacher of music is Maud Milvain in *New Grub Street* (1891) before she leaves home and goes to London. Maud's work as a music teacher was so irregular she didn't earn enough to support life. So she became an author where she found more irregularity and intense competition. Somewhat better off, though also victims of low salaries, are the women who teach in small private schools. Before her marriage Mrs. Hood in *A Life's Morning* (1888) taught in an obscure little school. James Hood *"married a schoolmistress, one Miss Martin, who was responsible for the teaching of some twelve or fifteen children of tender age."* After they marry Mrs. Hood continues her teaching to supplement their income, but within a few months most of her students go elsewhere.

At the time of her marriage she was twenty-five, fairly good-looking, and capable of exertion. Though superficially educated she was able to teach reading and writing and arithmetic with a fair degree of success. But after the birth of her first child, a little girl she names Emily, *"her moral nature showed an unaccountable weakening,"* and she loses interest in her teaching. From then on, as with so many women in Gissing's fiction, she finds the conditions of her life hard and growing harder. In *The Unclassed* (1884) Miss Rutherford operates a school in her home. Experienced and middle-aged, she is more competent than Mrs. Hood and more compassionate. Enrolled in her school are thirteen girls, the oldest fifteen and the youngest six. Most of them are the daughters of respectable tradesmen – Maud Enderby and Harriet Smales – but one, Ida Starr, is not. When she learns that Ida Starr is the daughter of a "fallen woman," for the sake of the school Miss Rutherford must dismiss Ida. Reluctantly she informs Lotty Starr, the girl's mother, that Ida must go.

In the same novel is the Tootle Academy, larger than Miss Rutherford's school and more pretentious. It is situated in *"a pleasant suburb of London,"* actually Brixton, a dingy locality with a mixture of shops and houses. It has it *"spacious playground and gymnasium,"* in reality a cluttered backyard and a vacant coach-house. As for education, the school offers *"either the solid foundation desirable for a commercial career, or the more liberal training adapted to minds of a professional bias."* The student body is made up of forty little boys crammed into very inadequate quarters: *"The marvel was how so many could be accommodated in so small a house. Two fair-sized bedrooms, and a garret in which the servants could not be persuaded to sleep, served as dormitories for the whole school; the younger sleeping two together."* Running the school is self-centered Dr. Tootle. His chief distinction is having *"grievously over-exerted his brain in literary labour."*

The parents of the boys are willing to accept this hearsay as proof of the doctor's fitness to fill his post, *"though it resulted in entire weeks of retreat from the school room under the excuse of fearful headaches."* His absence poses no problem, however, for when Dr. Tootle is suffering from "constitutional headache," Mrs. Tootle runs the Academy with an iron fist. The woman flits about classrooms during lesson time brow-beating the teachers and telling them how to teach: *"Don't you think it would be better to confine yourself to the terms of the doctor's little compendium?"* She's an offensive, domineering, formidable busy-body who keeps the school in an uproar day after day from morning till night. Just the opposite of Mrs. Tootle is Mary Abbott in *The Whirlpool* (1897). Once a high-school teacher, "very clever and successful," she has about her an air of superiority that comes from the classroom. Her friends know her as intelligent with many interests.

When Harvey Rolfe visits Mrs. Abbott, shortly before the death of her husband, he finds her reading Théodule Ribot's *L'Hérédité Psychologique* (1873), a book Gissing himself had perused. Her reading of Ribot is meant to show that she is not merely educated in the ordinary sense, but in tune with the intellectual currents of the time and able to read easily a French work in the original. She tells Rolfe she finds the book "intensely interesting" and returns to it as soon as he departs. During their conversation her remarks reflect Ribot's theories on heredity, but Gissing doesn't tell us that Ribot really had no training in this field. He was an artisan painting picture frames in Paris before becoming an artist painting realistic pictures showing members of his own family at mundane tasks. At the time of Rolfe's visit Mary Abbott is seen as a peevish woman, impatient when things go wrong. But when her husband, "groaning with neuralgia," dies of a medical overdose, the adversity she faces helps her to know herself better. Later she takes a house away from London and converts it into a successful school.

In *The Odd Women* (1893) the Madden sisters, Alice and Virginia, reap only a dumb perplexity from their suffering. They talk constantly of opening a school in the country with the eight hundred pounds left them by their father: *"We have made up our minds; that is to be our life's work. It is far, far more than a mere means of subsistence."* They mean well but are too weak to put the plan into practice. They can only dream of a handsome school owned and operated by themselves, bustling with subordinate teachers, and filled to capacity with eager, clean-faced pupils. Worn and discouraged, they are deathly afraid of losing the little money they have, and they lack the ability to manage a school for even the youngest of children. They must also consider the sad fate of three sisters who died before their time and a fourth who dies in childbirth as cautionary instruction .

Gissing's own unmarried sisters, Margaret and Ellen, didn't lack the courage to open a school or the ability to run it. At the beginning of 1898, Ellen complained that the stress of teaching was hurting her health and making her miserable. From Rome, Gissing replied on January 23, 1898: *"I grieve over your school troubles. Yes, it is a monstrous thing that you should work so hard for so little – a ludicrous thing. Yet I suppose people will not pay more."* Shortly afterwards the sisters decided to open a school of their own. A month later Gissing wrote to Ellen, expressing enthusiastic approval, and enclosing a contribution of five pounds. He even took the trouble to compose a lengthy advertisement for the new school: *"The misses Gissing, after some years' experience in private teaching, are about to open a Preparatory Day School. Their course of instruction will comprise the usual English subjects (grammar, history, geography), arithmetic, French & Latin. Extra Subjects: Music & Drawing. In all their teaching the Misses Gissing will aim at the thoroughness & method which are of prime importance in the education of children. It will be their endeavour to lay the foundations of a sound intellectual training."*

After some months of stumbling, the enterprise began to flourish. Gissing enrolled his son Walter in the school and sent whenever he could small checks to cover the boy's support. In 1902, when the sisters suggested that Walter's tuition be free, Gissing replied: *"Your school is large, & a splendid result of the intelligence & hard work you have both devoted to it; but it is far from profitable, & you have burdens enough of your own. So I send herewith a cheque for £3."* Gissing seems to have had little hope that his sisters would ever marry, and for twenty years he wrote them long letters in an effort to mold them into women capable of standing alone in the world. His efforts were not in vain. Even though he had his doubts as to whether their school would endure for any length of time, his sisters were able to support themselves and their school long after his death in 1903.

Mary Barfoot in *The Odd Women* (1893) is the kind of woman Gissing hoped his sisters would become. About forty, her mental and moral stamina has seen her through severe troubles, poverty among them, and her struggles have culminated in a staunch personal dignity: *"She was handsome, and her carriage occasionally betrayed a consciousness of the fact. According to circumstances, she bore herself as the lady of aristocratic tastes, as a genial woman of the world, or as the fervid prophetess of female emancipation, and each character was supported with a spontaneity, a good-natured confidence which inspired liking and respect."* She operates a commercial academy, or "business college" as such institutions were soon to be called, for young women who wish to earn their living in business. Her mission is to train girls for work in offices, teaching them shorthand, bookkeeping, the writing of business letters, and typing. She and her dedicated assistant, Rhoda Nunn, don't show an active interest in improving the lot of the lower classes. They wish to be of use chiefly to the daughters of educated people who could find themselves in a situation where they need to work.

Most of Gissing's teachers are associated with private schools, but at least two are with the "board schools" of the Education Department. In *The Odd Women* (1893) Isabel Madden, one of six Madden sisters, is trained to be an elementary teacher at a school in Bridgewater. She undertakes the rigorous preparation as described earlier in these pages, completes it, and because of her qualifications finds a job that pays well. But soon after she begins to teach, for reasons no one seems to know, she suffers a nervous breakdown and becomes ill. Her sisters believe the breakdown came from overwork but have no proof. Even so, they discourage their youngest sister from following in the footsteps of Isabel. In conversation with Rhoda Nunn, Monica says: *"Alice and Virginia were afraid of having me trained for a school; you remember that one of our sisters who went through it died of overwork."* It seems the young woman didn't die of overwork. Constitutional factors were involved. Isabel was simply unfit for work requiring mental labor. At twenty-two, "the poor hard-featured girl," suffered brain trouble and drowned herself in a bathtub. Years later her sister Monica would die in childbirth at twenty-two.

Another teacher in a board school, one stronger and smarter than Isabel, is Miss Rodney of "Miss Rodney's Leisure" (1903). She is one of Gissing's new women – bright, energetic, opinionated, forceful, and with a purpose. She works long hours, seldom gets to bed before midnight, and faces the challenge of the next day with enthusiasm and vigor. About twenty-eight and dressed in tailor-made clothes, she walks faster than anyone in Wattleborough yet never seems hurried. When she crosses a muddy street, she does it without thinking of long skirts, and yet they remain clean. She holds up her head proudly, and instead of casting her glance downward in a man's presence she looks him full in the face. A university graduate, she knows many important people and has a reputation for being remarkably clever. Taking up residence in the Turpin boarding-house, she makes plans, over their mother's objections, to send Mabel and Lily Turpin into service. Her story is a study of what an active mind can do among apathetic people. Though she is portrayed with broad strokes of irony, it's clear that Gissing likes her.

He concerns himself with her leisure time, making no mention of her duties at the high school. If he had chosen to do so, he could have placed her in an academic setting as well, for he himself had been a high-school teacher in America when quite young. He accepted a position for the winter of 1876-77 in the Waltham High School, Waltham, Massachusetts, to teach French, German, and English for a salary of eight hundred dollars. In a letter to Algernon at the beginning of 1877, he indicated that he was especially pleased with the way

Americans treated teachers: *"The perfect order that prevails and the respect with which the masters are treated is delightful. I never saw anything like it in England. A High School teacher is an important person here."* He seems to have found his work pleasant and rewarding, but for reasons unexplained he suddenly gave up his post and caught a train for Chicago, arriving there near the first of March in 1877. He wrote stories for a newspaper there and returned to England in the fall. It is doubtful whether anyone will ever know with certainty why he suddenly gave up his teaching post. In *The Unclassed* (1884), his second novel, three teachers find little satisfaction in their jobs and resign to become a rent collector, a grocer, and a waiter.

We know that at one time Gissing wanted to become a teacher on the university level with a specialty in Greek and Roman literature. At heart he was a classicist and would have loved nothing better than teaching classical literature to eager students. It was a long-held dream of his that was shattered by the Manchester debacle. In America to build a new life for himself, that dream of becoming a professor slowly shifted to the dream of becoming an influential novelist of ideas and opinion. Perhaps that's why he left Waltham to travel by train to Chicago. He wanted to be a writer and would have to channel his energy in that direction. So in *The Unclassed* (1884), a very early novel and only his second, a novel with many echoes of the recent past in his own life, not one but three teachers show displeasure in their work and resign to pursue work more satisfying.

Chapter 19

Female Nurses

Other young women of the middle class in England were skirting the teaching profession to become nurses. For centuries the job of nursing, particularly in demand during warfare, had been considered low, rough, crude, disreputable, and suitable only for males. The Greek physician Hippocrates, referred to as the father of western medicine, is said to have had male attendants providing skilled care of patients in sanitary conditions. On the battlefield those aiding the wounded were invariably male. During the middle ages, however, monks and nuns provided nursing-like care, but even though the nuns were female they lacked the necessary training to be called nurses. Even so, they began the tradition of religious organizations taking care of the sick, which continues today. Phoebe, mentioned in the Bible, has been described as "the first visiting nurse," but not until the middle of the nineteenth century did Florence Nightingale during the Crimean War, from 1853 to 1856, lay down the foundations of professional nursing. Her *Notes on Nursing: What It is and What It is Not* (1859) was a popular manual of 136 pages intended to guide those in the field. The last half of the long title was later dropped.

In 1844, in the person of Sarah Gamp, Charles Dickens could depict the average nurse as vulgar, loathsome, eccentric, and not very clean. In 1898 George Gissing published a critical study of Dickens in which he asked exactly who is Sarah Gamp, and made answer to his own question: *"Well, a so-called nurse, living in Kingsgate Street, Holborn, in a filthy room somewhere upstairs, and summoned for nursing of all kinds by persons more or less well-to-do, who are so unfortunate as to know of no less offensive substitute. We are told and can believe that in the year 1844, the date of 'Martin Chuzzlewit,' few people did know of any substitute for Mrs. Gamp; that she was an institution; that she carried her odious vices and her criminal incompetence from house to house in decent parts of London. In plain words, then, we are speaking of a very loathsome creature; a sluttish, drunken, avaricious, dishonest woman. Meeting her in the flesh, we shrink disgusted, so well does the foulness of her person correspond with the baseness of her mind."* Dickens knew her quite well, for she had officiated in his home during moments of domestic crisis, had brought his children into the world or kept one or two from leaving it. So his estimate of the woman was less bitter and more generous than Gissing's.

At the time Gissing wrote his book on Dickens, Sarah Gamp and her kind were vanishing. Charles Booth observed in 1896: *"Sairey Gamp still survives here and there with her love of 'something stronger than water,' and her hap-hazard rule of thumb. But slowly and surely her ways have been discovered by the district nurse, and the knowledge that something better is obtainable has practically stopped the demand for her services."*

Even as Dickens was creating Sarah Gamp, a movement was underway to elevate nursing to the status of a respected profession. Florence Nightingale supplied the proper impetus after 1854 and became the founder of modern nursing. Before the century ended the public image of the nursing profession had so changed that Booth was able to say: *"In no walk of life has the desire of certain women for independence and usefulness outside their homes found on the whole a more satisfactory expression than in the adoption of the profession of hospital nurse. Just as every boy has the wish to become a soldier or sailor, so does every girl at one period or other desire to take up nursing. The census at each decade shows an increase in the numbers of women so employed."*

Following the example of Miss Nightingale, women from every social class flocked into nursing. Some of the candidates, surprising the do-nothing aristocracy, were ladies by birth and education, the daughters of men with titles. Numerous candidates also belonged to the upper servant class and the middle class. Daughters of clergymen, military officers, doctors, lawyers, farmers, tradesmen, and artisans worked side by side in the hospitals of the day. Many of those who formerly would have sought places as music teachers or nursery governesses went into nursing. Most of them depended upon their profession for a living, though a few had private means. Nurses with a university education in medicine and the sciences were rare, for those women who went on to obtain university degrees usually did a little more work and study to become doctors. Nursing candidates had to be of good morals, sound of mind, in good physical condition, and not younger than twenty-three. As nurses they were expected to be clean and neat, cheerful and kindly, careful and trustworthy.

In *Born in Exile* (1892) Janet Moxey, an intelligent plain girl of eighteen, studies medicine at the Women's Medical School in London, becomes a physician, and develops into an admirable woman. In 1901, when Gissing was suffering from what he thought was tuberculosis, his doctors recommended the "open-air and over-feeding cure" at Dr. Jane Walker's newly opened sanatorium in Suffolk. Gissing went there near the end of June, ate stupendously, "got up to 10 stone 9 without clothing" (149 pounds), and left the first week in August. Dr. Walker – sensible, efficient, respected by her colleagues in a profession occupied almost solely by men – impressed Gissing as a fine example of the new woman making a genuine contribution: *"Dr. Walker makes a good impression. She has been invited, I hear, to read a paper at the forthcoming international congress on Tuberculosis – a distinction which must mean something."* He was also impressed by another new woman at the sanatorium, a patient name Rachel Evelyn White, who might have been the model for Miss Rodney in the story "Miss Rodney's Leisure." The piece was written in the early spring of 1902 when Miss White was still fresh in Gissing's memory.

The training to become a nurse was a time of trial. One supervisor remarked that not a single person went through the hospital mill unchanged: *"The nurse after her training is either a distinctly worse or distinctly better woman than when she entered. It is a trial as well as a training that is undergone."* The period of training considered necessary to produce a fully qualified nurse was generally stated to be three years, but it varied. Some hospitals granted a certificate after two years, others after three or four. In most cases, once the certificate was granted, a period of service was insisted upon. A nurse on day duty, according to Charles Booth, was awakened in her quarters at 5:45 or 6:00 a.m. and went to a common dining room for breakfast. At 7:00 she entered the wards. There she worked for two hours with the night nurse, sweeping the wards, emptying night pans, washing patients, and serving them breakfast. Near ten o'clock she was allowed twenty minutes to have a lunch of bread and milk in summer and soup in winter. Then she worked until one in the afternoon and later, after resting and perhaps a soothing bath, she went to dinner. It was the chief meal of the day, and she ate bread, meat, and cheese with milk or beer to drink and pudding for dessert.

In some hospitals a nurse had to sit at table for half an hour, whether eating or not, "for the sake of her digestion." Then came long hours of work in the wards, interrupted only by half an hour for tea, until 9:30 at night. At that hour she got off duty and went to a supper of cold meat and vegetables. An hour later, at half-past ten, she was in her bed with the lights out. Once a month the typical hospital nurse was given a day off and once every two weeks an evening. She got a yearly vacation of about three weeks, not always in the summer. Her dedication was rewarded by indigestion, anemia, sore throat, over-strain, flat feet, and sometimes a deadly disease caught from a patient. Her salary, which gradually improved as the years passed, ranged between twenty-six and forty pounds a year. It was the salary of a good cook or governess.

Gissing's opinions concerning the nursing profession were ambivalent. As he began his career he viewed the profession as a noble calling where ardent idealists could find a sense of worth and fulfillment. In *Workers in the Dawn* (1880) that attitude comes forward with the heroine of the novel, Helen Norman. When she is about to complete a two-years' term of intensive study, her period of Sturm und Drang in Germany, her friends believe she will become a hospital nurse. As Gilbert Gresham sees it, only in that way can she utilize in active life what she has learned from Schopenhauer, Comte, and Shelley. But Helen has other ideas. Instead of becoming a nurse, she takes up social work among the poor and dedicates herself entirely to that pursuit. In another novel of the slums, *Thyrza* (1887), Gissing implies that nursing and working among the poor are quite similar in nature. Both are selfless pursuits requiring the same qualities of zeal, determination, and dedication. In both the young woman works not merely for money, but for the good of others. Both aim to make existing conditions better, and both demand the energy of idealists.

Helen is an admirable young woman, as perfect as Gissing can make her, but not without her critics. After roundly condemning idealistic reformers, Mr. John Tyrrell, a philistine disliking change, speaks of nursing and "district-visiting" (his language for social work in the slums) in the same breath: *"The girls, I notice, are beginning to have the same craze. I shouldn't wonder if Paula gets an idea that she'll be a hospital nurse, or go district-visiting in Bethnal Green."* Gissing's readers knew that Bethnal Green was one of the most noisome slums in all of London and a very dangerous place for any outsider. Tyrrell goes on to say that "the real social reformers" are not the idealists like Helen and Walter Egremont, but the hard-headed, practical, and selfish men like James Dalmaine: *"Nothing solid has ever been gained in this world that wasn't pursued out of self-interest."* It's possible that Tyrrell has read Adam Smith and Thomas Malthus and the political economists who came later to postulate self-interest as the motivating force of all trade and human improvement.

If Gissing himself was coming to believe that only the realists get things done, he continued to view the hard-working nurse as representative in the broad sense of "the highest form of life." In *The Emancipated* (1890) Mallard is of the opinion that the lives of struggling artists are perhaps the most noble though not the highest: *"When I say that I believe this course is the highest I can follow, I mean that I believe it employs all my best natural powers as no other would. As for the highest in the absolute sense, that is a different matter. Possibly the life of a hospital nurse, of a sister of mercy – something of that kind – comes nearest the ideal. I do not speak contemptuously. I speak sincerely. In a world where pain is the most obvious fact, the task of mercy must surely take precedence of most others."*

Convinced that hospital nursing was dedicated to the selfless ideal of caring for the helpless, Gissing's admiration of the profession was as strong in 1890 as in 1880.

Five years later, perhaps because of the propaganda which lured young girls into nursing without mentioning the long hours, low wages, and exposure to disease, or because like Dickens he had always hated the workhouse, Gissing attacked with some violence the conditions of infirmary nursing in the nation's workhouses. In "The Beggar's Nurse," a story of 1895, a sick and destitute woman appeals to a friend for help. For more than a year she has been a nurse in a workhouse infirmary, a shadowy place where the poorest of people falling sick are sent to die, and the job has all but killed her.

> *"I remember," said Mrs. Hinton, "that you often spoke of nursing – thought you would like it. Did it prove too much for your strength?"*
>
> *Adeline shuddered, looked away, seemed unable to talk of this experience. But at length she forced herself to do so. In a low, unsteady voice, she gave answer: "It not only ruined my health – it made me a devil!"*

Adeline tells her friend that when she entered the workhouse infirmary she was sensitive and compassionate, but soon became base, cruel, and uncaring. The "moral poison" of having to nurse paupers until she went to sleep on her feet corrupted her: *"There were two of us nurses, only two. Often I have had forty patients to look after, and for twelve hours at a time. Ah! often for longer. I have sunk down and fallen asleep by dying people."* The toil, she asserts, was not the worst of it; that harmed only her body. Working and living under vile conditions taught her to hate: *"I suffered most from never having any privacy. I had no sleeping room to myself; two servants shared it with me when I slept at night, and when I had my rest in the daytime the other nurse kept coming in and out for things that were kept there. Later she did it just to annoy me, for we hated each other. She was the first I hated – a heartless, vile-minded woman."* Adeline exhausted herself in conscientious nursing because she thought it was the Christian thing to do and would keep her pure. It didn't.

Her fellow nurse, who had been there for a long time, was steadily corrupted by the vileness of the place, suffered from the ailments of over-worked nurses, and performed her duties as mechanically as possible: *"Poor agonising wretches would cry to her by the hour, and she wouldn't heed them – either because she hated them for the trouble they gave, or because it was cold and she wanted to sit by the fire."* And then Adeline found her own heart was hardening against the helpless patients. Even the doctor, who had taken an oath to do all in his power to comfort the sick, scorned the wretched beggars brought there to die. *"Rattle his bones over the stones,"* he would sing to himself with a sardonic smile while examining a patient. *"He's only a pauper whom nobody owns."* Mrs. Hinton can hardly believe her ears, exclaiming that what she has heard surely doesn't go on any longer. Adeline replies that such conditions exist in many of the workhouses in England.

One must be more than human to nurse professionally, she tells her friend, one must be a saint. Any girl in her right mind should think twice before even considering a nursing career. Charles Booth in 1896 confirmed the accuracy of this bleak assessment of nursing on the lowest level. Infirmary nurses in the workhouses seldom worked fewer than fifteen hours a day. They were paid a servant's salary of twenty to twenty-five pounds a year, and had almost no time to themselves. Some workhouses added to the salary three to four pounds "in lieu of beer." The allowance was meant to discourage the sisters of mercy from getting drunk on the job.

On the whole Gissing respected the fledgling nursing profession of his day and was glad to see hundreds of women in the last decade of the century flocking to newly established nursing schools to be trained as nurses. He was fully aware that only a couple of decades earlier those same women, as with his own sisters, would have had to become governesses at low wages in the houses of people who tended to view them as superior servants and showed them little respect. He was heartened to learn that wages in the nursing profession were steadily increasing year by year even though on the lowest level, as with infirmary nurses, they remained at a level comparable only to those of servants. When he read in the papers that some hospitals were abusing nurses with long hours, overwork, and low pay, he didn't hesitate to speak out with force and candor.

Chapter 20

Writers and Artists

Several young women in Gissing's work support themselves by writing. The earliest appears to be Ada Warren, an emancipated woman in *Isabel Clarendon* (1886). When she was quite young Ada came under the tutorship of Thomas Meres, a professional writer. He plotted for her a rigorous program of reading designed to develop her intellect to fullest capacity. Then he told her after she knew something of the world she could write about it. Growing up in surroundings of wealth and refinement, Ada was able to secure books of every description on every subject. She read just about everything she could get her hands on, and in time her voracious habit of reading became an urge to write. With some trepidation, after much hesitation, she allowed Meres to read one of her stories, asking him for criticism. He said the story showed promise but was too subjective. Later he advised her to write a story in which every detail was a product not of personal experience, but of pure imagination.

Whether she was able to do that or not, whether she even wanted to do it or not, we are never told. Even so, she continues her apprenticeship and eventually publishes a brief descriptive sketch she calls "River Twilight." It is not imaginative; it is something she has seen with her own eyes. In the autumn of 1883, as he wrote *The Unclassed* published the next year, Gissing himself penned a description very similar to Ada's "River Twilight" and called it "On Battersea Bridge." Years later his alter-ego, Henry Ryecroft, remembers: *"I loitered upon Battersea Bridge and there the western sky took hold upon me. Half an hour later, I was speeding home. I sat down and wrote a description of what I had seen and straightway sent it to an evening newspaper which, to my astonishment, published the thing next day. How proud I was of that little bit of writing!"* Ada, too, is proud of her descriptive piece. The sight of it in print prompts her to think of earning her living as a writer. Her apprenticeship over and having tested the waters, she relinquishes her claim to the Clarendon fortune and becomes a woman of letters.

Helen Norman, the heroine of *Workers in the Dawn* (1880), is a woman who could write if she wished but decides work among the poor is nobler. She thinks about the advantages of becoming a published writer but later changes her mind: *"Dr. Gmelin asked me the other day whether I did not intend to write at all on the subjects which interest me; write that is to say, in the periodicals and daily papers. On reflection, I think not. In the first place I am not by any means sure that I possess a spark of literary ability, and then it is my firm believe that such work is not woman's true sphere."* Helen has become a well-educated woman in this first novel by Gissing, but like Florence Nightingale in real life she craves action. Though

Nightingale became a prodigious and versatile writer, she once observed: *"I had so much rather live than write; writing is only a substitute for living. I think one's feelings waste themselves in words; they ought all to be distilled into actions which bring results."* The founder of modern nursing went on to live a very active life and leave behind a lasting legacy when she died at the advanced age of ninety in 1910.

Maud and Dora Milvain in *New Grub Street* (1891) eventually begin to write for money. When we first see them they are respectively a music teacher and a governess, earning not enough to support themselves. Fraught with worry about the future, they can talk only of "doing something" that will bring them a living. During a breakfast-table conversation their enterprising brother, Jasper, suddenly exclaims, *"Why don't you girls write something? I'm convinced you could make money if you tried. There's a tremendous sale for religious stories; why not patch one together? I am quite serious."* When his sister Maud asks why he doesn't do it himself, he replies: *"I can't manage stories, as I have told you; but I think you could. In your place, I'd make a speciality of Sunday-school prize books; you know the kind of thing I mean. They sell like hot cakes. And there's so deuced little enterprise in the business. If you'd give your mind to it, you might make hundreds a year."* When Maud protests that such writing is "an inferior kind of work," he reminds her she is no George Eliot and must do what she is capable of doing.

He advises her to get together "half a dozen fair specimens" of the kind of writing they will attempt, study each one for its essential points, hit upon something slightly new to hold a reader's attention, and go to work methodically. He says nothing at all about creative or imaginative writing. It is writing done by a standard formula others have developed and found successful. Simply follow the formula, introducing the necessary material when the formula calls for it. Later Jasper becomes more ambitious as he comes to believe his sisters can write just about anything that requires a little research. He boasts that before long he will "set my sisters afloat in literature," and he sounds out a publisher on the reception of a work to be called "A Child's History of the English Parliament." The publisher asks for a specimen chapter, which Milvain himself writes, and from that point onward his sisters continue the project.

Having come to know Marian Yule, described as "the modern literary girl," Dora Milvain writes to her with excitement to tell her about the book they hope to finish and get published as the beginning of a literary career. *"It will amuse you to hear that the literary project is really to come to something. We have a specimen chapter and Maud thinks she could carry it on in that style if there's no hurry. So perhaps our literary career will be something more than a joke after all."* As Jasper – already a professional writer churning out entertaining stuff for the masses – had predicted, it was no joke. They go to London and become writers similar to their brother and make a living at it. They write for money until both are able to find husbands, and Dora continues her literary career after marriage to supplement her husband's income. In London they are in almost daily contact with Marian Yule, who spends most of her time in the Reading Room of the British Museum.

A real-life model for Marian Yule was probably Miss Bradley, daughter of the Dean of Westminster and sister of the popular novelist Mrs. Woods, whom Gissing admired. He met Miss Bradley in 1887 through the family of his pupil, Walter Grahame. In July of that year he wrote to his brother Algernon: *"I dined with the Grahame's last night and had an interesting talk about the British Museum Reading Room with the daughter of Dean Bradley. She is working for the* National Biography *and goes to the museum daily."* Perhaps Gissing remembered this conversation when he began to outline the character and occupation of Marian Yule. The full title of the work he mentions in this letter is *Dictionary of National Biography*. It began to publish brief biographies of notable figures in 1885 under the editorship of Leslie Stephen, the father of Virginia Woolf, and continues to the present day. The new dictionary, now known as the *Oxford Dictionary of National Biography*, was published in September of 2004. It ran to sixty volumes in print and sold for a hefty £7,500 ($11,352). An Internet edition was also made available to subscribers. But what about Marian Yule?

Not yet a writer at the time we meet her, Marian does the reading and research for her father, Alfred Yule, who writes for the periodical press. She does the scut work while he takes the credit, and later she does most of his writing:

"Her task at present was to collect materials for a paper on 'French Authoresses of the Seventeenth Century,' the kind of thing which her father supplied on stipulated terms for anonymous publication. Marian was by this time almost able to complete such a piece of manufacture herself, and her father's share in it was limited to a few hints and corrections." The research her father requires her to do "in the valley of the shadow of books" is often unpleasant and sometimes even repellent: *"When you have time I want you to read Ditchley's new book and jot down a selection of his worst sentences. I'll use them for an article on contemporary style."* Marian would like to marry, believes she has "a right to happiness as well as other women," but since she is poor and plain there is little hope for her. Ultimately she escapes the grinding toil of New Grub Street to become an assistant in a country library.

Writing for the journalistic press as the amanuensis of her flinty and self-centered father, Marian Yule is miserable. A sensitive and intelligent girl, she wants to be her own person and live her life as she sees fit. Yet every day for many hours she must perform the drudgery he requires of her. Reading dusty volumes in the British Museum begins to strain her eyesight and damage her health. Like Miss Bradley in real life, she goes to the Reading Room every day and spends most of her waking hours there, but in time manages to escape. Nancy Lord of *In the Year of Jubilee* (1894) would like to publish the novel she has written for her own entertainment, but her husband sternly advises her to keep out of "the beastly scrimmage." Her novel is better than any of those cranked out on schedule by "the ordinary female novelist," but it isn't her place to earn money by writing: *"Leave that to the poor creatures who have no choice,"* he tells her. *"You are not obliged to go into the market."*

In a mood to resist, Nancy retorts: *"I never thought myself a Charlotte Brontë or a George Eliot. But so many women make money out of novels, and as I had spare time I didn't see why I shouldn't use it profitably."* Again her husband asserts that he doesn't want her competing in "the rough and tumble of the literary trade." She can do something useful by devoting herself to the important task of helping her little boy develop into a worthy man. For Charlotte Brontë, Gissing had high praise: *"She is the greatest English woman after Mrs. Browning,"* he said to his sister Margaret in 1887. *"George Eliot is poor in comparison with her. No page of her is without genius, and she wrote a style such as you find in no other writer. She strengthens me enormously."*

A few days later he wrote in similar vein to Bertz. *"Trollope? Ah, I cannot read him; the man is such a terrible Philistine. Indeed, of English novelists I see more and more clearly that there is only one entirely to my taste, and that is Charlotte Brontë. A great and glorious woman! George Eliot is miserable in comparison!"* Though he came to think of George Eliot as no match for Charlotte Brontë, at an earlier time he had studied Eliot's work carefully. He admired her fidelity representing country folk in her novels, and he was impressed by her "rare conscientiousness." He also liked the work of George Sand and that of a novelist whose name is lost in the mists of time,

Mrs. Woods. He wrote that her *Village Tragedy* (1887) was *"more remarkable in its way than anything since the Brontës."* Contemporary critics were not so enthusiastic. Again Gissing was expressing opinion that went against the grain.

Clara Collet and Edith Sichel were two women of literary talent whom he knew personally and admired. His admiration also went to a German, Eduard Bertz, whom he met quite early when he took up residence in London. Though Bertz soon returned to his native land, they formed a friendship that lasted many years. In Germany his old friend was struggling to gain a reputation as a novelist too, and having less success than Gissing. He often wrote to complain that few people were taking the time to read his books, and he doubted he could devote himself to literary labor much longer. He knew full well that only one man in England, his old friend from way back, was willing to read his convoluted German script and offer comments. Gissing was having trouble making a name for himself too, but wrote encouraging letters to Bertz asking him to persevere. Do the work for yourself, he said, and try to take pleasure in the art of putting words on paper; appreciate what you are doing at the moment and don't worry about an audience that may or may not come later. It was good advice, though Bertz seems not to have taken it.

In "The Honeymoon," a short story published in 1894, Gissing again took up the theme of the aspiring lady novelist discouraged by an unsympathetic husband. Phyllis Waldron, recently married, wants her novel to be published with her new name on the title page. Her stubborn husband insists that she not bring out the book: *"An escapade of this sort would shame us. I have a serious career before me and can't afford to be made ridiculous. The novel is as good as five thousand others that will see the light this year, but it isn't the kind of thing that you must have anything to do with."* The young woman strenuously objects, but as Nancy Lord in the end buckled to her husband's demand, so does Phyllis Waldron. If a curious person were to compare this story to the Nancy Lord plot of *In the Year of Jubilee* (1894), he or she would find many similarities. The likenesses may be accountable to the fact that the story was written at the same time as the novel.

A woman writer unhampered by a husband, and destined never to have one, is Bertha Childerstone of "Comrades in Arms" (1894). A mannish product of female emancipation, Bertha has chosen deliberately to make her way in a dog-eat-dog profession: *"For seven or eight years she had battled in the world of journalism, and with a kind of success which seemed to argue manlike qualities. Since he had known her, these last three years, she seemed to have been growing less feminine."* Bertha has pushed herself to the brink of exhaustion and has attained a certain degree of success in the field, but she has paid for it dearly with damage to her health. At lunch with her comrade in arms, Wilfrid Langley, she becomes ill and is sent home to bed. As the long days of convalescence creep by, Wilfrid falls in love with his colleague and proposes marriage. She would like to marry but can't accept him because she believes she has lived too long in the world of men: *"Look at this room, dirty and disorderly. This is all the home I care for."* Back on her feet, she plunges once again into her work. Months later the two bump umbrellas on the pavement of the Strand. They nod and smile and go in opposite directions. The tempo of separate lives in a very competitive world allows them only a moment.

A dominant theme of the story is that of an attractive woman, Bertha Childerstone, doing a man's job in a man's profession and slowly losing her femininity as the result. However, Charles Booth noted that *"a noticeable feature of modern journalism is the number of women who have entered the profession to find it rewarding."* This led to the establishment in 1894 of the Society of Women Journalists. In 1896 the Society had more than two hundred members, all of them *"professionally engaged in journalism, either as writers or artists."* A young woman in Gissing's work who gets her living as an artist in the field is Bertha Cross of *Will Warburton* (1905). Newspaper and book illustration in a time prior to the prevalent use of photography was lucrative for a few. However, most illustrators were paid very little. Even though Bertha gets steady work as an illustrator of children's books, she and her mother remain quite poor: *"Did you ever see any of her work? Children's book illustrating? It's more than passable, I assure you. But of course she's wretchedly paid."* After Bertha and Warburton eventually marry, it's implied she will soon give up a job that requires too much of her time and talent for too little money.

In *The Crown of Life* (1899) Miss Bonnicastle is an artist in the advertising industry. She paints "glaring grotesques" that are posted in conspicuous places throughout London. They advertise in the blatant language of the trade the newest commodities of a thriving materialistic society. The posters, influenced perhaps by the French school of Toulouse Lautrec, are done in colors that startle the eye – "catch the eye" in the trade – and the girl is said to be awfully clever at it. Her roommate, Olga Hannaford, earns a good deal less as a fashion illustrator for ladies' magazines. The dress fashions are already drawn when she gets them. She merely sketches in the heads, arms, and torso to make the apparel look as if a model were wearing it.

Irene Delph in *The Emancipated* (1890) is the daughter of a man of letters who worked hard but died of poverty. The girl is hopeful of getting enough training to become a genuine artist. She is known to have talent but is hard-pressed to stay alive long enough to develop her talent. In Paris, as Gissing had done in London, she goes to a public institution on a winter's day mainly to keep warm. On some days she has the chance to copy the masterpieces in the Louvre as Gissing was able to use the Reading Room of the British Museum. In Paris, Mrs. Lessingham comes upon the thin and anxious girl and persuades her and her mother to come live in London. A room in the house is fitted out as a studio for Irene, and the fledgling artist, restored to good health by good food, begins to specialize in portraits. It's suggested that she will soon be able to support herself and her mother by selling her work. It's also implied that as "an ornament of the drawing-room," she could marry and have a family and forget all about her dream of becoming a famous artist.

Another serious artist, the most outstanding female painter in Gissing's fiction, is Hilda Castledine in "A Victim of Circumstances" (1893). The wife of an artist with little talent, a patient apprenticeship has made Hilda a very good artist. Although she produces exquisite little water-colors, her husband sees them as worthless: *"Here were two men, both excellent judges, who declared the water-colours of value. Yet he had never suspected it. The fact was, his wife's work had been growing better and better by gradual stages."* When people begin to buy the water-colors, Horace Castledine tries to pass them off as his own: *"He could not bear to become altogether insignificant, subordinate even to his wife."* To keep the money coming in, the self-sacrificing wife urges her husband to continue the fraud. But as her talent matures, it becomes difficult to lose her identity as an artist in that of a wife and mother. And yet to save her marriage, renunciation of her art and artistic talent becomes the only solution. She packs up her materials, her colors and sketch books, and never draws again.

A sculptor in *Born in Exile* (1892) is a young woman who goes by the name Agatha Walworth. Marcella Moxey, visiting the Academy, sees a female head on display. It is catalogued as "A Nihilist," which she remembers as meaning one who rejects all religious and moral principles in the belief that life is meaningless. Intrigued, she discovers the creator of the head is a former schoolmate and later she goes to visit Agatha Walworth: *"Knowing little of life and much of literature, she pictured Miss Walworth as inhabiting a delightful Bohemian world where the rules had no existence and everything was judged by brain. She prepared herself for the first visit with a joyous tremor, wondering whether she would be deemed worthy to associate with the men and women who lived for art. The reality was a shock. In a large house at Chiswick she found a gathering of most respectable English people, chatting over the regulation tea-cup; not one of them inclined to disregard the dictates of Mrs. Grundy in dress, demeanour, or dialogue. Agatha Walworth lived with her parents and her sisters like any other irreproachable young woman. Of Bohemia she knew nothing whatever save by hearsay."* It was the opposite of what Marcella hoped to find. She left the residence feeling deeply disappointed.

From childhood Gissing had found good paintings and pictures delightful and maintained an interest in art all his life. Even during the hectic days in America he sketched in a notebook (now in the Yale Rare Book Room) a passable drawing of a gaff-rigged sailboat he may have seen on Lake Michigan while living in Chicago. He was not an accomplished artist, but it's clear he considered women just as capable of artistic achievement as men. In fact, virtually all the women in his fiction, whether pursuing art or something else to make their lives meaningful, prove that Gissing stubbornly resisted the Victorian myth of woman's inferiority to man. Fortunately, during the last two decades of the century, that old, cracked, time-worn myth was slowly disappearing. All that Gissing says about women shows he was glad to see it go. He lived long enough to welcome the more liberal attitude that eventually took its place.

Chapter 21

Women of Leisure

Though he was poor all his life and occupied even in his later years a social position only slightly above the shopkeeping class, one may find in Gissing's novels and stories a large number of upper-class women. Though largely not in sympathy with women of the middle class, he had a certain reverence dating from boyhood for women of the upper classes. In his novels he uses several epithets to describe them. Some he called "women of quality" and some were "women of leisure." A special group that he admired he called "women of the world." Those with titles are fewer than ten, but of more than four hundred female characters in all his writings – and my count may not be entirely accurate – at least one hundred move in surroundings of wealth and refinement. The number belonging to the leisured class becomes even more extensive when one includes those women who lead idle, frivolous lives on the incomes of hard-working husbands. These in spite of social class we may call women of leisure.

It is not unusual to find one man supporting six or more females "in idle dignity." The Reverend Mr. Whiffle in

Workers in the Dawn (1880) is burdened by an invalid wife and five daughters. Mr. Cartwright in *A Life's Morning* (1888) is another who must support a wife and five daughters. Mr. Denyer in *The Emancipated* (1890) is driven to desperation by the extravagance of a selfish wife and three parasitic daughters. In *Born in Exile* (1892) the five Moxey girls demand subsistence from hard-pressed parents, and in *Denzil Quarrier* (1892) we see four girls in the Liversedge family. Until his untimely death Dr. Madden in *The Odd Women* (1893) is the sole support of six daughters, and in the same novel a young man named Bevis supports his mother and three sisters. In *The Whirlpool* (1897) three women, appropriately named Leach, live in elegant leisure upon the earnings of a hard-working lawyer. Similar situations may be found in several short stories by Gissing.

While their men work themselves to an early grave, these women enjoy unlimited leisure and live in luxury. In *A Life's Morning* (1888) Mr. Cartwright is only a commercial traveler, but to provide six females with a daily round of good food, good clothes, and a good house for their pleasure, he has joined with this main pursuit "many odds and ends of money-making activity." The family had formerly occupied a larger dwelling in a more fashionable neighborhood, but a reduction in the breadwinner's fortunes necessitated a move. The Misses Cartwright, disposed to resist the change, peevishly complain that it's their father's sworn duty to maintain them "*in that station of life for which they were clearly designed by Providence.*" To the amazement of the whole community, even in humbler circumstances, the girls continue to live beyond their means. Ignoring Cartwright's cries of dire circumstances, they indulge in extravagances even more wealthy households can't afford. Mr. Cartwright is seldom at home.

Mr. Denyer, a hard-driven paterfamilias seldom seen in *The Emancipated* (1890), keeps in touch with his undeserving family chiefly by mail. *"There existed a Mr. Denyer, but this gentleman was very seldom indeed in the bosom of his family. Letters – and remittances – came from him from the most surprising quarters of the globe."* His profession is that of "speculator at large," and for many years he has toiled unceasingly in several parts of the world to provide his wife and daughters with moneyed leisure. They in turn also travel far and wide in the world, but not on business. They hop from one expensive resort to another, priding themselves on their cosmopolitanism and feigning intellectual interests far beyond their sketchy education. Time and again Mr. Denyer has warned them to cut down on expenses, but every warning has fallen on deft ears. They ignore his warnings because he has cried "Wolf!" too often. Then, with genuine sadness, he tells them the big bad wolf is as real as can be and has taken everything.

In the presence of his wife and daughters, even writing to them from afar, the kind little man is apologetic and abashed: *"I must warn you very seriously that I can't supply you with as much as I have been doing. I repeat that I am serious this time. I've brought you bad news, the worst I ever brought you yet. My dears, I can hold out no longer; I'm at the end of my means. I shall have to make a new start, new efforts. I'm going out to Vera Cruz again."* His long, contrived absences have put him almost on terms of ceremony with them, but over the years he has come to know how selfish his wife can be and has ceased to love her. He toiled that she might live in luxury but now devotes himself to his innocent girls, only to discover they are made of the same fabric as their mother. In Vera Cruz he begins to rebuild his fortune, sending money to his daughters whenever he can. But the climate doesn't agree with him; in a few months he contracts a fever and dies. His death reduces the three luxury-loving Denyer girls, parasites who have fed on him for years, to penury.

In a similar predicament is Mr. Leach of *The Whirlpool* (1897). A mild little man dreading discord and subservient to his wife, he has no function in life but to support in genteel leisure a family of spendthrift females who care only for themselves: *"For many years he had made an income of about £2,000, every penny of which, excepting a small insurance premium, had been absorbed by expenses of the house. At the age of fifty, prematurely worn by excessive labour, he was alarmed to find his income steadily diminishing, with no corresponding diminution – but rather the opposite – in the demands made upon him by wife and daughters."* In a moment of courage and prompted by desperation, he persuades his daughters to move with their mother into a smaller house. But the change of abode causes so much conflict between him and his wife that he is *"glad to fit up a sleeping room at his office and go home only once a week."* Living in this manner, he will work himself to death or die early because of inadequate food. Until then his wife will continue to loll on sofas, entertain lavishly, and quarrel with the servants. His daughters require a steady stream of money. Both are young ladies of leisure, enjoying the fruits of the vineyard without laboring there.

While the Leach girls ape the manners of high society, in spite of their father's wealth they don't belong to the society that spells itself with a capital S. One can't enter this exclusive little world on a ticket bought by a hard-working father. One has to be born there and breathe the perfume of luxury from infancy. In *Thyrza* (1887) Paula Tyrrell was born there. For generations the Tyrrell family has lived as wealthy land owners. They are smooth, suave, cultivated, complacent, and entirely "subdued to the social code." Paula's mother is *"one of those excellently preserved matrons who testify to the wholesome placidity of woman's life in wealthy English homes."* Her existence has taken for granted the perfection of the universe and her place in it. Never has she known a day of trouble; any little problem is quickly solved for her. Paula herself is a superlative product of this wealthy, do-nothing-but-collect-rents class. *"Her dress was a miracle and inseparably a part of her; it was impossible to picture her in any serious situation, so entirely was she a child of luxury and frivolous concern."* She prides herself on being able to go through life without becoming serious about anything. Her situation should be contrasted with that of the artificial flower-maker in Hoxton or the match-girl in Lambeth. A gap as wide as the Atlantic lies between.

As *Thryza* (1887) opens, Paula Tyrrell is *"suffering under a calamity; her second 'season' had been ruined at its very culmination by a ludicrous contretemps in the shape of an attack of measles. Just when she flattered herself that she had never looked so lovely, an instrument of destiny embraced her and she was a fright."* Fateful incidents of this kind are described by Biffen in *New Grub Street* (1891) to illustrate his theory of realism. One in particular is very similar to what happened to Paula: *"Let the pretty girl get a disfiguring pimple on her nose just before the ball at which she is going to shine."* Detailing Paula Tyrrell's unfortunate experience, Gissing was putting into practice one of Biffen's theories several years before the character and his theory were created. Though not an alter-ego, Biffen serves as a mouthpiece for Gissing in several places.

To elude the specter of boredom, most of the women of Paula's class fling themselves into a seemingly endless round of gaiety. During the season in London they are swept into a whirlpool of feverish activity. When the parties, suppers, dinners, musical Sundays, and informal "at homes" are over, they seek excitement on the Continent. Then later they withdraw to their stately country homes of many rooms where the social whirl begins again. To have something to talk about, the stalwart shoot lions in Africa or tigers in India, and even the meekest indulge in the new fad of traveling to faraway places. Some of the women pick up scraps of foreign languages to impress their friends back home. A few others actually learn the foreign language. Gissing called these more experienced among them "women of the world." Shortly after

The Unclassed (1884) was published, he met a true and real "woman of the world" in the person of Mrs. David Gaussen. *"At a time when the horror of his life was only partially mitigated by the preference of his mad and wretched wife for the dens and slums of the New Cut,"* writes Morley Roberts, *"this woman of the leisured class came to him like a star."* At the end of August in 1884, a nervous Gissing paid a visit to Broughton Hall, the country house of the Gaussen family in Gloucestershire.

He went there as a tutor to examine the children and set up a course of study for them. When their mother insisted, he remained for the weekend as their guest. It was the first time for him to be exposed to the upper-class way of life, and he thoroughly enjoyed his visit. He found Mrs. Gaussen "one of the most delightful women imaginable." Born in India, she was well-educated and well-traveled. She knew scores of interesting people and was on terms of intimacy with persons of rank and title. She spoke Hindustani and Armenian – how well we don't know – and at the time was entertaining two Armenian ladies. *"I was to have gone home on Saturday night, but they begged me to stay till this morning. There were two young Armenian ladies of English birth staying also, and we had lively times."* After the grub-street author returned to his lowly flat in London, Mrs. Gaussen sent him a bouquet of flowers from her garden.

Near the end of September she informed him in purple ink on engraved paper that she planned to take a house in London for a year. By October she was occupying the house in an upscale neighborhood some distance from his own, and her friendship with the young novelist progressed rapidly. One of her sons soon became Gissing's pupil, arriving at the apartment near Regents Park in mid-afternoon and leaving at eight in the evening. Gissing grew fond of the boy, but fonder still of his mother who impressed him as the most beautiful, most "womanly woman" he had ever known. At their first meeting Mrs. Gaussen appeared to be in her early thirties. She was in fact almost ten years older. Her life had always been an easy one, and though approaching middle age for that time, she was quite lovely. We know she was gracious, charming, apparently well-built, and brimming with vitality. Reared in India and married to a wealthy man when quite young, she held Gissing spellbound with tales of the things she had seen and done. Her husband David traveled a lot, was seldom at home, and the woman seems to have taken a genuine interest in developing a close friendship with the young writer.

She invited him to supper parties, dinner parties, tennis parties, all kinds of parties, and thus enabled him to see much of a world that as an outsider he had only glimpsed. To his sister Margaret he wrote at the end of October in 1884: *"Here is one for a tennis party next Monday, which I shall certainly not accept! There is a line to be drawn somewhere and tennis really cannot be submitted to."* Yet his description of Mrs. Bruce Page in *Isabel Clarendon* (1886) indicates that he went to at least one tennis party: *"She seemed about the same age as Mrs. Clarendon, and in some eyes probably excelled the latter in attractiveness. Her bodily activity was surprising; she walked with the grace and liveliness of a young girl, and as she shortly showed at tennis, could even run without making herself in the least ridiculous."* The character appears to be based on one of Mrs. Gaussen's friends, many of whom he met and liked. His friendship with the personable woman was made easier by the fact that her husband, an ardent sportsman, spent much of his time in Ireland.

The lady was left to do much as she pleased, and it was this freedom of movement that allowed her to visit Gissing in his rooms at 7K Cornwall Residences. He had taken the new lodgings mainly because in jest she had "threatened" to visit him, and he was ashamed to receive her at 62 Milton Street. In view of the fact that Gissing's most famous novel is called *New Grub Street* (1891), an interesting discovery is to know Milton Street was the new name of Dr. Johnson's Grub Street. The street was described by Johnson as *"much inhabited by writers of small histories, dictionaries, and temporary poems."* Though the new Grub Street was still in existence under the name Milton Street, "New Grub Street" was Gissing's felicitous phrase for the conditions under which writers as poor as himself lived and worked. Many of these writers lived near Tottenham Court Road, where Gissing himself settled on first arriving in London.

The headquarters of English journalism, however, was in the locality of Fleet Street. *"Within a half-mile radius of this thoroughfare,"* Charles Booth wrote, *"are produced the great bulk of the two thousand periodicals which are issued from*

London printing offices, more than five hundred of them being daily or weekly newspapers and journals." How often Mrs. Gaussen came to Gissing's apartment we don't really know. His letters tell us she was there on a number of occasions, vivacious as usual and talkative. She spoke anecdotally about some of the well-known people of the day, encouraged him to talk about his work and explain it to her, examined his photograph album, and said kind things about his mother. To his brother Algernon he wrote: *"I was rather struck with some remarks Mrs. Gaussen made about Mother's portrait the other day in looking over my album. She said it was a strikingly handsome face, and extraordinarily full of character. I amazed her by explaining that I was really quite unable to say whether the character was in reality there or not; so utterly a stranger, on reflection, do I find my own mother to be to me. A curious state of things."*

His letters in the autumn of 1884 had many references to Mrs. Gaussen – compliments on her beauty, breeding, and personality. He wrote to his family in Yorkshire, to Morley Roberts in America, and to Eduard Bertz in Germany. The extravagance of his language led Roberts, whose mind was often below his belt, to believe the friendship had become an ardent affair: *"She visited him often in his chambers, and though he told me but little I gathered what the result was."* By June of 1885 Gissing perhaps found himself in love with the woman. She seemed to be always on his mind, and yet he knew how truly impossible it would be to have a love affair with her. She was married and she was not of his class and he was too shy to make advances. He was thinking of ending the relationship never to see her again. He told himself she was taking up too much of his valuable time, and he was beginning to dislike some of her friends, finding them shallow.

It was characteristic of him to flee whenever a woman began to show too much interest in him. In 1876 he had fled from Nell, hoping to find a new life in America. In 1877 he fled perhaps from an incipient affair with a student in Waltham, Massachusetts and went to Chicago. In 1885, by refusing to accept her invitations, he fled as it were from Mrs. Gaussen. In 1889, when he found himself liking Edith Sichel – "I half think she is beautiful" – again he took a deep breath and ran. In August of 1890, when he thought he was in love with Connie Ash, a Wakefield girl, he quickly left the district and went back to London. With Clara Collet, whom he met in 1893, he seems to have formed no romantic attachment, and was thus able to remain her friend until his death. But for the fact that Gabrielle Fleury was a foreigner and outside the context of his fear, he would have likely fled from her. With Englishwomen of class and education he felt strangely inferior; so in 1891 he committed the bitter error of taking for the second time a wife from the working class.

As the summer of 1885 came and went he was ready to rid himself of Gaussen, her sophisticated and wealthy friends, and her world of leisure in which he knew he would never find comfort. To his sister Ellen he confided in June of that year: *"I have not seen Mrs. Gaussen since you left. No one person of course is like another, but her personality is remarkable in a degree you cannot perhaps sufficiently appreciate as yet. When you have been fatigued and disgusted through a few more years of life by commonplace, dreary people, shallow in heart and mind, you will get in the habit of resting in the thought of her."* For once he wasn't advising his sister on anything at all; he was talking about himself and his feelings. He was perhaps purging himself of troubling thoughts concerning the lady. In the next paragraph he wrote that he was thinking of giving up the "fruitless struggle" and returning to America. Perhaps in that country he would be able to get literary work, *"though I had rather end all that and work in a healthy way on a farm."* He complained that "this kind of life is too hard," and it was. He spent most of his waking hours in a stuffy little room struggling to write, and when a book was done and sent off to a publisher who took his own sweet time before presenting it to the public, few people bothered to read it.

At the end of August in 1885 he made it known that he would not accept another invitation to Broughton Hall. He was in the mood to withdraw entirely from the world of Mrs. Gaussen and get on with his work in a fictional world. By September he had rejected the leisured class as not being worth his time. Those who had seemed intelligent, affable, even fascinating at first were now revealed in their true colors. They were shallow, empty, superficial, and selfish people flitting across the surface of life without really touching its texture. Gissing was forced to admit, at length, that Mrs. Gaussen's friends fell short of his expectations. As Jack London said of such people who lived a life of leisure and didn't work, they were "milking the udders of papier mâché cows." Their interests were frivolous and their conversation seldom went beyond small talk. They were more concerned with style than with substance, or with anything solid.

In a letter to his sister Margaret, Gissing wrote that he was finding it difficult to maintain the tone of society nonsense. Earlier he had complained that the round of parties was stealing too much of his time: *"I used to suffer from loneliness; now the difficulty is to get any time at all to myself. I am beginning pugnaciously to refuse invitations."* He lacked "social nerve" as H. G. Wells called it, and when invitations pelted him like unwelcomed rain, he declined them all and crept into seclusion. Before the beginning of 1886 his excursion into the glittering world of high society was at an end. Yet thoughts of Mrs. Gaussen lingered on. At the peak of their friendship he deserted his chosen subject matter, hard life in the slums, and began a new kind of novel. In manuscript he called it "The Lady of Knightswell," but before its publication in 1886 he changed the title to *Isabel Clarendon* after the main character, an exemplary lady who stands out in a crowd in the same way clarendon type stood out on the printed page. It dealt with that new kind of life to which Gaussen had introduced him.

Before he met the woman he had only a dim conception of the leisured class and the way they lived their lives. In his first novel he had depicted them as stiff and "stagey" types – as saintly philanthropists (Helen Norman), cynical artists

(Gilbert Gresham), or insincere dilettantes (Maud Gresham). Now Mrs. Gaussen suggested a new set of standards: education without heavy intellectuality, a knowledgeable view of the world without cynicism, feminine vitality and charm without silliness, gorgeous clothing in excellent taste that accented a woman's body, subtle modulation of voice without shrillness, and easy, affable, idiomatic language. These standards were applied to Isabel Clarendon, and the result was the first of Gissing's upper-class women really to come alive. Isabel is Gissing's representation of the society woman before idle and polite society had disappointed him. Unmistakably, the model for Isabel Clarendon was Mrs. David Gaussen, a leisured woman who divided her time between a town house in London and a country manor in Gloucestershire.

Isabel is also Gissing's conception of the "womanly woman" as she approaches perfection. She isn't the highest among women, and she falls short of the noblest because her eyes are "too level on the surface of this world." But she has in perfect balance all the traits in a woman that combine to charm a man. She is simply *"woman womanly in every fraction of her being."* At thirty-six she enjoys the full bloom of her womanhood and takes pride in it. Resplendent in evening dress, her neck and shoulders gleaming above the dark richness of her town, she is *"a woman whom men of ripe experience, men of the world, would take for herself, asking no wealth but that of her matchless charm, a woman for whom younger and more passionate hearts would break with longing."* Her womanliness is said to express her sexuality in a hundred different ways: *"Isabel rose and stepped forward to meet him, In the act of greeting she was, perhaps, seen to greatest advantage. The upright grace of her still perfect figure, the poise of her head, the face looking straight forward, the smile of exquisite frankness, the warmth of welcome and the natural dignity combined in her attitude as she stood with extended hand, made a picture of fair womanhood which the eye did not readily quit. It was symbolical of her inner self, of the large affections which made the air about her warm, and of the sweet receptiveness of disposition which allowed so many different men to see in her their ideal woman."* Few men can resist her, and soon she makes a captive of Gissing's alter-ego, Bernard Kingcote.

So closely does Gissing identify with Kingcote that one is hard put to distinguish fictional character from author; both pay homage to Isabel Clarendon in the same ecstatic, excessive language. When Kingcote writes that *"Mrs. Clarendon is to me a new type of woman – new, that is in actual observation,"* a fictional character isn't saying this, but Gissing himself. The woman displayed in a very favorable light throughout the book – and by Kingcote in a long, confidential letter – is more than a product of the author's imagination. She is a woman in the flesh, a woman in real life, and warming the man's heart even as he writes. *"She is a woman of the world,"* Kingcote writes to a friend, *"perhaps even a worldly woman. I was never before on terms of friendly intercourse with her like, and she interests me extremely. She is beautiful and has every external grace."* The words seem to have been lifted verbatim from one of Gissing's own letters. It isn't unlikely that such a letter was received by his friend, Eduard Bertz. Following Bertz's return to Germany on Easter Sunday of 1884, a copious and lasting correspondence sprang up between them. We may be certain that Gissing gave Bertz the details of his friendship with Mrs. Gaussen. However, because the letters he wrote to Bertz before Nell's death showed little restraint, his friend thought it best to destroy all but one written before September 1888.

Kingcote's description of Isabel seems without doubt an accurate word-picture of Mrs. Gaussen: *"Though she is anything but intellectual, her mind has delicacy and activity; her judgments of people are probably not wide of the mark. Then her tenderness shows in every glance and in her bright, free gladness. A woman to the tips of her fingers, a womanly woman. Mrs. Clarendon will henceforth be to me the type of perfectly sweet womanhood."* In maturity she is more delightful than in girlhood, even more beautiful. In maturity she lacks the self-consciousness and rough edges of youth. Her lyric charm is easy and natural, never deliberate. Particularly striking is her frankness, her exquisite and honest openness. She seems to speak from the heart, to conceal nothing. She is kind and gentle without being weak, womanly without being womanish. The portrait of Isabel Clarendon, inspired by a rare woman he knew early in his career, is Gissing's tribute to all women.

Scattered throughout his novels are many such tributes. In his first novel he paid homage to womankind in his delineation of Helen Norman; in his second with Ida Starr; and here in his third with Isabel Clarendon. In *A Life's Morning*, written just after *Isabel Clarendon* in 1885 but not published until 1888, both Emily Hood and Beatrice Redwing are tributes to womanly perfection. In *Demos* (1886), his fourth novel, he created Adela Waltham as something of a paragon and fell in love with her. His sisters and his critics didn't see perfection in her, thought he was deceiving himself, insisted she was not so admirable as he thought, and they were right. As he fashioned Thyrza, the eponymous heroine of his fifth novel (1887), he wrote with "fever and delight," again falling in love with his own creation. In all his novels he demonstrated a steady, unwavering appreciation of females ranging from nubile girls in their teens to old women. A delightful portrait of a girl no older than fourteen or fifteen is that of Hilda Meres in *Isabel Clarendon* (1886). A vivid representation of a strong-minded old autocrat well into her seventies is Lady Ogram of *Our Friend the Charlatan* (1901). Oddly enough the female child is virtually forgotten in Gissing's fiction. Curiously, no particular child of either gender is fully realized in any of his stories or novels.

Though one may expect certain differences in character and development, most of Gissing's women of the world derive in some measure from Mrs. Gaussen. Mrs. Boscobel in *Demos* (1886) is such a woman, and subsequent novels have at least a score. They are usually in their late thirties, wealthy, leisured, active in polite society, intelligent, traveled, charming, and sometimes mischievous intruders in the lives of others. In the novels of the eighties most of these women are "well fitted to inspire homage," but in those of the nineties some of them, all wives or widows, take on ominous qualities. Several women, for example Mrs. Ormonde (1887), Mrs. Damerel (1894), Mrs. Strangeways (1897), Mrs. Borisoff (1899), and Mrs. Toplady (1901), seem to be consciously fitted into the Mephistophelean tradition. They bear a striking resemblance to some of Thomas Hardy's "Mephistophelian Visitants," and show at times, like them, a strange, preternatural power as they dabble in the lives of mortals. The change of attitude could have originated perhaps in Gissing's increasing disenchantment with London society, but Hardy's influence can't be ignored. Gissing maintained a casual friendship with Hardy from 1886, visiting him at Max Gate in 1895.

Mrs. Boscobel is the wife of a successful artist and the center of a brilliant social circle that includes famous people. She has lived for years in all the capitals of Europe and enjoys having young men of promise surrounding her. In several respects she is characteristic of Mrs. Gaussen, her archetype: *"Mrs. Boscobel was a woman of the world, five-and-thirty, charming, intelligent; she read little, but was full of interest in literary and artistic matters and talked only as a woman can who has long associated with men of brains."* The archetype also sets the pattern for Mrs. Boston Wright in *New Grub Street* (1891): *"She's had an extraordinary life. Was born in Mauritius – no, Ceylon – I forget; some such place. Married a sailor at fifteen. Was shipwrecked somewhere, and only restored to life after terrific efforts; her story leaves it all rather vague. Then she turns up as a newspaper correspondent at the Cape. Gave up that, took to some kind of farming, I forget where. Married again (first husband lost in aforementioned shipwreck), this time a Baptist minister, and began to devote herself to soup kitchens in Liverpool. Husband burned to death somewhere. She's next discovered in the thick of literary society in London. A wonderful woman, I assure you. Must be nearly fifty but looks twenty-five."* A very active woman, she edits *The English Girl* but finds time to entertain famous people.

Her magazine is not a social, religious, political, or feminist organ, but a polite little publication directed to the upper-class English girl. In the past Boston Wright – her first name recalling Gissing's American year – was considered more "advanced" than "womanly," but now gives her time to the social whirl. She is "a cyclopaedia of the day's small talk," and she has on the tip of her tongue all the latest gossip of London's literary colony. Her colorful life with its wild adventures seems an exaggerated version of Gaussen's earlier years. Another feature reminding one of Gaussen is the woman's perpetual youth. She also plays the role of mentor to promising young writers. "I'm quite a favourite with her," Milvain confesses.

Gissing himself had once considered the advantages of coming under the influence of an older woman. As a youth in America he wrote in his commonplace book: *"Very young man falls into society of an older lady who takes interest in and polishes him."* It's doubtful whether Mrs. Gaussen exerted a polishing effect upon the later Gissing, and yet she immediately assumed the role of tactful adviser. Later, almost every one of his worldly women enters into a teacher-student relationship with a young man. In *Thyrza* (1887) Mrs. Ormond, whose very name is suggestive of worldliness, wields a huge influence over Walter Egremont. In *A Life's Morning* (1888) Mrs. Baxendale becomes the gentle counselor of Wilfrid Athel, and *"in a day or two the confidence between them was as complete as if their acquaintance had been life-long."* Mrs. Damerel of *In the Year of Jubilee* (1894) has a similar relationship with young Horace Lord, who turns out to be her son. Finally, Lady Revill in *Sleeping Fires* (1895) is disturbed by Mrs. Tresilian's influence upon Louis Reed.

As with any good novelist, Gissing drew his materials from the life around him. When his main interest centered on the poor and the way they lived in the slums, he wrote about the nether world. As he came to know upper-class families, he made use of them in his novels. *"I am getting to like the atmosphere of cultured families,"* he said in one of his letters. *"I study the people, and they are of use."* While Gaussen meant more to Gissing than a mere literary source, there is little doubt she became the model for many of his women of leisure. As late as 1899 she informs the portrait of Mrs. John Jacks in *The Crown of Life*: *"Mrs. Jacks was of that tall and gracefully commanding height which has become the English ideal in the last quarter of our century. Consummate as an ornament of the drawing-room, she would be no less admirably at ease on the tennis lawn, in the boat, on horseback, or walking by the seashore. Beyond criticism her breeding; excellent her education."*

Chapter 22
Female Philanthropists

The women of wealth and polite society, as we have seen, concerned themselves mainly with a life of pleasure. Yet some of these women found themselves bored silly by the shallowness of their lives, were caught up in the "spirit of the times," and were persuaded to "do something." Influenced by the philanthropic movement that got under way early in the century, they ventured outside their comfortable drawing-rooms and found reality anything but comfortable. Children were dirty, diseased, and ragged; young girls barely in their teens were selling their bodies on the streets; wives were beaten and abused by drunken husbands; whole families lived in one squalid room with no privacy whatever; and thousands in a very wealthy nation were going hungry as they tried to live on starvation wages. Encouraged by professional philanthropy and by the biblical rhetoric of John Ruskin, it soon became quite suitable for idle women of the upper classes to "go among the poor."

In "Of Queens' Gardens" (1864), the second lecture in *Sesame and Lilies* (1871), Ruskin exhorted women to use their power of personal influence to improve social conditions.

Women, he said, particularly you women of means, have a pronounced responsibility to look after the wretched sufferers in society. With these ringing words he called on them to become aware of what they had to do: *"Oh, you Queens, you Queens! Among the hills and happy greenwood of this land of yours, shall the foxes have holes and the birds of the air have nests; and in your cities shall the stones cry out against you that they are the only pillows where the Son of Man can lay his head?"* With Ruskin urging them on, it became fashionable in the seventies, almost to the point of necessity, for wealthy women to engage in charitable work. While those more thoughtful took the work seriously and went about it methodically, some more frivolous were mere dabblers with a mania for "slumming."

In *New Grub Street* (1891) Mrs. Boston Wright devoted herself "to soup-kitchens in Liverpool," but growing tired of Liverpool and philanthropy, she was soon discovered "in the thick of literary society in London." Another dabbler is Beatrice Redwing in *A Life's Morning* (1888). A "being of inconsistencies and contradictions," the propaganda of the day has led her to various forms of missionary work in the slums. However, her most sincere alliance is with high society: *"She haunted vile localities, ministering alike to soul and body. At the same time she relished keenly the delights of the masquerading sphere, where her wealth and her beauty made her doubly welcome. From praying by the bedside of a costermonger's wife, she would speed away to shine among the brightest in phantasmagoric drawing-rooms. Once in the world from which thought is banished, she seemed as thoughtless as any."* Gissing is now viewing high society as peopled by puppets incapable of thought. It's a double life the lady is leading, and in two different worlds. Her missionary work allows her to escape the senseless seeking after pleasure so popular in her class to find a modicum of meaning in her life.

In *The Whirlpool* (1897) Lady Isobel Barker and Sibyl Carnaby also dabble in philanthropy without becoming seriously involved. Married to a millionaire, it is said of Lady Isobel that she "did a good deal of slumming at the time when it was fashionable" but later funded a home for "fallen women." Now seeking another way to help working-class women, she and her circle have let it be known to a newspaper exactly what they intend to do: *"Yesterday, at Lady Isobel Barker's house in Point Street, a meeting was held of ladies interested in a project for the benefit of working-class women in the West End. It is proposed to arrange for a series of lectures, specially adapted to such an audience, on subjects of literary and artistic interest. The ladies dwelt on the monotony of the lives of decent working-class women and showed how much they would be benefited by being brought into touch with the intellectual movements of the day."* The scheme is designed more to relieve these idle women from boredom than to help the poor. Concerning the quixotic project, Harvey Rolfe speaking for Gissing, asserts with tongue in cheek: *"Splendid idea! Any one who knows anything of the West End working-class woman will be sure to give it warm support."* Gissing has slipped into a satirical mode once again, and yet real women were actually trying projects like this.

A dabbler among the poor with similar impractical plans is May Tomalin in *Our Friend the Charlatan* (1901). One of the most delightful of Gissing's young women, she has a good heart but an empty head. *"I take a great interest in the condition of the poor,"* she informs pragmatic Lady Ogram. *"We have a little society for extending civilization among the ignorant and the neglected. Just now we are trying to teach them how to make use of the free library, to direct their choice of books. I must tell you that a favourite study of mine is Old English, and I'm sure it would be so good if our working classes could be brought to read Chaucer and Langland and Wyclif and so on. One can't expect them to study foreign languages, but these old writers would serve them for a philosophical training, which has such an excellent effect on the mind. I know a family – shockingly poor – living four of them in two rooms! They have promised to give me an hour every Sunday to 'Piers the Plowman" and I have made them a present of the little Clarendon Press edition, which has excellent notes."* Gissing was laughing as he created that bit of trenchant satire but certainlhy not at ease.

May Tomalin, the girl babbling all this, is like a wind-up doll. Once you get her going she doesn't want to stop. So Lady Ogram listens as she chatters onward: *"The other day I went, on the business of our society, into a dreadfully poor home where the people, I'm sure, often suffer from hunger. I couldn't give money – for one thing, I have very little, and then it's so demoralizing, and one never knows whether the people will be offended – but I sat down and told the poor woman all about the Prologue to the Canterbury Tales, and you can't think how interested she was, and how grateful! It quite brightened the day for her. One felt one had done some good."* Lady Ogram can hardly believe her ears: *"If anyone else had talked to her in this way, no vehemence of language would have sufficed to express her scorn."* But she indulges May and the girl chatters on: *"Next winter we hope to give a few concerts in a schoolroom. Of course it must be really good music; we shan't have anything of a popular kind – at least we shan't if my view prevails. It isn't our object to amuse people; it would be really humiliating to play and sing the kind of things the ignorant poor like. We want to train their intelligence. Some of our friends say it will be absurd to give them classical music, which will weary and discontent them. But they must be made to understand that their weariness and discontent is wrong."* With May Tomalin, whose mission it is to go forth and spread the light, Gissing rises chuckling to the peak of his satirical best.

May Tomalin can be compared to the young woman whose portrait Norbert Franks has painted in *Will Warburton* (1905). The artist has placed his "slummer" on a dirty, narrow street in a typical London slum. She is *"a tall, graceful, prettily-clad young woman, obviously a visitant from other spheres."* In one hand she carries a book, and with the other hand she strokes *"a ragged, crippled child, who gazed up at her with a look of innocent adoration."* Hard by stands a miserable creature with an infant suckling her breast, *"she too adoring the representative of health, wealth, and charity."* Behind them, sprawled on the curbstone and viewing the invader with a look of cold disgust, is an unemployed costermonger. But where the pretty face of the central figure should be shining with compassion and benevolence, the canvas remains blank. The artist hasn't found a model beautiful enough to help him capture the radiance his slummer's face must show. If Franks had the courage to paint "the right sort of face" for the slummer, he would paint it *"sharp-nosed, thin-lipped, rather anaemic, with a universe of self-conceit in the eye."* These are Gissing's thoughts, but the artist replies that slummers are not always that sort, and besides if he painted the picture that way, the Academy would never hang it.

Between his last novel and his first, Gissing's conception of the serious female philanthropist changed. He came to believe that individual efforts among the poor were of little use, and he deplored the trend that made slumming fashionable. In his commonplace book an incident recorded after rambling through the streets takes the place of abstract comment: *"As I went out today, I saw an old, old woman in conversation on the pavement with two smug middle-class females. 'I begin to be very tired,' she was saying. 'I'm quite ready to go. I'm only waiting for the Lord to take me.' Whereupon one of the listeners replied in a voice suitable to some triviality, 'Oh, that's very nice!'"* His critique of "The Slummer" is cynical and bitter in tone, although twenty years earlier in *Workers in the Dawn* (1880), his own portrait of Helen Norman was just as sentimental. Helen is beautiful, wealthy, cultured, highly educated, compassionate, serious, idealistic, and eager to do her part to alleviate the suffering of the poor. She's as perfect as Gissing can make her.

However, Helen is also an incorrigible bluestocking, who can hardly speak a sentence without sounding pompous: *"I shall endeavour to gain the personal confidence of these poor people, so that they will freely impart to me their difficulties, and allow me to help them in the most effectual way."* She is too severe to be human and too noble. She represents an early attempt to realize an upper-class woman, and because he had no living woman he could base her on, Helen is a failure. Later his upper-class women would trill an easy flow of sparkling, idiomatic language that delighted his readers. Of Mrs. Bruce Page in *Isabel Clarendon* (1886), he writes: *"Her greeting of the hostess was one unbroken articulate trill, lasting two minutes and a half; it embodied a series of inquiries, response, information, comments, forecasts, and ejaculation."* Equally adept at conversation are women in later novels.

Whatever she is, Helen Norman is not a slummer. She dedicates her life to bringing about lasting change, and she believes education is the answer. Once more in pompous language she explains what she has in mind: *"Then as I am firmly convinced that no radical change for the better can take place in these people's condition till they are educated, I shall endeavour to establish a free evening school for girls."* In time she opens a night school for factory girls and needlewomen. Their jobs require them to labor fifteen hours a day, but somehow they find the time and energy to attend Miss Norman's school and benefit from it. In the meantime they adore its founder and hang on every syllable she utters. As the school achieves its purpose Helen also begins to improve the living conditions of the poor, putting into effect any number of innovative ideas. But at twenty-two, hardly before her work has begun, she dies of tuberculosis. It's a touch of Victorian melodrama a beginning novelist couldn't resist.

In his second novel, *The Unclassed* (1884), Ida Starr, after inheriting a fortune, follows in the footsteps of Helen Norman. At first she begins to help the poor by replacing and repairing the run-down tenements left her by her grandfather. Then she turns her attention to the children, particularly the little girls: *"The children she came to regard as her peculiar care. Her strong common sense taught her that it was with these that most could be done. The parents could not be reformed; at best they might be kept from that darkest depth of poverty which corrupts soul and body alike. But might not the girls be somehow put into the way of earning a decent livelihood? Ida knew so well the effect upon them of the occupations to which they mostly turned, occupations degrading to womanhood, blighting every hope."* When Waymark tells her she is too good to be visiting the vile haunts of the poor, she bristles at the man's inverse flattery: *"Too good for it? How can any one be too good to help the miserable? If you had said that I was not worthy of such a privilege, maybe I could understand. But too good? Do you really believe I could live here in peace, whilst those poor creatures stint and starve themselves every week to provide me with comforts? Do I seem to you such a woman?"* She expresses an idea developed by H. G. Wells in *The Time Machine* (1895). The Morlocks live underground and support the idle Eloi who live in a perpetual garden.

To give the children of Litany Lane and Elm Court something to look forward to, something to bring fun into their lives, Ida uses her money to establish a series of garden parties. At each party the children eat their fill of wholesome food, receive new clothes (but no toys or doodads), and play games. Ida takes great pleasure in seeing all the children grow strong and happy. Healthy faces replace thin and drawn faces that have never known a smile, and silent children in a world better than they've ever known whoop and holler. Mrs. Jaffray of "The Peace Bringer" (1898) is another remarkable woman who finds satisfaction entertaining the children of paupers in her garden. And Mrs. Ormonde of *Thyrza* (1887) has turned her entire house into a convalescent home for emaciated girls eight to thirteen. So we have children on the scene here even though not one comes forward as a developed character. The women, however, are well developed with a full range of emotions. They feel rewarded by helping the poor, living for others instead of for themselves.

In *The Nether World* (1889) Miss Lant, the one upper-class woman in the entire novel, is like Norbert Franks's slummer "a visitant from other spheres," but far from beautiful. Of middle age and with very plain features, she has for several years devoted herself to philanthropic work among the poor. Even though her income is several hundred pounds a year, to save money for charitable expenditure she lives a Spartan existence. The energy she puts into this self-denying enterprise is excessive but rewarding: *"She was no pietist, but there is nowadays coming into existence a class of persons who substitute for the old religious acerbity a narrow and oppressive zeal for good works of purely human sanction, and to this order Miss Lant might be said to belong."* Her philanthropic projects have become her profession and her religion. Unfortunately, because she has trouble understanding the mentality of the poor, much of her work is ineffectual.

This is well illustrated by the episode of the soup kitchen. The society which established the kitchen entrusted its operation to very practical people, a couple themselves of the working class, and the enterprise has been running smoothly for several years. The stock forming the basis of the soup is wholesome and nutritious; the peas are excellent in quality; and the pittance they charge is twopence a quart. Later the poor, taking advantage of the kitchen, complain they want more than just soup. In response they are told to take it or leave it – *"an' none o' your cheek here, or you won't get nothing at all!"* Then several "philanthropic ladies of great conscientiousness" – one of whom is Miss Lant – inquire into the working of the kitchen and find fault with the management: *"No, no, these managers were of too coarse a type; they spoke grossly; what possibility of their exerting a humanising influence on the people to whom they dispensed soup? Soup and refinement must be disseminated at one and the same time over the same counter. Mr. and Mrs. Batterby were dismissed, and quite a new order of things began."* Trying to economize, the well-meaning ladies buy inferior ingredients for the soup, and immediately that becomes known to their clients.

The word leaks out to the paupers of Shooter's Gardens and causes much excitement: *"I need not tell you that the nether world will consume, when others supply it, nothing but the very finest quality of food, that the heads of sheep and bullocks are peculiarly offensive to its stomach, that a saving effected on sacks of peas outrages its dearest sensibilities."* And the result? The ragged poor, convinced that a heinous fraud has been practiced upon them, bring the tasteless soup back to the kitchen, and with "proud independence of language," pour it grandly upon the floor. When the soup kitchen is on the brink of failure, Miss Lant takes the advice of Jane Snowdon, a girl of the people, and restores the Batterbys to their position of management. Within days an orderly line stands waiting for hot and nourishing soup.

Two other women of wealth who engage in philanthropy are Mrs. Tresilian in *Sleeping Fires* (1895) and Lady Ogram in *Our Friend the Charlatan* (1901). Mrs. Tresilian lives among the poor in the same neighborhood to know them intimately, but Lady Ogram administers her bounty from a luxurious country house. Of humble birth, she doesn't agree with those landed aristocrats who want to maintain the status quo at any cost. A disciple of Thomas Macaulay in her full acceptance of all that he said in lengthy essays, particularly his praise of progress, she is a very practical-minded woman. Like Richard Mutimer in *Demos* (1886), she believes it better that the poor be fed and housed and given work to do than the rich to have a pretty landscape to view. In the picturesque village of Shawe, she has built a hideous paper mill to employ scores of people. The building may be ugly and at odds with the rural scenery, but what goes on inside is saving lives. Though of great help in a time of agricultural depression, the woman's philanthropy is motivated not so much by a zeal for good works, however, as by an earnest desire to perpetuate her name.

In Gissing's day numerous wealthy women were expending their zeal for good works on the human rather than religious level. It was a zeal that in former times had been reserved for the chapel, but in the last two decades of the century one organization after another came into existence to solve social questions, and the church was effectively relegated to the shadows. The different organizations covered an immense and complicated field, including the welfare of soldiers, sailors, domestic servants, factory workers and the working-class in general to the conversion of savages and heathens in faraway lands. Also included in the good works were the lame, prize-fighters, orphans, and lunatics. The organizations were directed toward "furthering the claims of humanity and religion," and they aimed high. Philanthropy lay at the heart of virtually all of them, and the female philanthropists were an important part of all that was going on.

During slightly more than twenty years between his first novel and his last, Gissing's opinions on a number of issues affecting the times in which he lived changed radically. Philanthropy was one of those issues. At the beginning of his career he believed that organized charity could work wonders among the poor in England, particularly through education. Later he considered the poor unresponsive to all but the simplest help. An earnest personal philanthropy could aid them perhaps in a small way, but it had to be at all times very practical. Schemes to elevate the poor were unrealistic, even ridiculous, and wide-open targets for satire. At the end of his career he had come to believe that even education was not the panacea he once thought it to be. Letting his thoughts be known in *The Private Papers of Henry Ryecroft* (1903), he wrote: *"Education is a thing of which only the few are capable; teach as you will, only a small percentage will profit by your most zealous energy. On an ungenerous soil it is vain to look for rich crops."* The tone is one of utter resignation. In his youth, gifted as a student, he had wanted to become a scholar and gain eminence as a well-known professor of classical literature. He dreamed of teaching at Cambridge or Oxford or some other prestigious university in England. By the time his life was nearing its end he had lost faith in the belief that education could bring enormous benefit to the masses. Faith in the centuries-old classical education he dearly loved as a boy with dreams he retained without doubt or question.

Chapter 23

A Backward Glance and Conclusion

The Woman Question

In the last two decades of the nineteenth century, England saw three basic types of women: the womanly woman, the woman in revolt, and the new woman. Though present as three distinct groups in the eighties and nineties, they came on the scene separately as the century unfolded. In the early years a torrent of feminine conduct books spelled out the ideal of the womanly woman, stressing self-repression, patience, and woman's natural inferiority to man. The daughters of England were told in preachey, bombastic language that only in marriage and the home life could a woman find happiness. Brought up on teachings of this sort, most young women looked forward to marriage and were afterwards duly submissive. But John Ruskin, rejecting the notion that woman owed her lord "a thoughtless and servile obedience," declared that a woman's true function in the home was to guide and uplift.

In harmony with Tennyson, Ruskin believed that woman's sacred duty was redemption of certain defects in man. Her place was not among the soul-soiling pursuits of men, but in the home. More than a mere house, the home was meant to be a place apart, a walled garden or sanctuary, a shelter for those values which the commercial and critical influences of the time were threatening to destroy. Reigning in this sacred place, the woman's prime duty was thought to be the moral elevation of man. This theoretical deification of woman accounts in part for the wide hostility to her emancipation. Most male opponents of the feminist movement wanted to prevent what they honestly believed would be the loss of a vital moral influence in their lives. If a woman left her home to rub shoulders with a tawdry world, she would inevitably lose those womanly virtues upon which man depended for his ethical and moral equilibrium.

The men of England differed as to what they wanted in a wife, but most agreed that ambition, achievement, and independence were attributes decidedly unfeminine. Obedience, humility, and unselfishness were the most desirable traits, to say nothing of purity. But even though young women competed earnestly in the marriage market, it was becoming increasingly difficult to find a husband. In 1860 it was said that only one girl in three, who was still single at twenty-one, could expect to marry. At twenty-five her chances had decreased to one in six, and at thirty to one in sixteen. As the century went along, this state of affairs became even worse so that by the 1880's large numbers of middle-class women were remaining unmarried. The result of all this was the existence of superfluous women. A girl could go on being some man's daughter only so long as he lived. After that, if she had not succeeded in becoming some man's wife, she was adrift, or as the saying went, "up the creek without a paddle."

In the first half of the nineteenth century in England, the legal position of a married woman was comparable to that of a child. The property, earnings, personal liberty, physical body, and even the conscience of a wife belonged to her husband. Moreover, even the children she might bear belonged to him. The first legislative attempt to improve the legal position of women was inspired by Caroline Norton. Following her example, the women in revolt – the "struggling sex" some called them – sought earnestly throughout the century to obtain equal rights for women. One group wanted equal educational opportunities. Another sought free entrance to the learned professions. Another demanded a share in the government of the nation. Another agitated for a new feminine morality – for greater freedom in dress, manners, and mode of living; while still another continued the agitation for legal emancipation begun by Caroline Norton.

In the 1890's the feminist revolt extended itself in many directions. New ideas and new methods were introduced, and the antagonism to male domination increased. In the propaganda of the nineties one found a tone of bitterness that to a large extent had been missing in earlier decades. There was also an element of emotionalism, sometimes bordering on hysteria, but this was characteristic of the more radical faction who came to be called "militants." By the nineties the feminist movement, referred to in these years simply as "the Cause," included many women who merely desired excitement. George Gissing died before this phase reached its climax, but he lived to see the meek Victorian woman become assertive and aggressive. Before his death more women were revolting than ever before, and against more things – against many issues of the time.

Nearly every home had at least one rebellious daughter, and the desire to escape male tyranny led to overt acts. But if the rebellious daughter ruffled the feathers of the late-Victorian paterfamilias, the rebellious wife was even worse. Some wives, according to Charlotte Yonge, began their rebellion with the marriage ceremony, refusing to pronounce the word "obey." Though murmurings of revolt began much earlier, it was generally stated that Ibsen's *A Doll's House*, produced in England in 1889, first incited wives to rebellion. Ibsen was hailed as a champion of the woman's cause (he was really concerned with broader issues), and his play was described as a powerful plea for the emancipation of women. Opponents of the feminist cause agreed with Henry Arthur Jones that Nora was the "the first of the tiresome hussies," and the play should have ended with the husband exclaiming, "Thank God she's gone!" Ibsen, of course, can't be said to have generated entirely the keen public interest in the rights and duties of married women in the 1890's, and yet his play seems to have served as a point of departure for much discussion.

In the last two decades of the century, the feminist revolt produced a woman of a new type. A person of so-called advanced views, she went about advocating the independence of her sex, defying convention, and generally calling attention to herself. The public, perceiving that she was thinking and acting in marked contrast to the traditional behavior of women, began to call her "the New Woman." Often plain to begin with and deliberately minimizing sexual features in long skirts, she was described as "looking like a man from the waist up." Moreover, her behavior was anything but womanly. At times she smoked cigarettes in public carriages, or dared to speak of female legs in print though never in public or the drawing-room. She made a lot of people angry when she called child-bearing females "cow-women," but that was her way of showing contempt of traditional values. As the century ended, however, she was becoming less extreme in her views and was winning acceptance. By then a new set of feminine ideals had been placed before English women, and the phrase "new womanhood" was commonly used.

Education and the new womanhood went hand in hand. To become "highly educated," to be termed "well-read" or "cultured" was the avowed ambition of every new woman. She was intellectual on the whole, or at least pretended to be, and she had a clever, quick, inquiring mind. She made herself au courant with the best that was being thought and said, and she was not averse to revealing how much she knew. Brightness of intellect and a tendency to display it were dominant traits of the new woman. She wanted to be known as "strong-minded" rather than "pure-minded," and she deliberately sought books that Mudie wouldn't stock. Even so, one can't suppose that all the new women were bluestockings; a large number were not. They read something about *mens sana in corpore sano*, and decided that in developing their minds, they must not neglect their bodies. As a consequence they began to engage in sports more strenuous than croquet, and in the nineties they were riding bicycles in the streets of London, where they scared the horses. At the end of the century sporadic attempts were made to reinstate the old ideal but to no avail. The new woman was on the scene to stay.

Gissing On the Woman Question

At the beginning of his career Gissing's conception of woman and her place in society was similar to that of John Ruskin. As a young man he was an idealist in his view of women, depicting them in his early books as either angel-women or bad-seed types. Ideal womanhood described by Ruskin in *Sesame and Lilies* (1871) Gissing accepted with no reservations. In his first novel Helen Norman was the measure of his woman-worship; in his third it was Isabel Clarendon, who became his fullest representation of the womanly woman. In his fourth, fifth, and sixth novels he imparted memorable qualities of the womanly woman to the chief female characters, confusing ideal womanhood with saintliness. By 1888 he believed his view of the womanly woman, when translated to paper, was too idealistic for a writer who prided himself on his realism. At that time he had become interested in the feminist movement. His next portrait would show the womanly woman with flaws that when corrected would leave her free of the old oppressive conventions – emancipated.

Miriam Baske in *The Emancipated* (1890) is an engaging young widow of narrow Puritan persuasion smitten by spiritual pride. In Naples, recovering from an illness, she gradually throws off the mantle of Puritanism and moves from strict Hebraism to enlightened Hellenism. She is a dynamic character in the process of changing from womanly to new. While her story is concerned with the spiritual aspects of female emancipation, that of the Madden sisters in *The Odd Women* (1893) shows Gissing's interest in the economic ramifications of the question. They are conventional women trained in the old ways and forced to support themselves when their father dies. Through them Gissing is saying that women of the middle class must be given an education that fits them for life in a changing world. Women who can't marry can become valuable members of society with proper training. The Madden sisters are superfluous because the old-order education for women has not prepared them for changing times. If Dr. Madden had given them a practical education as they were growing up, as grown women on their own they would have found good jobs and would not have suffered.

The informing idea of *The Odd Women* (1893) was first suggested in *Denzil Quarrier* (1892). There Quarrier spoke of the nation's superfluous women and the need for the more intelligent of them to train the rest. In *The Odd Women* (1893) Mary Barfoot and Rhoda Nunn are doing exactly that. Their position is clearly defined in a formal address delivered by Mary to several of her students. She is strenuously opposed to the Ruskinian view of woman. If woman is to become a human being of power and influence, she must first become militant, defiant. Out of this warfare, this struggle against men for equality, will come a new type of woman. The Ruskinian ideal of womanly perfection doesn't fit the times. It would have women remain dependent when they have only themselves to depend upon. But the time has come when women must have an ideal of strength, self-reliance, and independence set before them.

This new woman should be active in every aspect of life, sharing the world's work, but not at the expense of neglecting the home. In shaping a new ideal for guidance the best of the old ideal should be retained. The new woman must be a balanced mixture of manly and womanly traits, for that is what the world demands. Emulation of man will not diminish her sexuality any more than getting a college degree has done so. In fact the adoption of manly traits will be a vast improvement, not only to women but to society as a whole. Gissing is in full agreement with virtually everything Mary has said. At the beginning of his career he had been pro-Ruskin, and had held the womanly woman in high esteem. Now in the middle of his career he has shifted his position to the opposite pole. Later, as we shall see, he would return to a more conservative position.

His shifting views may be seen in his reaction to the new woman. In *Isabel Clarendon* (1886) his first new woman is set against a womanly woman and loses markedly in the comparison. Isabel is womanly and beautiful, gracious and charming while emancipated Ada Warren is plain and caustic. Most of the characters in the novel see Ada as "a strange specimen of womanhood." But when she proves to be a very worthy person, Gissing's sympathy is at once apparent. In the same novel Hilda Meres, who in time will become a new woman, delights her creator. Her new education is similar to Cecily Doran's in *The Emancipated* (1890). But Gissing suggests that Cecily's training has been too radical, based too much on the new principles while the best of the old were ignored. Change of this sort must come slowly, not only through education but also through experience. Even then one can't expect the process to be ameliorative at all times.

In *Born in Exile* (1892) he was of the opinion that most emancipated women were incomplete, and yet they seemed an improvement over conventional women. He believed at this time that education would eradicate much of the foolishness in women, but he was still undecided about the virtues of the new women. In 1893 he was convinced that no "social peace" could be achieved "until women are intellectually trained very much as men are." He was "driven frantic by the crass imbecility of the typical woman," and vehemently he declared that a new woman would have to take her place. By this time he had begun to admire and carefully develop in his fiction such women as Rhoda Nunn of *The Odd Women* (1893).

While gaining enormously on the intellectual side, they had lost no single good quality of their sex. Women were once empty-headed, but now a vast change was coming about to correct that fault.

By 1894 Gissing's marriage to Edith Underwood had fallen into ruin, and his attitude toward women of her class had become bitter. Also he found fault with the class slightly above hers and was beginning to believe the spirit of emancipation had taken a turn for the worse. Women were no longer interested in home, children, and husband; the domestic virtues were being lost. In 1890 as he published *The Emancipated* he could sympathize with a woman's "slavery to nature." With admiration he could say that lively Cecily Doran in that novel would have rebelled had she been constrained to "stay home and mind the baby." He could believe that her son demanded too much of her time, and in *New Grub Street* (1891) he could show Reardon disliking his little son. But at this time Gissing was between marriages and had no children of his own. By 1894 he himself had a son, and he expected his wife to love and care for the child with all the energy at her command. His change of mind is reflected in Arthur Peachey's tender parental affection in *Year of Jubilee* (1894). It may also be seen in *The Whirlpool* (1897), where Harvey Rolfe has intense love for the child his socialite wife has neglected.

In 1894 Gissing was also beginning to question his earlier view concerning woman's equality. He failed to convinced himself that woman in any way was inferior to man, but he now felt that female emancipation was undermining the husband's right to rule. In his own family, though his mother had a strong personality, his father wore the pants. He grew up thinking that arrangement was universal in all families. In *New Grub Street* (1891) he had shown that unless the husband is strong enough to dominate his wife, inevitably she will dominate him. And so Lionel Tarrant of *In the Year of Jubilee* (1894) makes it clear to Nancy Lord after marriage that he is her superior. What is more, Nancy is willing to accept this injunction with no show of disapproval. She has come to believe that a woman must be the slave of her husband and children or defy a basic law of nature. This, of course, is a far cry from what Gissing had said of Cecily Doran in 1890. It is in fact just the opposite of what he put in the mouth of Mrs. Wade in *Denzil Quarrier* (1892).

In *The Whirlpool* (1897) Gissing is clearly opposed to the wife and mother who neglects her family to engage in selfish pursuits. In this novel Alma Rolfe illustrates the woman who abuses her freedom, a type that Gissing thought was becoming all to plentiful in the England of his day. By way of contrast he praised the virtues of Mrs. Basil Morton, an old-fashioned wife and mother. His fear that Mrs. Morton represented a rapidly vanishing specimen of womanhood is revealed in "Out of the Fashion" (1896), the last story of *Human Odds and Ends* (1898). He believed that the simple, self-sacrificing woman of the old ideal had been replaced by a brash, selfish, bicycle-riding, bloomer-clad new woman. The Mary Claxtons were "out of harmony with the day that rules" because the Ada

Peacheys had taken over. The change that had produced rather admirable women in the beginning was now creating extreme specimens. He expressed this sentiment in his portrayal of three types: Linda Vassie who moves always "at high pressure"; Charlotte Grub who takes advantage of the system to live comfortably without working; and the "heroine of gun and pen" who slaughtered lions for amusement and wrote about it.

Having once sided with the aims of the feminist movement, by the end of the century Gissing had retreated to the ranks of the conservatives. At the beginning of the new century his position was similar to that of Martin Blaydes in *Our Friend the Charlatan* (1901): "Back with them to nursery and kitchen, pantry and herb-garden! Back with them or we perish." Less extreme were the thoughts of Lord Dymchurch on this one important subject, and those were more closely Gissing's: *"Frankly he said to himself that he knew nothing about women, and that he was just as likely to be wrong as right in any theory he might form about their place in the world."* As a youth in Manchester, Gissing knew nothing about women and so fell victim to one. Now at the end of his career he has come full circle to admit that in all his years of living and study he never learned to know women.

The Heart of the Matter

An important issue of the woman question was the work of women. Each year thousands of women found themselves unable to marry and were constrained to support themselves. But until the last three decades of the nineteenth century "woman's work" consisted mainly of duties in the home. Outside the home the only respectable occupation open to women of the middle class was teaching. It was the aim of the feminist movement to rectify this situation, to open for more and more women a greater variety of jobs. Early in his career Gissing considered the work of women important and sent letters to his sisters urging them to prepare themselves for work in the world. Virtually all his novels from the first to the last show this same concern even when the plot differs. A pertinent question confronting many of his female characters is "what shall I do in the world?" A cursory glance at his novels will show women at work at the bottom of the social latter, in between, and at the top.

In his proletarian novels one may find vivid pictures of destitute girls who turn as a last resort to the world's oldest profession. His poverty made him the neighbor of some of the women who worked the streets after nightfall, and we know he observed them carefully. During his early years in London he lived within easy walking distance of those streets and squares that for more than a century had been the center of London prostitution. For Gissing these women had none of the glamour that some attributed to them. They lived their lives on the fringes of society, often among criminals, and no one really cared whether they lived or died. Many forces brought a girl to the streets, and the love of frippery and finery wasn't the least of them. But Gissing thought seduction, poverty, and the indifference of people in power were the main causes. His portrayal of London's harlots grew out of his own experience, for as a youth he had loved just such a girl who in later years became his wife. Personal experience with Marianne Helen Harrison (referred to as Nell) led him to ponder the problem of the fallen woman. At first he thought of Nell as a victim of social and economic pressures, but when she disappointed him again and again he blamed hereditary factors.

Then in 1888, viewing Nell in death, he experienced a resurgence of pity that made him think of her again as a victim of society. In the heat of his emotion he wrote *The Nether World* (1889), a savage indictment of that upper world which allowed such a one as Nell to live and die in misery. Then he turned to other matters, but as late as 1894 he was still wrestling with the issue of what causes a woman to prostitute herself when other solutions are possible. His opinions on what he called "ladies of the town" fluctuated. At times they seem almost contradictory, but against those social and economic conditions that brought degradation to women he spoke loudly in protest.

Gissing viewed domestic servants as low on the social scale, but observed that within their ranks there was an upward gradation from domestic scut worker, or "domestic slave," to the respected housekeeper. He concerned himself with servants hired, and often abused, by the middle class, making no attempt to study those of upper and titled classes. Often he depicted the lower servant as grossly mistreated, and then he showed her in revolt against overwork, low wages, and poor working conditions. In the novels of the eighties he had little to say about servants, for he was too poor to hire one, but in several novels of the nineties he recognized a pervasive servant problem, tried to get at its roots, and offered a solution.

He placed needlewomen and factory girls slightly above the servants. Indeed, members of the working class, particularly women who operated lodging-houses, had their servants. Also a skilled artisan was able to hire a servant, but most working women did their own house work while working also for income. Gissing observed them closely, and the accuracy of his observation was corroborated by Charles Booth, a leading social investigator. But sometimes he exaggerated to drive home a point, emphasizing the long hours and low wages of needlewomen. He called them "silent victims of industrialism," and more than once he said overwork drove many to the streets and brothels. In his early novels he was savage in his condemnation of those economic forces that bought misery to working women. Yet while viewing the needlewoman as exploited and oppressed, he often looked at the factory girl with ironical amusement, depicting her as rough, boisterous, outspoken, warm-hearted, laughing, singing, and seldom overworked. The working woman who adjusted to her surroundings found a modicum of happiness. The ambitious one trying to leave her class for something higher sometimes reaped a bitter harvest of frustration and despair.

The shopgirls of Gissing's day belonged to the lower-middle class and haughtily considered themselves superior to working girls. In *The Odd Women* (1893), tracing the course of Monica Madden's career as a shopgirl, he gave his readers a vivid picture of the conditions under which these girls lived and worked. Their hours were interminably long and their wages rock-bottom low; their moral sense was suspect and soon corrupted. Monica is able to leave the hard life of the shop to marry, only to find her marriage to an older man unendurable. Other shopgirls in Gissing's fiction long to marry the clerks they come in contact with but often miss their chance and live without hope. Polly Sparkes of *The Town Traveller* (1895), a novel that focuses entirely on shop-keeping and shop-people, has all the qualities of the shopgirl good and bad. Beatrice French of *In the Year of Jubilee* (1894) represents a new type of woman moving away from the ordinary shop to more complicated business.

Governesses were at the bottom of the professional class. Even though they belonged to a social rank somewhat higher than shopkeepers, many earned less in a year than superior servants. To test the truth of Gissing's remarks on salary, I compared classified advertisements in the *Times* (London) for the first week in 1880 with the first week in 1900. The results indicated that a sweeping change in the position of governesses had occurred during those twenty years. Like the Milvain sisters in *New Grub Street* (1891), near the end of the century many English girls were no longer interested in becoming governesses. Those who would have done so in 1880 were in 1900 becoming bookkeepers, secretaries, stenographers, typists, journalists, hospital nurses, and even doctors. Gissing's novels present at least sixteen governesses, three of whom are central characters in long novels. All of them are grossly underpaid. The low pay was supported by the advertisements of 1880. By 1900, when the supply was less than the demand, salaries had risen considerably.

His teachers usually operate small private schools, but at least two are associated with the "board schools" of the new Education Department. One of these, Miss Rodney, meets the challenge of her job with strength and enthusiasm. She is obviously a new woman in sleek tailored clothes and creating a stir in the town in which she teaches. Most of the teachers, however, are old-fashioned in their view of life. Teachers in Gissing's fiction, like the servants, fall into social and economic ranks. At the bottom is a lowly music teacher who must teach music to the children of working people at whatever they are willing to pay. At the top is the university graduate teaching in one of the new high schools. For many long hours on the job she receives enough pay to live on but not enough for extravagances.

Gissing's nurses belong to a new school of nursing that was replacing the lowly, unsanitary, hit-or-miss practice of earlier generations; but his attitude toward nursing was ambivalent. In 1880 he looked upon the profession as a noble calling. Ten years later in 1890 he believed it offered a woman one of the highest forms of life, dedicating herself to help those who needed her most. Then in 1895 he penned a violent attack upon infirmary nursing in the workhouses. Even though it showed horrendous conditions under which the poor nurse lived and worked, the attack was directed more at the workhouse than at hospital nursing. Charles Booth supported him in deploring the low salaries, long hours, and undesirable working conditions of even the best nurses in top-notch hospitals.

Those women who chose not to go into teaching or nursing often attempted to write for a living, and some did all right. A number of lady novelists whose names are now lost in the mists of time earned more at their writing than Gissing ever did. He once said he would give up literary labor altogether rather than join the ranks of "the petty scribblers" as he called these women. In that respect history was kind, for today he is seen as one of the better novelists writing in the last two decades of the nineteenth century. Though several young women in his novels support themselves as writers, on the whole he believed the "rough and tumble" of the literary profession was no place for women. Yet some he admired and openly admitted warm admiration for Charlotte Brontë, George Eliot, George Sand, and a woman called Mrs. Woods. She was the sister of a woman who went daily to the British Museum, and Gissing used her as the model for Marian Yule in *New Grub Street* (1891). Among lady novelists Charlotte Brontë was his undisputed favorite.

In addition to writers one finds also female artists who use their talent mainly to earn a living, for example Miss

Bonnicastle in *The Crown of Life* (1899) who paints "glaring grotesques" for the advertising industry. However, Hilda Castledine in "A Victim of Circumstances" (1893) discovers lurking somewhere within herself a genuine artistic talent. She develops her art to surprising maturity until it comes in conflict with that of her husband and she has to abandon it. Her example is clear indication that Gissing considered some women fully capable of genuine artistic achievement. Others, as with philanthropic slummers, he saw as dabblers, women who took up painting mainly to impress their friends. From childhood Gissing was interested in art. His notebooks contain original sketches and he loved the paintings of Hogarth. The talented woman artist he admired as much as the talented woman writer.

Though most of his fictional women eventually find work to do, an indeterminate number are women of leisure and privilege without a thought of work. They are wealthy and belong to the upper class of British society, and they spend their time seeking pleasure. A few, becoming bored with their shallow lives, take up philanthropy and tell themselves they are helping the poor. As early as 1886 with the publication of his third novel, Gissing wrote sympathetically of the upper classes. The women of the leisured class he admired, but his vision was not so blurred as to prevent him from seeing that some were not contributing anything to the world around them and were little more than parasites. He called the more experienced among them "women of the world," of whom the archetype was a lady in his own life, Mrs. David Gaussen.

In *Isabel Clarendon* (1886) he presented a paragon of English womanhood based on Mrs. Gaussen. In time she moved out of his life, possibly without knowing the adoring tribute he had paid her. And in time he met the woman meant for him, a woman who lived in Paris name Gabrielle Fleury. His four years with her were the happiest of his entire life.

The novels of George Gissing, dealing prominently with "the Woman Question" in England near the end of the nineteenth century, portray women of three basic types: the womanly woman, the woman in revolt, and the new woman. These types go hand in hand with the women on many social levels in a rigidly class-conscious society who work for a living. The novels reveal also, in dialogue rather than diatribe, Gissing's shifting position in regard to the woman question. Rather than presenting propaganda that professed to solve the woman question, his novels defined it in the lives of individual women, raising in the minds of his readers the significant issues on which any solution had to rest.

The Novels of George Gissing

1880	Workers in the Dawn
1884	The Unclassed
1886	Isabel Clarendon
1886	Demos: A Story of English Socialism
1887	Thyrza: A Tale
1888	A Life's Morning
1889	The Nether World
1890	The Emancipated
1891	New Grub Street
1892	Denzil Quarrier
1892	Born in Exile
1893	The Odd Women
1894	In the Year of Jubilee
1895	Eve's Ransom
1895	The Paying Guest
1895	Sleeping Fires
1897	The Whirlpool
1898	The Town Traveller
1899	The Crown of Life
1901	Our Friend the Charlatan
1901	By the Ionian Sea (autobiographical)
1903	The Private Papers of Henry Ryecroft
1904	Veranilda (historical and posthumous)
1905	Will Warburton (posthumous)

Other posthumous writings were published later.

A George Gissing Chronology

1857 — Born November 22 in Wakefield, Yorkshire, England, son of a chemist. Christened George Robert Gissing.

1870 — Father, Thomas Waller Gissing, died suddenly in December, leaving behind a young wife, three sons, and two daughters.

1871 — With his two brothers, William and Algernon, entered a Quaker boarding school, Lindow Grove, at Alderley Edge, Cheshire.

1872 — In October matriculated at Owens College, Manchester on a scholarship that provided free tuition for three years. Continued to live at Lindow Grove until he went off to college.

1875 — Moved to private lodgings in Manchester, winning honors in English and Latin and distinguishing himself as a gifted student.

1876 — Met Marianne Helen Harrison (Nell), a young prostitute he attempted to rehabilitate and reform. Her picture shown to Morley Roberts. On May 31 arrested for stealing planted and marked money in college cloakroom. On June 6 convicted and sentenced to a month in prison at hard labor. On June 7 expelled from Owens College. In August sailed for United States to start a new life. In America wrote sentimental poems idealizing Nell.

1877 — Taught briefly in high school at Waltham, Massachusetts. Went by train to Chicago and published first fiction, "The Sins of the Fathers," in *Chicago Tribune* on March 10. Published several stories before leaving Chicago in July for east coast. Sailed from Boston in September, arrived in Liverpool October 3, found himself living in London lodgings by end of October.

1878 — Lived at 22 Colville Place, London, between January and September. Continued to use American notebook for plot outlines. On birthday, November 22, received his share of a trust fund (about £500) left by his father. Begins to advise two sisters on reading and the fundamentals of a good education.

1879 — In January met Eduard Bertz, a German intellectual who returned to Germany but who became an enduring friend to whom he wrote many letters. Married Marianne Helen Harrison on October 27. Earned a living as a tutor and worked on first proletarian novel.

1880 — In March *Workers in the Dawn* published at own expense. Friendship with Frederic Harrison. Brother Willian died April 16 of tuberculosis.

1881 — In February moved to Worthington Road, earned 45 shillings a week tutoring children of wealthy families. In August moved to 15 Gower Place. Lived in rented lodgings with Nell who was often ill. Worked on his second novel, hoping against hope that a publisher would accept it.

1882 — Tutored ten pupils from 9 to 6 and wrote in the evenings. "Mrs. Grundy's Enemies" completed in September and accepted for publication but never published. Nell, alcoholic and sick, sent to an invalids' home in Battersea. Returned in October, soon left. Gissing moved to 17 Oakley Crescent, Chelsea, where he lived two years.

1883 — Nell back on the streets, involved in street disturbance in September. Gissing lived alone, worked on next novel, tried and failed to get a divorce, never saw Nell again until after she was dead.

1884 — Moved to a single room at 62 Milton Street near Regents Park. Bertz left London in April. *The Unclassed*, his second novel, published in June. In summer met Mrs. Gaussen, visited her home in September, began to tutor her son at 7K Cornwall Residences.

1885 — In the spring spent a week with the Gaussens along with sister Ellen. Worked on next novel, begun in 1884 and influenced throughout by Mrs. Gaussen. Also completed *A Life's Morning* in this year, both a departure in subject matter from earlier novels.

1886 — *Isabel Clarendon* published in February. *Demos*, a return to his "special line of work," published a month later. Reviewed favorably.

1887 — *Thyrza* published in April. Colorful scenes of lower-class life dominated by girls and women. Main character, a lively working girl, idealized and supplies the title.

1888 — *A Life's Morning*, written before *Demos*, published in February. Nell died February 29. Gissing viewed her body on March 1. Began work on *The Nether World* and completed novel in four months. On way to Italy stopped briefly in Paris, attended a speech by a leading feminist. In Italy five months. Loved the country, climate, people.

1889 — *The Nether World* published in March. Completed Italian trip. Began trip to Greece and Italy. Met Edith Sichel in September.

1890 — *The Emancipated* published in March. In April visited Paris with his sisters. On September 24 met Edith Underwood in London. Made rapid progress on next novel after he met her and completed the novel in December.

1891 — Married Edith Underwood on February 25 and moved from London to Exeter in the county of Devon, noted for its scenery. Son, Walter Leonard, born December 10. Edith suffered from neuralgia, showed first signs of sour temper. *New Grub Street,* his best-known novel, published in April.

1892 — Two novels published in this year, *Denzil Quarrier* in February, *Born in Exile* in April. Living in pleasant surroundings away from London and better off financially, but a year of "domestic misery and discomfort."

1893 — *The Odd Women* published in April and well reviewed. In September some newspaper publicity when he accused a parson of stealing a long passage from *The Nether World* and publishing it as his own. The parson blamed the printer. Met Clara Collet in July, visiting her in Richmond.

1894 — *In the Year of Jubilee* published in October. Finished *Eve's Ransom* in June and moved to Somerset. Complained of isolation and uncertain health and low income in spite of never-ending work.

1895 — Three short novels published in this year. *Eve's Ransom* ran serially in *Illustrated London News,* out in book form later in year. *The Paying Guest* and *Sleeping Fires* published near end of year. Domestic turmoil increased.

1896 — Second son, Alfred Charles, born January 20. By the end of year, as he finished his latest novel, Gissing's troubles with Edith had convinced him he would have to abandon his family. Worried about welfare of sons.

1897 — In February driven from home. Published *The Whirlpool* in spring. Returned to Edith in June and moved in July to Yorkshire. In September he fled from Edith and domestic conflict again, making the separation final. Italian trip of six months provided materials for *By the Ionian Sea*.

1898 — Returned to England April 18. Met Gabrielle Marie Edith Fleury on July 6 at home of H. G. Wells. Saw wife Edith and son Alfred for last time on September 7. Published *Human Odds and Ends*, a collection of short stories, *The Town Traveller*, and *Charles Dickens, A Critical Study*. Influenced by Gabrielle, began work on what he thought would be his best novel.

1899 — Began to live with Gabrielle Fleury in France after a mock marriage ceremony on May 7. Finished *By the Ionian Sea* and "Among the Prophets," but destroyed. Published *The Crown of Life* in October.

1900 — In April visited his family in Wakefield. Worked through the summer on "The Coming Man" published in 1901 as *Our Friend the Charlatan*. In autumn *Private Papers of Henry Ryecroft* written in less than two months.

1901 — With Gabrielle visited Wells in May. In June went alone to Dr. Jane Walker's sanatorium in Suffolk, stayed there a month. In August joined Gabrielle in Autun, living there until October 12. Later for health reasons moved southward to Arachon. Published *Our Friend the Charlatan* and *By the Ionian Sea*.

1902 — In February Edith Underwood Gissing committed to insane asylum. With Gabrielle Fleury and her mother, he moved to St. Jean de Luz in June to take advantage of the climate. Worked on historical novel and other projects in spite of steadily declining health.

1903 — Published *The Private Papers of Henry Ryecroft.* Completed *Will Warburton* in March. During summer and fall worked on historical novel, *Veranilda*. Fell ill with five chapters yet to be written and was not able to finish it. Moved to Ispoure in St. Jean Pied de Port and died there of double pneumonia at forty-six on December 28. Buried at St. Jean de Luz.

1904 — Unfinished historical novel *Veranilda* published.

1905 — *Will Warburton* published.

1906 — *The House of Cobwebs*, a collection of short stories, published.

1917 — On February 27 Edith Underwood Gissing, his second wife, died at forty-five of "organic brain disease" in a lunatic asylum.

1954 — In April Gabrielle Fleury Gissing, (his third wife in name only) was injured in a street accident in Paris and died several months later.

Gissing's Female Characters

Mary Abbot	The Whirlpool (1897)
Mrs. Allchin	Thyrza (1887)
Mrs. Argent	Victim of Circumstances (1927)
Miss Armitage	The House of Cobwebs (1906)
Amy Baker	The Paying Guest (1895)
Mary Barfoot	The Odd Women (1893)
Mrs. Tom Barfoot	The Odd Women (1893)
Lady Isobel Barker	The Whirlpool (1897)
Amelia Barmby	In the Year of Jubilee (1894)
Lucy Barmby	In the Year of Jubilee (1894)
Miriam Baske	The Emancipated (1890)
Mrs. Batt	Human Odds and Ends (1898)
Mrs. Batterby	The Nether World (1889)
Mrs. Batty	Stories and Sketches (1938)
Mrs. Baxendale	A Life's Morning (1888)
Mrs. Bellamy	In the Year of Jubilee (1894)
Bevis sisters (3)	The Odd Women (1893)
Mrs. Bevis	The Odd Women (1893)
Mrs. Blatherwick	Workers in the Dawn (1880)
Mrs. Bloggs	Human Odds and Ends (1898)
Mrs. Bolsover	The Town Traveller (1898)
Mrs. Bolt	Isabel Clarendon (1886)
Miss Bonnicastle	The Crown of Life (1899)
Mrs. Borisoff	The Crown of Life (1899)
Mrs. Borrows	Stories and Sketches (1938)

Mrs. Boscobel	Demos (1886)
Mrs. Bower	Thyrza (1887)
Mary Bower	Thyrza (1887)
Mary Bowes	The House of Cobwebs (1906)
Mrs. Bradshaw	The Emancipated (1890)
Mrs. Breakspeare	Our Friend the Charlatan (1901)
Constance Bride	Our Friend the Charlatan (1901)
Agnes Brissenden	The Odd Women (1893)
Mrs. Brookes	Stories and Sketches (1938)
Mrs. Bubb	The Town Traveller (1898)
Budge sisters (4)	Stories and Sketches (1938)
Mrs. Budge	Stories and Sketches (1938)
Mrs. Budge	Victim of Circumstances (1927)
Bessie Bunce	Thyrza (1887)
Mrs. Buncombe	The Whirlpool (1897)
Mrs. Butterfield	Thyrza (1887)
Mrs. Byass	The Nether World (1889)
Evelyn Byles	Victim of Circumstances (1927)
Jessie Byles	Victim of Circumstances (1927)
Mrs. Byles	Victim of Circumstances (1927)
Emily Cadman	Born in Exile (1892)
Maria Candy	The Nether World (1889)
Pennyloaf Candy	The Nether World (1889)
Sibyl Carnaby	The Whirlpool (1897)
Edith Carter	New Grub Street (1891)
Amy Cartwright	A Life's Morning (1888)
Barbara Cartwright	A Life's Morning (1888)
Eleanor Cartwright	A Life's Morning (1888)

Geraldine Cartwright	A Life's Morning (1888)
Jessie Cartwright	A Life's Morning (1888)
Mrs. Cartwright	A Life's Morning (1888)
Hilda Castleldine	Victim of Circumstances (1927)
Mrs. Catterick	Human Odds and Ends (1898)
Mrs. Charman	The House of Cobwebs (1906)
Mrs. Chattaway	Demos (1886)
Bertha Childerstone	Human Odds and Ends (1898)
Mrs. Chittle	In the Year of Jubilee (1894)
Winifred Chittle	In the Year of Jubilee (1894)
Mrs. Christopherson	New Grub Street (1891)
Mrs. Christopherson	The House of Cobwebs (1906)
Isabel Clarendon	Isabel Clarendon (1886)
Mary Claxton	Human Odds and Ends (1898)
Kate Clay	Demos (1886)
Lucy Cliffe	Human Odds and Ends (1898)
Hannah Clinkscales	Workers in the Dawn (1880)
Lizzie Clinkscales	Workers in the Dawn (1880)
Miss Cloud	Victim of Circumstances (1927)
Louisa Clover	The Town Traveller (1898)
Minnie Clover	The Town Traveller (1898)
Mrs. Conisbee	The Odd Women (1893)
Florence Cootes	Isabel Clarendon (1886)
Mrs. Cope	Workers in the Dawn (1880)
Mrs. Cosgrove	The Odd Women (1893)
Bertha Cross	Will Warburton (1905)
Mrs. Cross	Will Warburton (1905)
Curate's wife	Human Odds and Ends (1898)
Mrs. Cumberbatch	Workers in the Dawn (1880)

Mrs. Damerel	In the Year of Jubilee (1894)
Grace Danver	The Nether World (1889)
Alma Dawson	Stories and Sketches (1938)
Irene Delph	The Emancipated (1890)
Mrs. Delph	The Emancipated (1890)
Barbara Denyer	The Emancipated (1890)
Madeline Denyer	The Emancipated (1890)
Zillah Denyer	The Emancipated (1890)
Mrs. Denyer	The Emancipated (1890)
Louise Derrick	The Paying Guest (1895)
Irene Derwent	The Crown of Life (1899)
Rachel Donne	Victim of Circumstances (1927)
Cecily Doran	The Emancipated (1890)
Effie Dover	Stories and Sketches (1938)
Amy Drake	The Odd Women (1893)
Mrs. Ducker	The House of Cobwebs (1906)
Maggie Dunn	Victim of Circumstances (1927)
Miss Eade	The Odd Women (1893)
Mrs. Egremont	Thyrza (1887)
Mrs. Ellerton	Stories and Sketches (1938)
Mrs. Elderfield	Human Odds and Ends (1898)
Mrs. Eldon	Demos (1886)
Mrs. Elgar	The Emancipated (1890)
Rosamund Elvan	Will Warburton (1905)
Winifred Elvan	Will Warburton (1905)
Mrs. Emerson	Thyrza (1887)
Emily Enderby	The Unclassed (1884)
Maud Enderby	The Unclassed (1884)
Jenny Evans	Stories and Sketches (1938)

Muriel Featherstone	The Paying Guest (1895)
Sally Fisher	The Unclassed (1884)
Mary Fleetwood	Victim of Circumstances (1927)
Mrs. Fletcher	Human Odds and Ends (1898)
Beatrice French	In the Year of Jubilee (1894)
Fanny French	In the Year of Jubilee (1894)
Mrs. Frothingham	The Whirlpool (1897)
Mrs. Thomas Gale	Born in Exile (1892)
Mrs. Gallantry	Our Friend the Charlatan (1901)
Sarah Gandle	Thyrza (1897)
Ivy Glazzad	Denzil Quarrier (1892)
Mrs. Goldthorpe	The House of Cobwebs (1906)
Mrs. Gorbutt	New Grub Street (1891)
Mrs. Grail	Thyrza (1897)
Maud Gresham	Workers in the Dawn (1880)
Charlotte Grub	Human Odds and Ends (1898)
Mrs. Gulliman	Demos (1886)
Mrs. Gully	The Nether World (1889)
Mrs. Gunnery	Born in Exile (1892)
Mrs. Halliday	Victim of Circumstances (1927)
Mrs. Hammer	A Life's Morning (1888)
Olga Hannaford	The Crown of Life (1899)
Mrs. Hannaford	The Crown of Life (1899)
Hannaford's sister	The Crown of Life (1899)
Mrs. Handover	The Whirlpool (1897)
Miss Harrow	New Grub Street (1891)
Winifred Haven	The Odd Women (1893)
Mrs. Hefron	Victim of Circumstances (1927)

Polly Hemp	Workers in the Dawn (1880)
Amy Hewett	The Nether World (1889)
Clara Hewett	The Nether World (1889)
Margaret Hewett	The Nether World (1889)
Cissy Higgins	The Paying Guest (1895)
Mrs. Higgins	The Paying Guest (1895)
Emily Hilliard	Eve's Ransom (1895
Mrs. Hinks	New Grub Street (1891)
Mrs. Hinton	Human Odds and Ends (1898)
Mrs. Hitchin	Denzil Quarrier (1892)
Lady Honeybourne	Our Friend the Charlatan (1901)
Mrs. Hood	A Life's Morning (1888)
Mrs. Hopper	Will Warburton (1905)
Mrs. Humplebee	The House of Cobwebs (1906)
Miss Hurst	The Unclassed (1884)
Miss Hurst	Human Odds and Ends (1898)
Mrs. Ireton	The House of Cobwebs (1906)
Mrs. John Jacks	The Crown of Life (1899)
Bella Jacox	Born in Exile (1892)
Lily Jacox	Born in Exile (1892)
Mrs. Jacox	Born in Exile (1892)
Mrs. Jaffray	Stories and Sketches (1938)
Mary Jalland	Isabel Clarendon (1886)
Mrs. Jarmy	Stories and Sketches (1938)
Mrs. Jedwood	New Grub Street (1891)
Mrs. Jenkins	A Life's Morning (1888)
Mrs. Jephson	Human Odds and Ends (1898)

Rosamund Jewell	Victim of Circumstances (1927)
Sukey Jollop	The Nether World (1889)
Miss Jupp	Human Odds and Ends (1898)
Mrs. Jupp	Human Odds and Ends (1898)
Winifred Kay	Stories and Sketches (1938)
Mrs. Keeting	The House of Cobwebs (1906)
Lady Kent	Isabel Clarendon (1886)
Miss Kerin	Stories and Sketches (1938)
Kate Kirby	Stories and Sketches (1938)
Mrs. Lane	New Grub Street (1891)
Miss Lant	The Nether World (1889)
Mrs. Lanyon	Stories and Sketches (1938)
Mrs. Ascott Larkfield	The Whirlpool (1897)
Mrs. Larrop	Thyrza (1887)
Mrs. Lashmar	Our Friend the Charlatan (1901)
Dora Leach	The Whirlpool (1897)
Gerda Leach	The Whirlpool (1897)
Mrs. Leach	The Whirlpool (1897)
Mrs. Ledward	The Unclassed (1884)
Mrs. Lessingham	The Emancipated (1890)
Laura Lindon	Sins of the Fathers (1924)
Liversedge sisters (4)	Denzil Quarrier (1892)
Mrs. Liversedge	Denzil Quarrier (1892)
Nancy Lord	In the Year of Jubilee (1894)
Lumb sisters (2)	Born in Exile (1892)
Alice Madden	The Odd Women (1893)

Gertrude Madden	The Odd Women (1893)
Isabel Madden	The Odd Women (1893)
Martha Madden	The Odd Women (1893)
Monica Madden	The Odd Women (1893)
Virginia Madden	The Odd Women (1893)
Mrs. Maddison	Isabel Clarendon (1886)
Eve Madeley	Eve's Ransom (1895)
Mrs. Mallard	The Emancipated (1890)
Mrs. Rayner Mann	The Whirlpool (1897)
Mrs. Marshall	Human Odds and Ends (1898)
Mrs. Maskell	The Whirlpool (1897)
Mrs. Mayhew	Human Odds and Ends (1895)
Miss Medwin	Will Warburton (1905)
Mrs. Mewling	Demos (1886)
Hilda Meres	Isabel Clarendon (1886)
Rhoda Meres	Isabel Clarendon (1886)
Fanny Michelthwaite	The Odd Women (1893)
Mrs. Middlemist	In the Year of Jubilee (1894)
Dora Milvain	New Grub Street (1891)
Maud Milvain	New Grub Street (1891)
Mrs. Milvain	New Grub Street (1891)
Carrie Mitchell	Workers in the Dawn (1880)
Sylvia Moorhouse	Born in Exile (1892)
Jessica Morgan	In the Year of Jubilee (1894)
Mrs. Morgan	In the Year of Jubilee (1894)
Mrs. Morton	Born in Exile (1892)
Mrs. Basil Morton	The Whirlpool (1897)
Moxey sisters (5)	Born in Exile (1892)
Janet Moxey	Born in Exile (1892)

Marcella Moxey	Born in Exile (1892)
Serena Mumbray	Born in Exile (1892)
Emmeline Mumford	The Paying Guest (1895)
Mrs. Murch	In the Year of Jubilee (1894)
Alice Mutimer	Demos (1886)
Mrs. Mutimer	Demos (1886)
Totty Nancarrow	Thyrza (1887)
Annabel Newthorpe	Thyrza (1887)
Helen Norman	Workers in the Dawn (1880)
Lilian Northway	Denzil Quarrier (1892)
Rhoda Nunn	The Odd Women (1893)
Mrs. Oaks	Workers in the Dawn (1880)
Mrs. Ogle	The Unclassed (1884)
Lady Ogram	Our Friend the Charlatan (1901)
Mrs. Orchard	The Odd Women (1893)
Mrs. Ormonde	Thyrza (1887)
Bridget Otway	The Crown of Life (1899)
Mrs. Jerome Otway	The Crown of Life (1899)
Mrs. Paddy	Human Odds and Ends (1895)
Mrs. Bruce Page	Isabel Clarendon (1886)
Constance Palmer	Born in Exile (1892)
Ada Peachey	In the Year of Jubilee (1894)
Charlotte Peak	Born in Exile (1892)
Mrs. Peak	Born in Exile (1892)
Clem Peckover	The Nether World (1889)
Mrs. Peckover	The Nether World (1889)

Pettindund sisters (4)	Workers in the Dawn (1880)
Mrs. Pettindund	Workers in the Dawn (1880)
Phoebe	Stories and Sketches (1938)
Martha Pimm	Human Odds and Ends (1895)
Mrs. Pole	Workers in the Dawn (1880)
Polterham ladies	Denzil Quarrier (1892)
Mrs. Pool	Human Odds and Ends (1895)
Mrs. Poole	Thyrza (1887)
Miss Pope	Denzil Quarrier (1892)
Mrs. Poppleton	The Odd Women (1893)
Mrs. Potter	Stories and Sketches (1938)
Miss Pye	Isabel Clarendon (1886)
Mrs. Quodling	The Town Traveller (1898)
Amy Reardon	New Grub Street (1891)
Beatrice Redwing	A Life's Morning (1888)
Mrs. Redwing	A Life's Morning (1888)
Lady Revill	Sleeping Fires (1895)
Patty Ringrose	Eve's Ransom (1895)
Mrs. Rippingille	Victim of Circumstances (1927)
Tilly Roach	Thyrza (1887)
May Rockett	The House of Cobwebs (1906)
Mrs. Rockett	The House of Cobwebs (1906)
Clara Rodman	Demos (1886)
Miss Rodney	The House of Cobwebs (1906)
Alma Rolfe	The Whirlpool (1897)
Mrs. Roots	Born in Exile (1892)
Edith Rossall	A Life's Morning (1888)

Bella Royston	The Odd Women (1893)
Miss Rupert	New Grub Street (1891)
Miss Rutherford	The Unclassed (1884)
Mrs. Rutland	Human Odds and Ends (1895)
Rutland sisters (3)	Human Odds and Ends (1895)
Ryecroft's servant	Henry Ryecroft (1903)
Mrs. Rymer	The House of Cobwebs (1906)
Miss Saxby	Victim of Circumstances (1927)
Mrs. Shaklewell	Victim of Circumstances (1927)
Hilda Shale	The House of Cobwebs (1906)
Lady Shale	The House of Cobwebs (1906)
Miss Shepperson	The House of Cobwebs (1906)
Emma Shergold	The House of Cobwebs (1906)
Mrs. Shufflebotham	Our Friend the Charlatan (1901)
Lotty Simpson	Stories and Sketches (1938)
Mrs. Simpson	Stories and Sketches (1938)
Harriet Smales	The Unclassed (1884)
Mrs. Smallbrook	The Odd Women (1893)
Pauline Smith	The Whirlpool (1897)
Caroline Snapshall	Stories and Sketches (1938)
Henrietta Snapshall	Stories and Sketches (1938)
Jennie Snapshall	Stories and Sketches (1938)
Mrs. Humphrey Snell	Victim of Circumstances (1927)
Mrs. Snickers	Human Odds and Ends (1895)
Jane Snowdon	The Nether World (1889)
Polly Sparkes	The Town Traveller (1898)
Eleanor Spence	The Emancipated (1890)
Sarah Sprowl	The Unclassed (1884)

Ida Starr	The Unclassed (1884)
Lotty Starr	The Unclassed (1884)
Mrs. Strangeways	The Whirlpool (1897)
Mrs. Stratton	Isabel Clarendon (1886)
Lady Teasdale	The House of Cobwebs (1906)
Letty Tew	Demos (1886)
Mrs. Tichborne	A Life's Morning (1888)
May Tomlin	Our Friend the Charlatan (1901)
Geraldine Toplady	Our Friend the Charlatan (1901)
Mrs. Travis	The Emancipated (1890)
Lydia Trent	Thyrza (1887)
Thyrza Trent	Thyrza (1887)
Mrs. Tresilian	Sleeping Fires (1895)
Mrs. Tubbs	The Nether World (1889)
Lily Turpin	The House of Cobwebs (1906)
Mabel Turpin	The House of Cobwebs (1906)
Mrs. Turpin	The House of Cobwebs (1906)
Paula Tyrrell	Thyrza (1887)
Mrs. Tyrrell	Thyrza (1887)
Linda Vassie	Human Odds and Ends (1895)
Lucy Venning	Workers in the Dawn (1880)
Mildred Vesper	The Odd Women (1893)
Emma Vine	Demos (1886)
Jane Vine	Demos (1886)
Lucy Vissian	Isabel Clarendon (1886)
Mrs. Wade	Denzil Quarrier (1892)

Minnie Wager	The Whirlpool (1897)
Carrie Waghorn	The Town Traveller (1898)
Phyllis Waldron	Victim of Circumstances (1927)
Mrs. Walker	Denzil Quarrier (1892)
Adela Waltham	Demos (1886)
Mrs. Waltham	Demos (1886)
Agatha Walworth	Born in Exile (1892)
Jane Warburton	Will Warburton (1905)
Mrs. Warburton	Will Warburton (1905)
Ada Warren	Isabel Clarendon (1886)
Sidwell Warricombe	Born in Exile (1892)
Mrs. Weare	The House of Cobwebs (1906)
Annie West	Thyrza (1887)
Stella Westlake	Demos (1886)
Whiffle sisters (5)	Workers in the Dawn (1880)
Mrs. Whiffle	Workers in the Dawn (1880)
Rose Whiston	The House of Cobwebs (1906)
Lady Whitelaw	Born in Exile (1892)
Frau Wholgemuth	The Emancipated (1890)
Mrs. Wick	Will Warburton (1905)
Mrs. Luke Widdowson	The Odd Women (1893)
Mrs. Wilcox	Victim of Circumstances (1927)
Mrs. Willard	The Emancipated (1890)
Mrs. Wilson	Denzil Quarrier (1892)
Miss Winter	Will Warburton (1905)
Henrietta Winter	The Whirlpool (1897)
Mrs. Winter	The Whirlpool (1897)
Miss Withers	Human Odds and Ends (1895)
Ada Wolstenholme	An Heiress on Condition (1923)

Mrs. Wolstenholme	An Heiress on Condition (1923)
Mary Woodruff	In the Year of Jubilee (1894)
Iris Woolstan	Our Friend the Charlatan (1901)
Mrs. Boston Wright	New Grub Street (1891)
Mrs. Alfred Yule	New Grub Street (1891)
Mrs. Edmund Yule	New Grub Street (1891)
Marian Yule	New Grub Street (1891